THE
ORIENTAL GEOGRAPHY
OF
EBN HAUKAL
AN
ARABIAN TRAVELLER OF THE TENTH CENTURY

Translated from a Manuscript in His Own Possession, Collated with one Preserved in the Library of Eton College

BY

SIR WILLIAM OUSELEY

Elibron Classics
www.elibron.com

Elibron Classics series.

© 2005 Adamant Media Corporation.

ISBN 1-4021-7684-8 (paperback)
ISBN 1-4021-2437-6 (hardcover)

This Elibron Classics Replica Edition is an unabridged facsimile
of the edition published in 1800 by the Oriental Press,
London.

Elibron and Elibron Classics are trademarks of
Adamant Media Corporation. All rights reserved.

This book is an accurate reproduction of the original. Any marks, names, colophons, imprints, logos or other symbols or identifiers that appear on or in this book, except for those of Adamant Media Corporation and BookSurge, LLC, are used only for historical reference and accuracy and are not meant to designate origin or imply any sponsorship by or license from any third party.

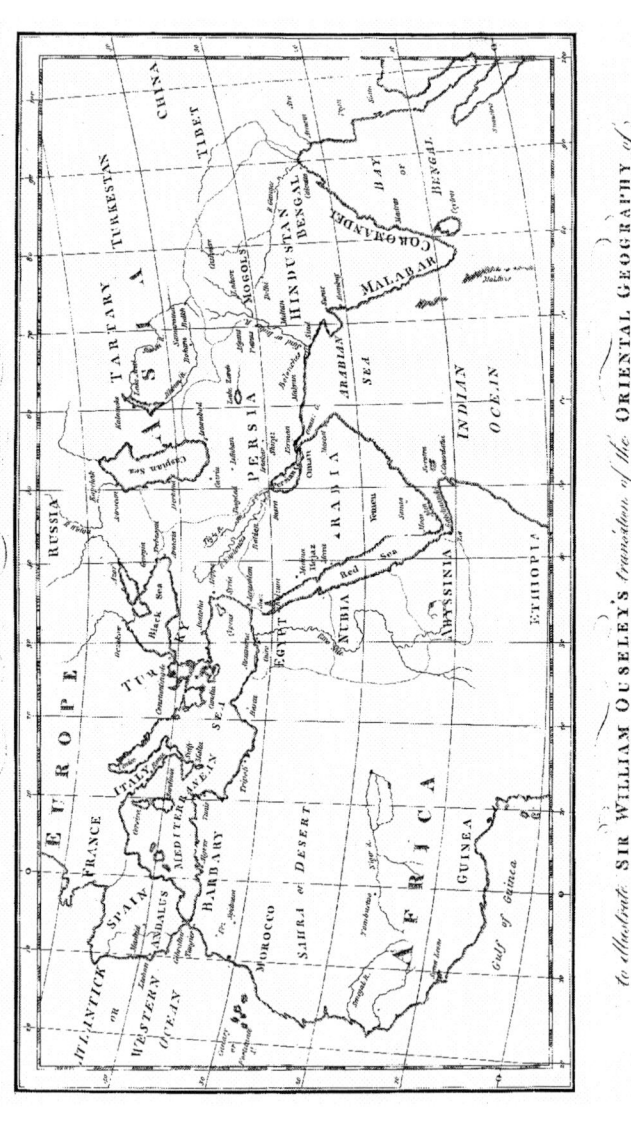

كتاب
مسالك و ممالك تصنيف ابن حوقل

THE

ORIENTAL GEOGRAPHY

OF

EBN HAUKAL,

AN

ARABIAN TRAVELLER OF THE TENTH CENTURY.

Translated from a Manuscript in his own Possession, collated with one preserved in the Library of Eton College,

BY

Sir WILLIAM OUSELEY, Knt. LL. D.

ORBIS SITUM DICERE AGGREDIOR, IMPEDITUM OPUS ET FACUNDIÆ MINIME CAPAX.
POMP. MELA.

London,

Printed, at the ORIENTAL PRESS, by *Wilson & Co.*
WILD-COURT, LINCOLN'S INN FIELDS,

FOR T. CADELL, JUN. AND W. DAVIES, STRAND.

1800.

TO

THE KING,

THIS ATTEMPT

TO IMPROVE OUR KNOWLEDGE

OF

THE EASTERN WORLD

IS HUMBLY DEDICATED,

BY

HIS MAJESTY'S

MOST DUTIFUL SERVANT, AND MOST

FAITHFUL SUBJECT,

WILLIAM OUSELEY.

PREFACE.

In compiling, from the Manuscript Works of several Persian and Arabian Authors, whatsoever they had written on the Geography of the Eastern World, I found that, in a variety of detached extracts, I had imperceptibly translated almost half of that treatise which I now offer to the Publick as complete in an English version as the obscurities and imperfections of the original would admit.

Besides the intrinsick merits of the work, its authenticity and antiquity induced me to regard it as the most important of all compositions on the subject of Oriental Geography. ABULFEDA *informs us, that* EDRISI, EBN KHORDADBAH, *and many other writers of high reputation, have only traced, on*

ii   PREFACE.

paper, the footsteps of EBN HAUKAL*, *who, it appears from his own words, had actually visited most of the places which he describes.*

Although the exact epoch of his birth and death is still unknown to me, I have not hesitated to announce EBN HAUKAL *as an author of the tenth century. That he wrote* before *the building of* Cairo, *we learn from his account of Egypt in the following work, page* 30; *and after the accession of* ABDARRAHMAN, *who, in his time, governed* Andalus, *or* Spain, *appears from p.* 28. *The foundation of modern Cairo was laid in the year* 968 *of the Christian Æra, and* ABDARRAHMAN *assumed the government of Spain in the year* 902 *of the same Æra, or of the Hegira* 290. *Thus we may ascertain, that* EBN HAUKAL *flourished before the year* 968, *and after the year* 902; *and we cannot err considerably if we place him in the middle, or, perhaps, in the beginning, of the tenth century* †. *He is styled, by* EDRISI *and* ABULFEDA, *simply*

---

* *Chorasmiæ et Maweralnahr descriptio, ex tabulis Abulfedæ, &c.* Quarto, London, 1650, *p.* 2.

† *This date is confirmed by another passage in our Author's description of* Maweralnahr, *or* Transoxania, *page* 235. *He there informs us, that he conversed with a respectable personage, who had served in the armies of* NASSER AHMED. *This Prince, of the*

PREFACE.

حوقل Haukal, *or* ابن حوقل Ebn Haukal: *But it appears, from one copy of his work deposited among the Oriental manuscripts in the Library at Leyden*, that his name was* ابي القاسم ابن حوقل Abi l'Cassem Ebn Haukal.

The work itself, in the original Arabick, according to the Catalogue of the Leyden Library, above quoted, is called كتاب المسالك الممالك Kitab al Mesalek al Memalek. *The Persian translation which I have used, and the copy preserved at Eton †, bear the same title, with the omission of the Arabick article, and (in my copy) the addition of the copulative, thus:* كتاب مسالك و ممالك. *Under this name the ancient Tarikh, or Chronicle of* Tabari, *quotes it in a passage which I shall hereafter adduce.*

Samanian *family, became Sovereign of* Maweralnahr, *Anno Hegiræ* 301, *(A. D.* 913.) . *If* Ebn Haukal *could have spoken with a contemporary of* Nasser Ahmed, *one who had been of sufficient age to attend him in his battles, we cannot, reasonably, assign a later date to the composition of this work than the middle of the tenth century.*

* *See No.* 1704, *page* 478, *of the Catal. Libr. tam impress. quam manuscriptor. Biblioth. publ. Universit. Lugduno-Batavæ, folio, Lugd. Bat.* 1716.

† *Eton Oriental MSS. No.* 418.—*This manuscript is an octavo volume, containing above three hundred pages, written in an uniform, but very difficult and inaccurate hand; most of the proper names wanting their diacritical points. My own copy, which I purchased*

PREFACE.

It is probable, however, that it bore a second, or more descriptive and ample title; for Mons. D'HERBELOT *mentions the work of* EBN HAUKAL *as entitled* " Giagrafiah fi Marefat al Boldan*: *And in the Leyden Catalogue, we find, after* Al Mesalek al Memalek, *these additional names:*

و البغاوزو البهالك و ذكر الاقاليم و البلدان

The words Mesalek Memalek *seem to form either the whole or part of the titles to many other Geographical manuscripts. Among the various original treatises which furnished materials to* HAMDALLAH MUSTOUFI, *the celebrated Persian geographer, in the composition of his* Nozahet al Coloub, *he*

with many other MSS. about three years ago, is a large and thin octavo volume, containing two hundred and twelve pages: it is imperfect at the end; but on a collation with the Eton MS. appears only to want the last leaf. The character is sufficiently neat; but the proper names are most inaccurately written, and whole lines, in various places, are without a diacritical point.

* *Bibliot. Orient. art.* Haucal. *As this article contains a very just account of our Author's defects, I shall give it entire:*—" Haucal,"—Ebn Haucal,—" *Auteur d'un livre intitulé* Giagrafiah fi Mârefat al Boldan. *C'est une Geographie fort prolixe;* Abulfeda *qui ie cite souvent, se plaint de ce qu'il n'a pas designé assez clairement les noms propres des lieux, faute de sétre servi des voyelles qui servent à en fixer la prononciation. Cet Auteur est aussi fort defecteux en ce qu'il ne marque ni les longitudes ni les latitudes des lieux dont il parle, defaut qui lui est commun avec la plûpart de geographes de l'Orient, qui ont laissè ce soin aux astronomes.*"

PREFACE.

enumerates, in the Preface to that most excellent work, the " Mesalek al Memalek, *by* Abi Cassem Abdallah ben Khordad, of Khorasan *."

A geographical book, entitled Al Mesalek ou al Memalek *(of which* Mons. D'HERBELOT *thinks the author may have been* ABOU ALI, *surnamed* MARAKSHI), *is quoted by* EBN AL VARDI, *in his* Kheridet al Ajaieb †.

The learned GRAVES, *who published* ABULFEDA's Chorasmia and Maweralnahr ‡, *mentions the celebrated composition of* EDRISI, *whom we generally style the* Nubian Geographer, *as entitled* Memalek al Mesalek, *although it bore many other names, which* HARTMANN *enumerates in his admirable commentary on this work* §. *Indeed the name* Mesalek al Memalek *seems to have signified an* Universal Geography, *or, rather, a* Work

---

* مسالك الممالك بتاليف ابي قاسم عبدالله بن خرداد خراساني

† *Bibliot. Orient. article* Marakeschi; *yet I suspect, that in this place, the learned author of the Bibliotheque Orientale has fallen into some error: he seems, however, to have corrected it in another article. See* Mesalek.

‡ *Before quoted. See note, p.* ii. " *Nobilis al Edrisi* الشريف الادريسي *in libro* المالك المسالك *de regnis et imperiis, urbium locorumque situs, &c.*

§ *Edrisii Africa, cura* J. M. HARTMANN, Gotting. 1796, *octavo, p.* lxvii. &c.

vi PREFACE.

describing several Countries; *for* ABULFEDA *complains,* " *That* " *the greater number of those books which are called* Al " Mesalek ou al Memalek *(of Countries and Kingdoms) treat* " *only, with accuracy, of those regions wherein the Mussul-* " *man religion is established,*" *&c.* *

Such were the observations I made, while uncertain to whom I should ascribe the composition of a manuscript treatise which fell into my hands about three years ago, bearing the same title, but without any author's name. Although the copy preserved in the publick Library at Leyden furnished the name of ABI L'CASSEM EBN HAÙKAL, *yet I was not, when visiting that magnificent collection in the year* 1794, *interested in a minute examination of any particular volume, and therefore could not afterwards ascertain whether my manuscript was a Persian translation of his work; and the copy deposited in the College Library at Eton, wanted, like my own, the author's name. But a comparison of the various extracts given by* ABULFEDA *in his account of*

---

* *Abulfedæ Chorasmiæ et Maweral. descript. &c. p.* 3.

و غالب كتب للمسالك و الممالك انما حققوا بلاد الاسلام *&c.*
The plan of EBN HAUKAL'S *work will be found to correspond exactly with this description. See p.* 1, 2, 3, 4, *&c.*

PREFACE.

Khorasmia and Maweralnahr, from EBN HAUKAL's book, with those which describe the same places in my manuscript, sufficiently demonstrates the identity of their author. I shall refer the reader, in particular, to ABULFEDA's account of تونکت Tuncat, the chief place of Ailak, near Chaje or Shash; its numerous gates; water running in the city; its wall to prevent the incursions of the Turks, reaching from the mountain called شابلغ Shabaleg, to the valley of Chaje; the river named Ailak *, &c. All these the reader will find more fully described by EBN HAUKAL in the following work (pages 266, 267); with a variation occasioned merely by the different collocation of diacritical points in the names of Tuncat and Shabaleg. The account of Naksheb and of Kash, as extracted by ABULFEDA† from EBN HAUKAL's book, will be found to correspond exactly with the description of those cities given in the following translation, pages 259, 260, &c. A comparison of these passages will convince the reader, that the Mesalek al Memalek, of which an English version is now before him, must be the work of EBN HAUKAL, so often quoted by ABULFEDA.

---

* *Chorasm. et Maweraln. p.* 49.   † *Chorasm. &c. p.* 43.

PREFACE.

But there are some more striking passages, which (as the work of ABULFEDA *may not always be at hand) I shall present in the original Arabick, with a literal translation.*

ABULF. PAGE 19.

قال ابن حوقل و في جبل من بعض جبال البتم غار و يستوثق من ابوابه و كواه فيجتمع في ذلك البيت من الغار بخار يشبه النار بالليل و الدخان بالنهار و يتلبد ذلك البخار و هو النوشادر و لا يتهيها للحد ان يدخل ذلك البيت الا ان يلبس لبودا و يربطها و يدخل بسرعة و ياخذ من النوشادر قال وهذا البخار ينتقل من مكان الي مكان فيحفر عليه حتي يظهر و اذا الم يكن عليه البيت لينبع من التفرق الم يضر من قاربه

" EBN HAUKAL *relates, that in the mountains of Al Botem*
" *there is a certain cavern, in which, when every passage for air*
" *is stopped up, a thick vapour arises, resembling fire by night*
" *and smoke in the day-time; and this is the* nushader *(or sal*
" *ammoniac.) Nobody, with safety, can enter this cave,*
" *unless covered with thick garments fitting close to his body,*
" *and he must be expeditious in taking away the nushader.*
" *The vapour moves from place to place, and they seek for it*
" *by digging until it appears. This vapour would not be*

PREFACE.

" *noxious to those who approach it, if there were not an*
" *arched house or vault erected, to prevent its evaporation.*"

The reader who is acquainted with the very vague and inaccurate manner of Eastern writers, both in their quotations and translations, must acknowledge this to be the same passage given in the following work, page 264.

Another extract will be sufficient to prove the identity of our author with the EBN HAUKAL, *quoted by* ABULFEDA, *page* 45.

قال ابن حوقل و رايت علي باب من ابواب سمرقند يسمي
باب كش صفحة من حديد و عليها كتيبت يزعم اهلها انها
بالحميريه و الباب من بنا تبع ملك اليمن فان من صنعا الي
سمرقند الف فرسخ وان ذلك مكتوب من ايام تبع قال ثم
وقعت فتنه بسمرقند في ايام مقامي بها و احترق الباب و
ذهبت الكتابه ثم اعاد محمد بن لقمان بن نصير بن احمد
الساماني عبارة الباب و لم يعد الكتابة

" EBN HAUKAL *says*—I *saw on a gate at Samarcand,*
" *which is called the Gate of Kash, an iron plate with an*

" inscription. The people report this to have been in the
" Hamariah character, and that the gate was erected by the
" Tobba, the king of Yemen, (Arabia Felix); that (the in-
" scription signifies) " From Sanaa to Samarcand is a thousand
" farsang." This was written in the days of the Tobba. Then,
" says he (EBN HAUKAL), a riot or tumult having happened
" at Samarcand, during my stay there, the gate was burnt
" and the inscription destroyed. After that, MOHAMMED EBN
" LOCMAN EBN NASIR EBN AHMED, the Samanian*, caused
" the gate to be rebuilt, but did not restore the inscription."

In page 254 of the following work, this passage will be found with less variation from the original than Persian translations generally exhibit: and as it leads to a curious anecdote in Oriental history, an article of the Appendix is devoted to its illustration.

The Author of the Ajaieb al Boldan (Fifth Climate) also quotes EBN HAUKAL on this subject; and he seems to have

---

* For some account of the Samanian dynasty, see the Appendix, No. IV.

PREFACE.

used the original work in Arabick rather than our Persian translation: his words are,

ابن حوقل گويد که نوبتي بسمرقند رسيدم و بر بابي از ابواب شهر که آنرا باب کش کفتندي صفحهٔ از حديد ديدم و بر آن صفحهٔ کلمهٔ چند منقوش بود و اهل سمرقند کمان داشتند که آن کلماترا اهل حِمیَر نکاشته اند و باني باب تبع ملک يمن است و همو گويد که در آن مدت در سمرقند ساکن بودم فتنهٔ روي نمود و آن بابرا باحراق معدوم ساختند

EBN HAUKAL says, "Once I went to Samarcand, and upon one of the Gates of that city, which they call the Gate of Kash, I saw a plate of iron, and on it were inscribed some words; and the people of Samarcand were of opinion that this inscription had been written by the people of Homer (or the Hamyarites), and that the builder of that gate had been the Tobba, or King of Yemen." The same person (EBN HAUKAL) also says, "at the time when I resided in Samarcand, a tumult or riot happened, and that gate was destroyed by fire."

Having mentioned in the beginning of this Preface, that the Mesalek Memalek is quoted in the ancient Chronicle of Tabari,

PREFACE.

it may be necessary to account for a seeming anachronism; as the reader who learns from Pococke*, D'Herbelot†, *or* Ockley ‡, *that the venerable historian died early in the tenth century* §, *will not readily believe that he could have quoted the work of* Ebn Haukal, *whom I have assigned to the middle of the same century, and consequently supposed to have existed several years after* Tabari, *although it is possible that they might have been contemporaries. But the Chronicle of* Tabari *underwent a Persian translation; which work, as it was performed by a man of learning and ingenuity, (vizier to one of the Samanian princes), and enriched by him with much curious additional matter,* M. D'Herbelot *prefers to the original Arabick* ‖. *This, indeed, is not*

---

* *Specimen Hist. Arabum,* 383, *Oxford, quarto,* 1650.
† *Bibliot. Orient. article Thabari.*
‡ *History of the Saracens. Vol. II. p.* 350.
§ *Anno Hegiræ* 310, *(A. D.* 922.)
‖ *On remarquera encore ici que ce vizir n'a pas seulement traduit le texte de Thabari, mais qu'il y a encore ajouté tout ce qu'il a cru pouvoir l'enricher, et ce sont pour la plûpart des remarques et des faits qu'il à tirez, comme il le dit lui même dans sa Preface, des Livres des Astronomes, et des Historiens des Ghebres, ou anciens Persans, adorateurs du feu, des Juifs et des Musulmans : de sorte que cette traduction est beaucoup plus curieuse que le texte Arabique."* *Bibliot. Orientale, art. Thabari.*

It was this passage which gave occasion to the following note in Mr. Gibbon's History of the Decline and Fall of the Roman Empire.—Chap. li. note 33.

PREFACE. xiii

to be found complete in any library. *Of the Persian translation, however, there are many copies in Europe**: it was made in the year of the Hegira 352, (A. D. 963), probably very soon after the time of* EBN HAUKAL. *To the Persian translator I would attribute that quotation from the* Mesalek al Memalek, *which thus occurs in* TABARI's *History of the Virgin* MARY; *and of her flight, with the infant* JESUS, *to a village in the territories of Damascus.*

گویند که آن دیه هم از شام بود از غوطهٔ دمشق و اندر
کتاب مسالک و ممالک ایدونست اندر خبر شهرها که در
جهان نزهت و خرمي چارجایست یکي شهر سغد سرتند و
دیگر غوطهٔ دمشق و سیوم نهر الیله و آن بصره‌ست و چهارم
شعب بوان و این پارس است از روستاهاء شهر شیراز پس این
دیه که مریم عیسی را آنجا بپرورد از روستاهاء غوطهٔ است
دهیست بر سر بلندي

" *Amidst our meagre relations, I must regret that* D'HERBELOT *has not found and used a Persian translation of Tabari, enriched, as he says, with many extracts from the native historians of the Ghebers or Magi.*"

* *In the Publick Libraries of Paris, Oxford, &c. Of this most valuable work I am fortunate in possessing three fine copies; one of which, uncommonly correct in the handwriting, was transcribed A. D.* 1446. *From this manuscript, which the learned Tychsen, in a letter from Rostock, entitles a* Phœnix Librorum, *collated with the other two copies, a*

xiv   PREFACE.

" It is said that this village also belonged to Syria, one of the
" villages of the Ghoutah of Damascus; and in the book Mesalek
" ou Memalek it is thus related among the descriptions of va-
" rious countries, that in the world of pleasantness and
" beauty there are four places most remarkable; one, the
" Soghd of Samarcand; another, the Ghoutah of Damascus;
" the third, Nahr Ailah*, which is Basrah; and the
" fourth, Shaab Bouan; this is in Persia, one of the terri-
" tories belonging to Shiraz. Now the place in which Mary
" nursed Jesus, was a village of the Ghoutah (of Damascus)
" situated on the summit of a rising ground," &c.

From the following passage of ABULFEDA†, it appears
that EBN HAUKAL must have been the author of that Mesalek

---

perfect and accurate text might be obtained; this, if correctly translated and illustrated from
other Asiatick compositions, the Biblical records, the classicks of Greece and Rome, and the
more modern productions of European writers, would form a complete body of Oriental
History and Antiquities; since it comprehends not only the Persian and Arabian annals, but
the most ancient traditions of the Jews, the Egyptians, and the Greeks.

* ايلة With two diacritical points under the second letter, for ابلة Ablah with one. By
a mistake also, of the transcriber, the word بصرى Basrah, in one copy of Tabari, is written
مصر Misr.
† Chorasm. p. 8.

PREFACE.

Memalek *alluded to in the preceding extract from* TABARI'S *Chronicle.*

سغد سمرقند وهواحد من نزهات الدنيا هي سغد سمرقند وغوطة دمشق ونهر الابله عند البصرة وشعب بوان بفارس قال بن حوقل و سغد سمرقند بماوراالنهر و هو انزه الاربع المذكورات

" The Soghd of Samarcand is one of those places esteemed
" the most delightful in the world; these are the Soghd of
" Samarcand, the Ghoutah of Damascus, the Nahar al Ablah,
" or river Ablah*, near Basrah, and Shaab Bouan in Persia;
" but EBN HAUKAL says that the Soghd of Samarcand is the
" pleasantest of all the four places above enumerated."

It would be surprising to find a passage from any Oriental manuscript remain uncorrupted or unaltered through different translations. My copy of the Mesalek al Memalek (see p. 237.) gives this in the following words:

---

* *I have followed* GRAVES, *the translator of* ABULFEDA, *in writing* Ablah: *but it is properly called* Ubbullah, *being thus accented* أُبُلَّه.—*According to the* تقويم البلدان Takouim al Boldan *or Tables of Longitude and Latitude, by* محمد صادق اصفهاني

xvi PREFACE.

و گویند که در همه جهان خوشتر از سه جایگاه نیست یکی سغد سمرقند و یکی رود ابله وسه دیگر غوطهٔ دمشق

"*They say that in the whole world there is not any place
more delightful than these three; one, the Soghd of Samarcand; another, the Rud-i-Aileh (or* Ablah*); and thirdly, the
Ghoutah of Damascus.*"

The reader will find in page 237 of this work, that EBN HAUKAL *prefers the Soghd of Samarcand (as in* TÁBARI'S *Chronicle, and* ABULFEDA*) to the rival Tempes, and describes those points in which its superior beauty consists. Why the Shaab Bouan has been omitted, I cannot pretend to have discovered*. The deplorable inaccuracy of Oriental transcribers, as well as translators, has been so often noticed, that it is unnecessary for me to dwell on the difficulties attending*

MOHAMMED SADUK ISFAHANI, *the* Nahr Ubbullah *is within four farsang of* Basrah.

* *Similar omissions (though not so important) may be detected in other passages.* EBN HAUKAL, *as quoted by* ABULFEDA, *tells us, that the Hamyaritick inscription before mentioned in this Preface, was on the* Gate of Kash *at* Samarcand.—*Our Persian translator has omitted the name of the gate; but we find, in some places, that he has retained more of* EBN HAUKAL'S *particular descriptions than* ABULFEDA.

PREFACE.

any endeavour to reconcile the various readings, and to supply the deficiencies, or to correct the errors of manuscripts. The instances, however frequent, of incorrectness and variations which occur in the present work, do not by any means surprise me. After a close application to Eastern literature for nine or ten years, during which I have turned over some thousands of written volumes, and attentively collated passages in several hundreds, I no longer expect to find in Arabick, Persian, or Turkish manuscripts (the Koran always excepted), either accuracy of transcribing, fidelity of translation, or exactness of quotation. Thus, a heavy cloud of uncertainty and confusion still hangs on the Geography of Edrisi, *notwithstanding the learned labours of* Kurzmann *and of* Hartmann, *who notice the numerous defects of the printed editions, the variations of the manuscript copies, the different titles of the same book, the uncertain age and country of the author, &c.*

Of Ebn Haukal's *work, had there been found a perfect copy in the original Arabick, it is most probable that the pleasure of offering this translation to the Publick would not have been reserved for me.* " *We must lament,*" *says the in-*

genious KOEHLER*, " that no better copy of the Mesalek al
" Memalek† exists, than the manuscript preserved in the Library at Leyden, which is exceedingly imperfect and very badly written." It seems, indeed, the lot of EBN HAUKAL's work, in whatsoever form it appears, to be censured for incorrectness and defects, by writers of different ages, and of different countries; for to the passage above quoted, we may add the following from ABULFEDA:

كتاب ابن حوقل و هو مطول ذكر فيه صفات البلاد مستوفيا غير انه الم يضبط الاسماء وكذلك لم يكثر الطوال و العروض نصار غالب ما ذكره مجهول لاسم و البقعة

" The book of EBN HAUKAL is a work of considerable
" length, in which the different countries are described with
" sufficient exactness. But neither are the names of places
" marked by the proper points, nor are their longitudes or
" latitudes expressed; this frequently occasions an uncer-
" tainty respecting the places, proper names, &c."

* " EBN HAUKAL, de quo dolendum modo non integrius exemplum extare illo quod in Bibliotheca Leidensi asservatur, valde mutilum ac pessimè scriptum," &c. Proem. ad Abulfedæ Tabul. Syr. p. 11. Leips. 2d edition, 1786.

† See the Leyden Catalogue before quoted.

PREFACE.

These are censures of the original Arabick. I must now bear testimony against the Persian transcripts which I have used.

Of the difficulties arising from an irregular combination of letters, the confusion of one word with another, and the total omission, in some lines, of the diacritical points, I should not complain, because habit and persevering attention have enabled me to surmount them in passages of general description, or sentences of common construction; but in the names of persons or of places never before seen or heard of, and which the context could not assist in deciphering, when the diacritical points were omitted, conjecture alone could supply them, or collation with a more perfect manuscript. The former I have seldom indulged, and the latter has enabled me, in several instances, to ascertain the true reading; and even the few names in which I have supplied the diacritical points from conjecture, are pointed out to the reader by a note, or otherwise.

Notwithstanding what I have just said, and although the most learned writers on Hebrew, Arabick, and Persian Literature, have made observations on the same subject, it may perhaps, be necessary to demonstrate, by a particular example, the extraordinary influence of those diacritical points, which, as they are essential parts of letters, must not be confounded with the vowel points or accents.

One example will suffice—Let us suppose the three letters forming the name تبت Tibbet to be divested of their diacritical points, and thus written ٮٮٮ—The first character may be rendered, by the application of one point above, an N, thus, ں— of two points a T, ں—of three points a TH or S, ڽ ; if one point is placed under, it becomes a B ٮ—if two points, a Y ٻ—and if three points, a P ٮ. In like manner the second character may be affected, and the third character may be, according to the addition of points, rendered a B, P, T, and TH, or S.

Thus, amidst the multiplicity of names which may be formed of those three characters, it would be almost impossible, without the aid of context, or previous consideration, to ascertain the true reading: and, to use the words of GOLIUS, that most learned Orientalist, on a similar occasion, one must act the part of a diviner before he can perform that of an interpreter*.

* As the whole passage, in which Golius apologizes for the mistakes of Erpenius in his

PREFACE.

Of the terms used in mensuration, or the computation of distances by time, I must here notice the extreme uncertainty which still pervades them, although many ingenious Orientalists have endeavoured to remove it.

We are sometimes informed that one place is distant from another one month's journey: the extent of this could be easily ascertained, were the number of miles or leagues in a day's journey (یک روزه راه) *exactly known; but we cannot expect precision in this computation, since much depends on the particular mode of travelling, the state of the roads, the nature of the country, and other circumstances. Equally vague and uncertain are the terms* مرحله *merhileh and* منزل *menzil which occur in the following pages.*

Graves, *in his Preface to* Abulfeda's Chorasmia, *translates* merhileh *by* statio, diæta, mansio. *According to* Edrisi's Geo-

---

translation *of* Elmakin, *is much to my present purpose, I shall give it here.* " Nam licet
" Niloticus hunc Codicem Calamus exaraverit, nimium tamen festinantis incuria eundem
" pessimè deformârat, crebra imprimis omissione orthographicæ punctuationis: quod quidem
" vitium in metris præsertim et propriis nominibus commissum, dici haud potest quam omnia
" luxet et incerta reddat: ita ut sæpenumerò vatem priùs agere debuerit quam interpretem
" possit." *Golii Præfat. ad Erpenii Hist. Saracen. Arab. Lat. folio.*

graphy *, *the merhileh consisted of thirty miles* (مرحله ثلثون میلا), *but* ABULFEDA *considered it as various and undetermined. Both* merhileh *and* menzil *signify a stage or halting place, after a day's journey* †.

Of the parasang or farsang (فرسنک) *of Persia we can speak with greater certainty and accuracy, although it appears, from the Greek and Roman, as well as the native writers, that this measure was not always exactly ascertained, even among the Persians. Xenophon computes the pharsanga at thirty* stadia; *and Pliny informs us, that, like the* schænos, *it was a measure variously determined* ‡.

HAMDALLAH MUSTOOFI, *the celebrated Author of the* Nozahet al Coloub §, *prefaces his account of the roads and stages of* Iran *by some observations on the several measure-*

---

* *Clim. V. Sect. I.*

† *But the number of miles or farsangs in a day's journey is not ascertained; and we accordingly find mention in the following work of a* short merhileh, *and a* long merhileh; *perhaps thirty miles may be the average.*

‡ *Persæ schænos et parasangas alii alia mensura determinant.*

§ نزهت القلوب *A most valuable work, frequently quoted by* D'HERBELOT, *who styles the author* (κατ'εξοχην) " Le Geographe Persan."

PREFACE. xxiii

ments in different provinces. *The farsang or parasang (he says), in the time of the* Caianians, *or second dynasty of Persian sovereigns, contained, according to ancient writers, three miles of twelve thousand feet. According to Malek Shahi, the farsang of* Khuarezm *consisted of about fifteen thousand yards,* (کم). *In* Azerbaijan, Armenia, *and the neighbouring provinces, it contained only twelve thousand yards; while in the two* Iraks, *in* Curdistan, Laristan, Khuzistan, Fars, Shebangareh, Diarbekre, &c. *the farsang was reckoned to contain only six thousand yards; in other places it consisted of eight thousand, but may be generally computed at twelve thousand cubits,* (زرع). *The following passage, however, from the Borhan Kattea seems to fix the measure with precision:*

فرسنگ ـــــ بغتح اوّل و ثالث بروزن سرچنک قدري باشد
معيّن از راه و آن بقدار سه ميل است و هر ميلى چهار هزار
کز که مجموع فرسنک دوازده هزار کز باشد و طول هر کزي بقدر
بيست و چهار انگشت دست باشد که بعرض در پهلوي هم
کزرند. و آن شش تبضه است يعنى شش مشت

" Farasang, *with the vowel accent* fatha *over the first and
" third, equivalent (in rhyme or metre)* to Sar-i-chang, *is a cer-
" tain fixed measure for roads, consisting of about three* miles,

xxiv   PREFACE.

" *each mile containing four thousand guz; so that the farsang*
" *altogether consists of twelve thousand guz: the length of each*
" *guz is equal to twenty-four fingers measured in breadth*
" *(sideways), and making six* handfuls, *or six measures of the*
" *clenched fist.*"

In another excellent Dictionary, the کشف الغات Kashf al
Loghat, *we find the following article :*

فرسنگ بالفتح و کاف فارسي سه کروه زمین که بتازیش
فرسخ خوانند

" *Farasang, with the vowel accent* fatha, *and the Persian*
" *letter* gaf, *three krouhs of ground. In Arabick they call it*
" *farsakh.*"

The کروه krouh, *according to the* Borhan Kattea,

سه هزار کز است و بعضي گویند چهار هزار کز و زیادة از
این نیست

" *consists of three thousand guz, or, as some say, of four*
" *thousand, but it does not exceed this number.*"

PREFACE.

The guz (as above described) may be computed from twenty to twenty-four inches. Mr. RICHARDSON* informs us, that the parasang, or league, contains about eighteen thousand feet; and Captain FRANCKLIN†, whose computation I would adopt, makes it nearly equivalent to four English miles.

These and many other matters, which in the following work appear obscure or difficult, it was my intention, when I undertook this translation, to investigate with minute research, and to illustrate with ample explanations. On those subjects, also, which seemed of the most curious and interesting nature, I collected a variety of notices, and extracted from several other Oriental Manuscripts, and from the works of European Antiquaries, Historians and Travellers, every passage that could contribute information.

I endeavoured, by examining the most ancient traditions preserved in Persian records, to ascertain whether the celebrated Ruins of Istakhar, often mentioned in the course of this work, exhibit any monuments of the scriptural עילם *Elam ‡, Ελυμαίς,*

---

* *Arab. and Persian Diction. art.* فرسخ

† *Tour to Persia, quarto edition, Calcutta,* 1788, *p.* 17; *Lond. edit. octavo,* 1790, *p.* 41.

‡ *Jeremiah, xlix.*

xxvi   PREFACE.

Elymais * : *whether it was the Persepolis of classick history* †, *the palace of Darius; or whether, according to one most learned Orientalist* ‡, *an edifice of more recent date, constructed by the Arsacides. But so much did my inquiries on this subject exceed the limits of a note, that they formed, rather, a distinct essay.*

The various Languages of Persia and other countries, noticed by EBN HAUKAL, were also the subject of laborious research: through the modern Deri and Parsi, the ancient Pehlavi and Zend, I have traced every vestige that remains of the dialects used in Iran during the earliest ages §; and I have collected, rather as an Antiquary than an Etymologist, many hundred Greek and Persian words, of which the identity cannot be disputed, and must have originated from some other cause than accidental resemblance: that interchange of

---

* *Macc. Lib. I. cap. vi.*
† *Diodor. Sicul.—Arrian.—Quint. Curt. &c.*
‡ *Tychsen de Cuneatis Inscriptionibus Persepolitanis. Rostoch.* 1798.
§ *In this research I have availed myself of the learned* Burton's *aid (see his " Veteris Linguæ Persicæ* ΛΕΙΨΑΝΑ"), *the more powerful assistance of* Reland *(see his Dissert. de Vet. ling. Pers. &c.), and that of* Wahl *(in his "Allgemeine Geschichte der Morgenländischen Sprachen und Litteratur"); but I have had access to original sources unexplored by them.*

PREFACE. xxvii

*nations and of people, to which Seneca * alludes, must naturally have occasioned a confusion of languages; and the intermixture of Greek and Persian dialects would be a probable consequence of the Macedonian conquest.*

Several pages, also, were filled with observations on EBN HAUKAL's *account of the* Magi, *or* Fire-worshippers: *one passage, which, for obvious reasons, I have translated into Latin, will be found to bear testimony in favour of Anquetil du Perron.*

On another part of this volume I was induced to bestow some inquiry, since it serves to illustrate, and is itself confirmed by, a Rabbinical work of high reputation. I allude to EBN HAUKAL's *description of the* Land of Khozr; *and to the Hebrew composition, entitled,* ספר כוזרי Sepher Cosri, *written about the year* 1140 *of the Christian æra, by* ר' יהודה הלוי

---

* *Consolat. ad Helviam. cap. vi.* " *Videbis gentes populosque mutasse sedem. Quid sibi volunt in mediis Barbarorum regionibus Græcæ urbes? Quid inter Indos Persasque Macedonicus sermo? &c. Atheniensis in Asia turba est.*" *I have already had occasion to quote these passages in the Preface to the* " Oriental Collections."

e 2

Rabbi Iehudah the Levite, *in honour of the Jewish monarch of that country* *.

From a multiplicity of Eastern traditions concerning the land of Yajouge *and* Majouge *(or Gog and Magog), I collected whatever could illustrate that subject, over which a veil of obscurity still hangs, notwithstanding the endeavours of* Bochart † *and* D'Herbelot ‡ *to remove it. It is unnecessary to mention any other European writer, however ingenious, since, if not skilled in the languages of Asia, or not having better sources of information than those eminent Orientalists above named, all that he can offer is mere conjecture.*

EBN HAUKAL's *account of* Spain *afforded subject for many observations, and my remarks on the* Pyramids of Egypt *occupied several pages. The vestiges of* Jewish *and* Christian *establishments pointed out by our Author in various parts of the following Work, appeared worthy of being examined with*

---

* *This work was published by the learned* Buxtorf, *with a Latin translation, at Basil,* 1660, *quarto; and in his* Bibliotheca Rabbinica, *p.* 298 *(Basil. duod.* 1613*), he celebrates it as* Liber multiplicis doctrinæ ac multæ laudis.

† *Geograph. Sacr. Lib. III. cap. xiii.*

‡ *Bibliot. Orient. article Iagiouge.*

PREFACE. xxix

attention: and I took some trouble in comparing his account of many natural curiosities with the descriptions given us by travellers.

I found, however, that these illustrations, whether to be printed in the form of notes, or as an appendix, would retard considerably the publication of my book, and render it doubly expensive by the addition of so much as another volume of equal size would scarcely contain. I therefore resolved to content myself with offering to the Publick a mere translation of EBN HAUKAL's *work, retaining what the Geographer and Critick will probably esteem the most essential part of the original, all names of places in the proper character; and so exactly have I followed the orthography of my manuscript, that in many pages the same word will be found spelt differently, and even erroneously* *. *Some of the most obscure, difficult, or doubtful passages, I have remarked in short notes, or endeavoured to illustrate in the Appendix, where many are given in Persian.*

---

* *Thus we find; in p.* 48, طبريه Tiberiah *and* طبرثه Tiberthah—*in several places,* Isfahan, Sfahan, Ispahan, &c. *The Pyramids of Egypt (properly written* اهرام *or* الاهرامان Ahram *or* Elheraman) *are styled, in page* 33, هومان Houman *or* الهومان Elhouman.

PREFACE.

The chief obscurity, as well as importance, consists in the proper names. From my accuracy, therefore, in observing the original orthography of these, every advantage which could result from a perusal of the manuscript is presented to the reader; for the passages merely descriptive or narrative contain few difficulties, and these few are noticed.

The illustrations and notes above mentioned, as I have reason to hope that the time and labour spent in collecting them were not employed in vain, shall soon be offered to the Publick. They will form part of a Work in which I propose to examine the Geographical System of the Asiaticks—to extract, from a multiplicity of Arabick and Persian Authors, their descriptions of Countries and Cities, Rivers, Mountains, Seas, Islands, &c.—to give exact imitations of many original Maps preserved in rare and curious manuscripts; and to inquire how far the Geographers of Asia agree with those of ancient Greece and Rome, and with modern Europeans. I shall collect all the traditions that can illustrate local History and Antiquities; and construct Maps, according to the best authorities, not only of the Asiatick regions, but of Africa and Europe, as described by Eastern writers **.*

---

* *Besides the Geographical Treatises of* Abulfeda, Edrisi *and others, well known to the*

PREFACE.   xxxi

In preparing for publication the Geography of EBN HAU-KAL, *had I solicited, I would most probably have received, assistance from many learned friends; and I should, in this place, with equal pride and pleasure, have followed the example of those writers who appropriate a department of their Prefaces to a publick acknowledgment of their numerous obligations.*

But on this subject I shall not long detain the reader; for

publick, I have used, in compiling materials for this Work, a variety of Oriental Manuscripts but little known in Europe. Among these are the هفت اقليم Heft Aklim, or Seven Climates, by Emir Rauzi; the شيرازنامه Shiraz Nameh, by Sheikh Zarkoub; the نزهت القلوب Nozhat al Coloub of Hamdallah Mustoufi, so often quoted by D'Herbelot; the عجايب البلدان Ajaieb al Boldan, or "Wonders of Regions; the تحقيق الاعراب Tahkik al Irab, a Geographical Dictionary, by Mohammed Saduk Isfahani; the تحفت العراقين Tohfut al Irakein, or Poetical Description of the two Iraks, Arabian and Persian provinces, by the celebrated Khakani; the عجايب الغرايب Ajaieb al Gheraieb; the عجايب المخلوقات Ajaieb al Mahkloucat; the صور الاقاليم Sour al Akalim; the سيرالبلاد Seir al Belad; the Geographical Index at the end of Mirkhond's Rozet al Sefa, &c. These, with the assistance of EBN HAUKAL'S work, have enabled me to construct a Map of Persia and the adjacent provinces, on so large a scale as to admit a multiplicity of names not found in any other. It comprehends (on a sheet measuring six feet by five) nearly the same extent as Mr. Wahl's celebrated Map, prefixed to his " Altes und Neues Vorder und Middel Asien;" and the names of places are written, not only in European characters, but respectively in Arabick, Persian, Armenian, &c.

my debt of gratitude is single. To the Provost and Fellows of Eton College *I am indebted, not only for frequent opportunities of collating their manuscript with my own, but for the most liberal hospitality and the most polite attention. Through their indulgence I have been enabled to supply some deficiencies, and correct several errors, which must otherwise have disfigured this translation: whatever imperfections still remain, would probably have been removed by the collation of a third copy with the two which I have used. A third copy, however, I sought in vain; although, from information, communicated by an ingenious friend, I have reason to believe that* EBN HAUKAL's *work is among the manuscripts belonging to a certain learned Society: but I must regret that it is not found in any other library of this metropolis to which I have been admitted. Such as it is, I am not without hopes that this work will prove acceptable to the Orientalist, the Antiquary, and the Geographer. If their approbation be withheld, I shall acknowledge that I have toiled in vain; for the result of my former labours has taught me to expect no other recompense than praise, and the hopes of substantial profit have been extinguished by successive disappointments.*

CONTENTS.

	Page
INTRODUCTION	1
The Author's Design, and the Plan of his Work	2
General Outlines of the Countries he proposes to describe	5
Description of the Seas	6
Of the Sea of Roum, or the Mediterranean, and other matters	7
Yajouge and Majouge, Cheen, Africa, Caspian Sea, Franks	8
Cheen, Maweralnahr, Nubians, Constantinople, Canouje, Siklab, Yajouge	9
Tibet, Rous, Jews turned into Monkies	10
Dejleh, or Tigris, Yemen, Oman	11
Of Bajeh, Abyssinia, and Nubia	13
Of Magreb (or the West) Part of Africa, its Distances and Stages	16
Andalus, or Part of Spain	18
Account of Egypt	29
Sham or Syria	37
Distances of Places in Sham and Jezireh	47
Mediterranean Sea	51
Jezireh, or Mesopotamia	54
Distances of Places in Jezireh	55
Towns and Districts of Jezireh	55
Description of Diar Modhar	58
Irak Arabi	61
Cities and Towns of Irak Arabi	63
Province of Khuzistan	72

CONTENTS.

	Page
Description of Pars, or Farsistan	81
The Kourehs of Pars	82
Joums of the Curds	83
Rivers of Pars	84
Lakes of Pars	84
Fire-temples	85
Districts of the Koureh of Istakhar	86
Ardeshir Koureh	87
Ardeshir Khereh	88
Account of the Territories of Darabgird	89
Koureh Shapour	89
Koureh Arghan	90
Account of the Zems	92
Of the Fortresses and Castles of Pars, and Fire-temples of Pars	95
Rivers of Pars	96
Lakes of Pars	98
Great Cities and remarkable Edifices	100
Koureh of Shapour	103
Koureh of Darabjird	104
Distances of Places in Pars	105
Road from Shiraz to Jenabah	106
Road from Shiraz to Sirgan	107
Road from Shiraz to Kattah	108
Road from Shiraz to Isfahan	109
Road from Shiraz to Arjan	110
Stages and Distances between the principal Towns of Pars	111
Of the Water, Climate, and Soil of Pars	112
Of the Persons, Manners, Languages, Religions, and chief Families of the People of Pars	114
Account of the most extraordinary Edifices in Pars, and other Curiosities	128
Commodities and Productions of Pars	132
Money, Weights, and Measures of the People of Pars	134
The Gates of Wealth, or the Manner of raising the Revenue	136
Of the Province of Kirman	138

CONTENTS.

	Page
Mountains, Inhabitants, and chief Cities of Kirman	140
Distances of Places in Kirman	144
Of the Country of Sind, and Part of Hind	146
The Cities and Towns	147
Distances of Places in Sind	153
Rivers of Sind	155
Description of Armenia, Aran, and Azerbaijan	156
Rivers and Lakes of those Countries, and other matters	161
Distances of Places	163
Description of Kouhestan, or Irak Ajemi	165
Road from Hamadan to Deinour	167
Cities and Towns in Irak Ajemi	168
Provinces of Deilman and Taberistan	174
Stages and Distances	180
Road from Rey to Khorasan	181
From Taberistan to Gurkan	182
From Amol to Deilem	183
Of the Sea of Khozr, or the Caspian	183
Roads and Stages of Khozr	191
Deserts between Pars and Khorasan	192
Route from Rey to Isfahan	195
From Mabein to Khorasan	196
Road of Shour	197
Road of Ravan	198
Road of Khebeis	199
Stages and Distances from Yezd to Khorasan	200
The New Road	202
Account of Seiestan, or Sejestan	203
Rivers of Sejestan	205
Distances and Stages	209
Road from Sejestan to Bost	209
From Bost to Ghizni	210
From Sejestan, by the Desert	211
Road from Sejestan to Kirman and Fars	211
Account of the Province of Khorasan	212

CONTENTS.

	Page
Roads and Stages of Khorasan	227
——————of Meru	230
——————of Balkh	230
Distances and Roads of the Towns in Kuhestan	231
Account of Maweralnahr, or Transoxania	232
City of Kash	259
City of Naksheb	260
Setroushteh	261
Road from the River Jihoun to Ferghaneh	273
Distances of Stages on the Road of Chaje	274
Road from Samarcand to Balkh	275
Distances and Routes of the principal Cities of Maweralnahr,	276
Distances and Stages of Termed and Cheghanian	277
Distances and Routes of the Towns of Bokhara	278
Distances and Stages of the Towns of Soghd and Samarcand	279

كتاب مسالك و ممالك تصنيف ابن حوقل

THE ORIENTAL GEOGRAPHY

OF

EBN HAUKAL.

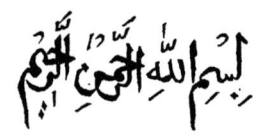

بسم الله الرحمن الرحيم

In the name of God, the Clement, the Merciful!

PRAISE be to God, the origin of all good! and may the blessing of God be on Mohammed, the Prince of Prophets! Thus says the author of the work: "My design, in the composition of this book, is to describe the various climates and regions of the face of the earth, comprised within the circle of *Islam*, or Mohammedanism, and their several divisions, in such a manner that every remarkable place belonging to each region shall be noticed, and all the boundaries and territories depending on them, their districts, cities, mountains, rivers, lakes, and deserts."

(2)

But as the particular details of all these seemed unnecessarily prolix, they are here compressed within a small compass; and in the present volume, which is entitled *Mesalek u Memalek*, our plan is to describe, and to delineate on maps, the various seas or oceans which surround the land, the inhabited and the desert islands, and every climate and region of the earth; affixing the name of each, so that it may be known in the maps; and confining ourselves to those countries which are the seat of *Islam*, and the residence of true believers.

We begin with *Arabia*, because the Temple of the Lord is situated there, and the holy *Kaaba** is the Navel of the World; and Mecca is styled, in the sacred writings, "*the Parent City*," or "*the Mother of Towns*†. Then we proceed to describe the درياي پارس *Deryai-Pars*, or Persian Sea, which bounds a portion of Arabia: then we speak of the western countries, زمين مغرب *Zemeen-i-Magreb* (part of Africa); then we describe the land of Egypt, مصر *Misr*; then Syria, شام *Sham*; then the درياي روم *Deryai Roum*, or Mediterranean Ocean; then the province of جزيره *Jezireh*, Mesopotamia; then عراق عرب *Irak Arabi*; then خوزستان *Khuzistan*, Susiana; then پارس *Pars*, or *Farsistan*; then كرمان *Kirman*; then منصوره *Mansoureh*, the places bordering on سند و هند *Sind* and *Hind*, the confines of

---

* كعبه The square Temple at Mecca; built, according to Mohammedan tradition, by Abraham.

† *Omm'al kura.* ام القري

Hindoostan, and such towns of these as contain Mussulman inhabitants: then we describe اذربايگان *Azerbaigan*, and its territories; then کوهستان *Kouhestan*; then دیلمان *Deilman*; then the دریای خزر *Deryai Khozr*, or Caspian Sea, and the various nations surrounding it; then the deserts between خراسان *Khorasan* and *Fars*; then the province of سیستان *Seiestan*; then *Khorasan* and ماوراالنهر *Maweralnahr*, or Transoxania.

(Here, in the original manuscript, a blank page occurs, on which was to have been delineated a general Map of the World, or the Eastern Hemisphere.)

The author of this work informs us, that such is the form of the earth, its various parts, inhabited and uninhabited. We have divided it into empires or states, ممالک *memalek*: and the signification of this word is پادشاهها *kingdoms*; in the singular, مملکت *memleket*, one kingdom or state. Of all the regions of this earth, none is more populous, cultivated, or flourishing, than the empire of ایران *Iran*, or Persia; the chief glory of which, in former times, was بابل *Babel* (Babylon.) This is the country of پارس *Pars*: and the extent of this empire, in the time of the ancient Persians, is well known; but the Mussulmans have since possessed themselves of the countries above enumerated; such as روم *Roum,* Natolia; and شام *Sham,* Syria; and مصر *Misr,* Egypt; and اندلس *Andalus,* Andalusia or Spain; and مغرب *Magreb,* the west (part of Africa), and part of *Hindoostan;* and the territories of منصوره *Mansoureh,* as far as ملتان *Multan;* and كابلستان *Kabulistan;* and the borders of تخارستان *Tokharestan;* and of چين *Cheen,* China or Tartary; and ماوراٴ لنهر *Maweralnahr,* or Transoxania. The author says, that he reckons, as belonging to روم *Roum,* the borders of سقلاب *Siklab,* Sclavonia; of روس *Rous,* Russia, سرير *Serir,* and الان *Allan,* and ارمن *Armen,* Armenia, where the Christian religion is professed; and he places, as belonging to *Hindoostan,* سند *Sind,* and كشمير *Cashmere,* and part of تبت *Tibet.* "As for the land of blacks, in the west (Africa), and the زنكيان *Zingians,* Æthiopians, and such tribes (says the author), I make but slight mention of them in this book; because, naturally loving wisdom, ingenuity, religion, justice, and regular government, how could I notice such people as those, or exalt them by inserting an account of their countries? Yet one race of them has some degree of civilization and religious observance, the نوبيان *Nubians,* and حبشيان *Habbeshians,* Abbyssinians: the reason of this is, their vicinity to the other more polished countries; thus نوبه *Nubia* and حبشه *Habbesheh,* Abyssinia, are situated on the borders of the درياي قلزم *Deryai Kolzum,* the *Sea of Kolzum,* or Red Sea. Nothing farther can be said in their favour."

The region of *Islam* is superior to the others, because it is more extensive; from south to north, and from the western bay or gulph, connected with the ocean, to the borders of چین ماچین *Cheen Macheen* (the southern parts of China), and another bay or gulph, likewise joining the ocean, from the west (Africa), to اندلس *Andalus*, Spain. The author informs us that he has drawn a line through this map, dividing it into two parts, and passing from the *Persian Sea* to the land of *Hindoostan*, through the midst of the region of *Islam*; likewise from the land of Egypt to the west of Africa. The inhabitants of the northern parts of these countries are of a fair complexion; those who dwell still farther north are more fair skinned, and their climate is cold. The inhabitants of the south are of a dark complexion, and the blackness of their skins increases as they dwell farther to the south.

On the east of the land of *Islam* are the regions of *Hindoostan* and the دریای پارس *Persian Sea*; to the west lie روم *Roum*, and ارمن *Armen*, and الان *Allan*, and سریر *Serir*, and خزر *Khozr*, and روس *Rous*, and بلغار *Bulgar*, and سقلاب *Siklab*, and part of ترکستان *Turkestan*. The land of Islam has to the north the empire of چین *Cheen*, and its various territories from the borders of *Turkestan*; and to the south the *Persian Sea*, and the region of سند *Sind*. The *Ocean* bounds it to the west and to the south.

ذکر دریاها

Description of the Seas.

The chief Seas are the دریای پارس *Persian*, and دریای روم the Sea of *Roum*, or the *Mediterranean*, which are nearly opposite: both join the great ocean. The Persian Sea is more extensive in length and breadth, reaching to the land of چین *Cheen*, and to the دریای قلزم *Sea of Kolzum*. From *Kolzum* to *Cheen*, in a streight line, is a distance of about two hundred *menzil**; and from Kolzum to عراق *Irak*, by the way of the desert, is a journey of two months. From the جیحون *Jihoun*, or Oxus, to the extreme boundary of *Islam*, on the borders of فرغانه *Ferghanah*, is above twenty *merhileh**; and, from those places to the coast of *Cheen*, is a very tedious way, because in these seas are various windings and turnings.

* See the Preface.

ذكر دريا روم و غيره

Of the Sea of Roum, or the Mediterranean, and other matters.

THIS sea comes from the ocean, and extends from that narrow bay, or pass, between the west (Africa), and the land of اندلس *Andalus*, Spain, to the coast of شام *Sham*, Syria, a distance of seven months journey. This sea is of a more regular and even outline than the *Persian*; for, after you pass the mouth of that bay before mentioned (*Gibraltar*), it is protracted in one line to the end.

From مصر *Egypt* to the extremity of the west مغرب *Magreb*, is a distance of an hundred and eighty merhileh. From the extremity of the east to that of the west, is near four hundred merhileh. From روم *Roum*, one comes to شام *Sham* (Syria) in the course of sixty merhileh. From *Sham* to مصر *Egypt* is thirty merhileh. The distance of the journey between the land of ياجوج *Yajouge* and بلغار *Bulgar*, and the country of سقلاب *Siklab*, is about four hundred merhileh; and from *Siklab* to روم *Roum*, to the borders of *Sham*, sixty merhileh. From *Roum* to the extreme boundary of the زمين نوبيان land of the *Nubians*, about eighty merhileh.

Between ياجوج و ماجوج *Yajouge* and *Majouge,* and the northern ocean, and between the deserts of the Blacks and the other limits of the ocean, all is desolate and waste, without any buildings. I know not what are the roads or stages of those two deserts which are on the coasts of the ocean, because it is impossible to travel in them on account of the excessive heat, which hinders the building of houses, or the residing there. Thus, also, in the south, no animal can exist, so excessive is the heat, nor any person dwell there. But between چين *Cheen* and the west مغرب *Magreb,* all is inhabited, and the ground cultivated, and the ocean surrounds the land like a collar or necklace.

From this ocean proceed the درياي فارس *Deryai Fars,* Persian Sea or Gulph, and درياي روم *Deryai Roum,* Mediterranean, but not the درياي خزر *Deryai Khozr,* or Caspian Sea. If any person wish to make a circuit round this sea, he must set out from *Khozr,* and proceed through the land of ديلمان *Deilman,* and طبرستان *Tabaristan,* and گرکان *Gurkan,* and, turning by the desert, in the vicinity of سياه کوه *Siah Kouh,* or the Black Mountain, thus come back to the place from which he had set out, as nothing would impede him but the river which falls into the Caspian Sea.

The Franks, in general, we speak of as belonging to روم *Roum* (Europe), because they have the same religion and king, though speaking various dialects.

The empire of چین *Cheen* extends, in length, a distance of four months journey; and in breadth, three. And when one comes from the mouth of the bay or gulph خلج to the land of Mussulmans, the borders of ماورا لنهر *Mauweralnahr*, Transoxania, it is a journey of three months. And when one comes from the east, and wishes to proceed to the west, by the land of نوبیان *Nubians*, and the land of خرخیز *Khurkhiz*, and of غرغز *Ghurghez*, and by کیماک *Kaimak* to the sea, it is a journey of about four months. In the regions of *Cheen* there are various dialects: but all ترکستان *Turkestan*, and غرغز *Ghurghez*, and عصه *Assah*, and خرخیز *Khurkhiz*, and کیماک *Kaimak*, and غرنه *Ghurneh*, and خرنجیه *Khurnjiah*; the people of all these have the same language, and are of one kind. The chief place of the empire of Cheen is called حمدان *Humdan*, as تصطنطینه *Costantineh*, Constantinople, is of Europe, or بغداد *Bagdad*, of the land of *Islam*, or قنوج *Canouge*, of Hindoostan; but the land of *Turk*, ترک زمین is separately situated. غز *Ghuz* is the boundary of it from خزر *Khozr* to کیماک *Kaimak*, and to خرنجیه *Khurnjiah* and بلغار *Bulgar*, and the borders of the land of Mussulmans from کرکان *Gurkan* to باراب *Barab*, and to سنجاب *Senjab*.

When you pass from the territories of *Kaimak*, then it is the land of خدرج *Khederje*, lying to the north, between غز *Ghuz* and خرخیز *Khurkhiz*, and behind سقلاب *Siklab*; and the land of یاجوج *Yajouge* is situated in the north, when you turn from

Siklab, and pass the bounds of *Kaimak*; but the extent of *Yajouge,* and the number of its inhabitants, are known to God Almighty alone. There is a place of *Khurkhiz,* situated between *Ghuz,* and *Kaimak,* and the ocean, and the land of خدرج *Khederje.* The country of تبت *Tibet* is situated between *Khurkhiz* and the empire of *Cheen. Cheen* lies between the sea and the land of *Ghuz* and *Tibet*; and *Cheen* itself constitutes this climate (or division); but the other parts of Tibet were annexed to it, as in Europe the lesser places depend on Constantinople, and in the region of Islam on *Iran,* which is the land of بابل *Babel.*

Of سقلاب *Siklab,* the extent is about two months journey; بلغار *Bulgar* is a small town, which has not many territories, and for that reason the places belonging to it have been well known. The روس *Rous* are a people between whom and *Bulgar* is a tribe of ترکان *Turks*; in one place here some fishermen reside, and there are a few date trees, as far as ثاران *Saran,* and چیلاق *Cheilak,* and opposite the mountains to ابله *Ableh. Ableh* is a small town, well inhabited, with a little tilled and cultivated land. " In that place were some Jews; those to
" whom it was forbidden to hunt on the Sabbath (or Sunday):
" and God transformed them, and caused them to become
" monkies*.

* و انجا جهودان باشند انارا که صبد روز شنبه برایشان حرام شد و خدای ایشان مسخ کرد و بوزینه کردانیه

As for مداين *Madaein*, and its territories, as far as يمن *Yemen* (Arabia Felix), and to عمان *Oman*, and بحرين *Bahrein*, (islands in the Persian Gulph), as far as عبادان *Abadan*; of all these we describe the roads as belonging to Arabia: but *Abadan* is a small fort or castle, inhabited, on the sea-coast, and the waters of the دجله *Dejleh* (or Tigris) come up there. This is a *rebat*, or station, where sentinels used to be placed, that they might watch the دزدان دريا *robbers of the sea*, or pirates. The river دجله *Dejleh*, or Tigris, passes here; and thence we come by the sea-shore to ماهي رويان *Mahi-rouian*, on the borders of *Pars*, or Persia. On this journey it is necessary in most of the places to go by water; because the river of خوزستان *Khuzistan* winds about دورق *Daurak*, and flows to حصن مهدي *Hysn Mohdi*, and رامنان *Ramnan*, and then falls into the sea at ماهي رويان *Mahi-rouian*; and this *Mahi-rouian* is a small town, well-inhabited, and pleasant, the port for ارغان *Arghan*, or the pass to it. Then we come to سينير *Sinir*, which is larger than *Mahi-rouian*; and this Sinir is the port of all *Pars* or Farsistan. From thence the sea-shore winds on to بجرم *Bijerm*. Between جنابه *Jenabeh* and *Bijerm*, there are groves, and meadows, and villages; and the air becomes very warm here. From this you proceed to سيراف *Siraf*, one of the most ample harbours in all *Pars*. Siraf is a large town از اعيان شهرهاي فارس *one of the eyes of the towns of Fars*. Here there is not any husbandry or cultivation of ground; and they bring water from a distance.

(12)

Passing from this along the shore, by places where there are hills and deserts, you come to the حصن ابن عبارّه *Hysn ebn ómarreh*. This is a very strong castle: in all Pars there is not any fort more strong, or in better condition; and it is thought that there is an allusion to the lords of this castle in that passage of the Koran, where it is said,

وَ كَانَ وَرَآءَ هُمْ مَلِكٌ يَأْخُذُ كُلَّ سَفِينَةٍ غَصْبًا

" *And there was, behind them, a king who forcibly seized on* " *every (sound) ship**.

From this place you proceed to هرموز *Hormuz*, which is the port of کرمان *Kirman*. *Hormuz* is a well-inhabited and flourishing city: it abounds in dates, and the air is exceedingly warm. From this you go to ديبل *Daibul*, where there are merchants, who trade in all places. This is the port of the land of سند *Sind*: and *Sind* is the same as منصوره *Mansureh*; and the region of لطيان *Lattian*, as far as چين *Cheen*, extends along the coast of *Hindoostan*, to تبت *Tibet*, and چين ماچين *Cheen Macheen*, beyond which no one passes.

---

* *Koran*, سورت الكهف *Chapter of the Cavern*. This king, according to some Mohammedan commentators, reigned in *Oman*. See SALE's Koran, Chap. xviii.—POCOCKE's Specim. Histor. Arab. p. 42. &c.

ذكر بجه و حبش و نوبه

Of Bajeh, and Abyssinia, and Nubia.

FROM كلزم *Kolzum*, on the west of the sea (the Red Sea), the dry deserts stretch very far, to the land of بجه *Bajeh*. The inhabitants of *Bajeh* are blacker than the Abbyssinians, like the Arabs*; and they have not either cities, villages, nor cultivated land---nothing but what they bring from *Yemen, Abbyssinia, Egypt*, or the land of the *Greeks* زمين يونان.

This country *(Bajeh)* is situated between حبش *Habesh*, Abbyssinia, the land of نوبه *Nubia*, and *Egypt*. In it are gold mines, which extend from near the borders of Egypt to a certain castle on the sea-coast, which they call عسات *Assat*†; a distance of about ten merhileh. Among these mines is a place called علامي *Allami*, situated on a level ground. There are not in any quarter of the world such gold mines as these. In *Bajeh* they worship idols, or any thing that seems pleasing to their eyes. Those who immediately border on the land of Abbyssinia are Christians, and of the same complexion as Arabians.

* Probably it should have been "Blacker than the Arabs, and like the Abbyssinians."

† This word is so equivocally written in the MSS. that it may be *Assab*, &c.

On the sea-coast there is a place called زيلع *Zeilaa*, which is the port for those who go to *Yemen* and حجاز *Hejaz*. Then begin the deserts of نوبه *Nubia*. The *Nubians* are Christians; and their country is wider than that of the Abyssinians; and " the Ægyptian Nile passes through their territories, and goes on " to the land of the *Zingians* (Æthiopia); and one cannot proceed " beyond that *."

The sea continues to the land of زنكبار *Zingbar*, Æthiopia, opposite عدن *Aden*: thence it departs from the regions of Islam. Æthiopia is a dry country, with few buildings, and very little cultivated ground. The leopard skins, and other spotted skins which are brought into *Yemen*, come from this place. The inhabitants are at war with the Mussulmans. There is in *Zingbar* a race of white people, who bring from other places articles of food and clothing. This country produces little: the inhabitants are not much inclined to the cultivation of arts or sciences.

So far we have spoken of those countries bordering on the Persian Sea: Now we proceed to describe the regions of the West.

* نيل مصريان بناحيت ايشان گذرد و بزنكبان رسد و بعد از آن نتوان رفتن
The last sentence (which seems obscure) is literally, " and after that it is impossible to go on."

ذكر ديار مغرب

Of Magreb (the West), or part of Africa.

THIS western region is situated along the روم درياي *Mediterranean Sea*, and is divided into two parts---one, the eastern ---the other, western. To the eastern division belong برته *Barkah*, and افرنقيه *Afrinkeieh*, and تاهوث *Tahouth*, and ملنجه *Melinjeh*, and سوس *Sus*, and زويله *Zouilah*; and all on the sea. The western division extends to اندلس *Andaluṣ*.

The sea, to the east, reaches as far as Egypt. From Egypt we proceed to مهديه *Mohediah*, and جزيره بني ربهي *Jezireh Beni Rebehi* (or رعي *Raai*), and بصيره *Basireh*, and اربله *Arbleh*, and سوس *Sus*, where are deserts without any sort of habitations. To the south of these places is sand.

(Map of the West.)

Alhakem ben Hesham ben Abdarrahman ben Moawiyah ben Hesham ben Abdalmulk ben Merwan ben Alhakm*. The first of those who passed over to اندلس *Andalus* was *Abdarrahman ben Moawiyah*; he conquered it in the beginning of the reign of the sons of *Abbas* (Abbasides); and the government of it remains still in his family.

Magreb (the west) or Africa, is chiefly remarkable for the black slaves: it is the land of blacks. The white slaves come from the quarter of *Andalus*; and damsels of great value, such as are sold for one thousand *dinars* or more; and mules fit for the saddle; and the coarse woollen stuff, called نبد مغربي *Nemed Magrebi*; and coral, and ambergris, and gold, and honey, and silk, and seal-skins.

ذكر مسافات ديار مغرب

The Distances and Stages of Magreb, or part of Africa.

From مصر *Misr* to برقه *Barkah*, twenty merhileh; from *Barkah* to طرابلس *Trablis* (Tripoli), twenty merhileh; from *Trablis* to قيروان *Kirouan* and شطيف *Shatif*, sixteen merhileh;

---

* الحاكم بن هشام بن عبد الرحمن بن معاوبه بن هشام بن عبد الملك بن مروان بن الحكم

from *Shatif* to تاهوث *Tahouth,* twenty merhileh; from *Tahouth* to فاس *Fas* (Fez), fifty merhileh; from *Fas* to سوس اقصي *Sus-aksi,* or *Sus* the boundary, near thirty merhileh; from *Kirouan* to *Sus-aksi,* about one hundred and sixteen merhileh. The whole distance from *Misr* to the boundary of the eastern division of the west, on the Mediterranean Sea, is about six months journey.

From *Kirouan* to زويله *Zouilah,* is a journey of one month; from *Kirouan* to *Mohadieh,* two days journey; from *Kirouan* to the town of لولس or بوس * three merhileh; from that to طرفه *Tarfah,* ten merhileh; from *Tarfah* to تنيس *Teneis (Tunis?)* about sixteen merhilch; from *Teneis* to the جزيره رعي *Jezireh Rahey,* five days journey; from تاهوث *Tahouth* to باكور *Bakour,* thirty merhileh; from Tahouth to سجلماسه *Se-jelmasah,* fifteen merhileh; and from فاس *Fas* to بصيره *Basireh,* six merhileh; and from *Fas* to ارمه *Armeh,* eight merhileh: and from *Kirouan* to سجلماسه *Sejelmasah,* by way of the desert, is a journey of near fifty merhileh.

* This name is so equivocally written in the MSS. that it may be *Lules, Tules, Boules, Nules,* &c. or *Boutes, Nubes, Tunis,* &c.

ذكر ديار اندلس

Of *Andalus*, or part of *Spain*.

FROM قرطبه *Cortubah* (which is the chief town of Andalus) to سبليه *Sebiliah*, is a journey of three merhileh; from *Cortubah* to سرفصه *Sarfassah* or *Sarkassah*, five days journey; and to بطيله *Batilah*, thirteen days journey; from *Batilah* to ارده *Ardah*, four merhileh; from *Cortubah* to مكبا *Mekiah*, three or four days journey; from *Cortubah* to توريه *Kourieh*, twelve days journey; from *Kourieh* to مارده *Mardah*, four days journey; from *Kourieh* to ناحيه *Nahiah*, six days journey; from *Cortubah* to طليطيه *Toletiah*, six days journey; from *Toletiah* to وادي الحجار *Wadi al hejar*, two days journey; from ماحيه *Mahiah*, or ماجه *Majeh*, to سيرين *Sirin*, twelve days journey; and to the extremity of the district of *Sirin*, كوره سيرين five days: from *Cortubah* to فحص البلوط *Fahas-alilout*, or *Kahas-alilout*, to the town called غافث *Ghafek*, one day's journey; from *Fahas-alilout* to بلبله *Bilbilah*, four days journey; from *Cortubah* to فرنويه *Fernouiah* (or ترنويغه *Kornouifah*), in the west, four days journey. Between ماجه *Majeh* and سبليه *Sebiliah*, on the road to مارده *Mardah*; from *Farmouiah* (or ترموره *Carmourah*), to *Sebiliah*,

(19)

twelve days journey; from اسبيجه *Asijeh** to مالغه *Malaca*, near ten days journey; and from *Malaca* to the *Jezireh*, الجزيره *Aljezireh*, of the كوه طارق *Mount-Tarek* (Gibraltar), four days journey; from *Cortubah* to ملسه *Melisah*, twelve days; from طرسوسه *Tarsousah* to *Melisah*, twelve days journey.

(Here is a sudden transition to the African coast, not marked in the original Manuscript by any Division, or Head of a new Section.)

برقه *Barkah* is a town of a middling size, neither great nor small, with an improved and well-inhabited neighbourhood, all about which, on every side, is the desert wherein the بربريان *Barbarians* reside. A Collector of Revenues, or Tax-gatherer, used to come here annually from Egypt, until the time that *Abdallah* assumed the government of the West.

طرابلس *Trabolis* belongs to the region of افريقيه *Africa*. It is a town built of stone, on the coast of the Mediterranean Sea, and a very strong place.

مهديه *Mahadiah* is a small town, which was built by *Abdallah*

---

* Probably for اسبيليه *Asebiliah*, as the name of *Seville* is sometimes written.

when he conquered the West: he gave it this name after himself*. It is situated on the sea coast. From طيروان *Kirouan* to this place is a journey of two days.

طبريه *Tiberiah* is a small town, which produces deadly scorpions, like those of *Leshkur*†; and here, out in the sea, coral is found, such as no other part of the world affords.

The جزيره بني ربهي *Jezireh Beni Rebehi* is a populous and well-supplied town, inhabited by the بربر *Berbers*. باكور *Bakour* is a considerable town on the sea-coast, well-inhabited and strong. بصيره *Basireh* is also a large town, and well-supplied, situated opposite جزيره *Jezireh*, or the place which they call جبال طارق *Jebal-tarek*, Gibraltar. Between this place (Basireh) and *Jezireh*, the breadth of the sea is twelve farsang‡.

اربله *Arbilah* is a large town on the sea-side: *Arbilah* and *Basireh* belong to the district of طنجه *Tanjiah*, Tangiers.— سوس اقصي *Sus-aski* is a considerable and fertile district, inhabited by بربريان *Berbers*. طنجه *Tanjiah* is an extensive district,

* This founder of the Fatemite Dynasty assumed the title of *Mehedi*, or Director of the Faithful; and began to reign Anno Hegiræ 296, (Anno Domini 908.)

† شهر لشكر The town of *Leshkur*, or *Asker Mokrem*, in the province of *Khuzistan*, in Persia;—a considerable city of the third climate—according to the *Nozhat al Coloub*, از همه ولايت خوزستان خوشهواتر و اما در او عقارب بسياراست
" Of more salubrious air than any other place in Khuzistan, but abounding in scorpions."

‡ On the subject of this, and other measures, see the Preface.

(21)

in which are cities, villages, and deserts on the borders of بربر *Berber*, Barbary. The capital of this country is فاس *Fas*, Fez, in which resides يابحي فاطمي *Iahia the Fatemite*; for عبدالله فاطمي *Abdallah the Fatemite* has not yet conquered that place*.

Bakour, and *Jezireh Beni Rel'ehi*, which we have before mentioned, and about ten other towns in the vicinity of *Tahouth*, are considerable. تاهوث *Tahouth* is the chief: it is a large town, well inhabited and supplied. The inhabitants practise agriculture:---they have been conquered by a people called باصنا *Basna*.

سجلماسه *Sejelmasah* is a town of middling size, belonging to the territories of *Tahouth*. One cannot enter *Sejelmasah* but by the way of the desert, which the sand renders difficult. This town is situated near the gold mines, between them and the land of the Blacks, and the land of زويله *Zouilah*. These mines are said to be of the most pure and excellent gold; but it is difficult to work them, and the way to them is dangerous and troublesome. They say that the district of *Tahouth* is reckoned as belonging to افريقيه *Africa*.

---

* The Fatemite Dynasty commenced in the year of the Hegira 296, (A. D. 908,) and lasted 172 years.---*See* D'Herbelot, Art. *Fathemiah*.

شطيف *Shateif*, is a considerable town, and well-inhabited, between *Tahouth* and تيروان *Kirouan*. The inhabitants are a tribe of *Berbers*, and called كنامه *Kenamah*. *Abdallah* has subdued them; and *Abu-Abdallah*, who was a servant of *Abdallah*, resides among them, and governs them.

تيروان *Kirouan* is the largest of all the towns. The tribes of *Magreb* all resided there; and it was their chief place until the decline of their government, when *Abu-Abdallah* came forth, and conquered them; since which time *Abdallah* dwelt at *Kirouan*, until he built the town of مهديه *Mohediah* on the sea-coast, and removed to that place.

زويله *Zouileh* is a town of middling size, with many territories belonging to it: it is situated near the country of the Blacks. This land of the Blacks is a very extensive region, but extremely dry. In the mountains of it are to be found all the fruits which the Mohammedan world produces; but they do not eat of them; they have other fruits and natural productions for their food. Their skins are of a finer and deeper blackness than that of any other blacks, whither حبشي *Habeshis*, Abyssinians, or زنكي *Zingians*, Ethiopians. And their country is more extensive than that of any other nation of Blacks: it is situated on the coast of the ocean to the south: to the north they have deserts which extend towards the deserts of Egypt: from behind واح *Wahh* the desert reaches to near the *Nubians*; then to the desert in the vicinity of زنكبار *Zingbar*. Whatsoever they get, comes to them from the western side, because of the difficulty of entering their country from any other quarter.

Now we proceed to speak of the West, and begin with an account of اندلس *Andalus*, or Spain. *Andalus* is an extensive and considerable country, with many large and flourishing cities, the chief of which is called قرطبه *Cortubah* (Cordova), situated in the midst of the country. The ocean is on one side of Andalus, and the درباي روم *Sea of Roum* (the Mediterranean) on the other, as far as the زمين فرنك *Land of the Franks* (France.) The first of the cities is سرين *Serin*; then حسينيه *Husiniah*, اسبليه *Asebiliah* (or *Sebilah*, Seville), سدونه *Sedounah*, Sidonia, مالغه *Malaca*, to the country of مولسه *Moulsah*, and to طلسه *Tolsah*, and طرطوسه *Tartousah*; where there is باريس *Baris*, a town on the sea-side. Thence along the sea, belongs to the land of the Franks; and on the dry side belongs to the country of علجكس *Aljekes*. This country is inhabited by a race of Christians, and as far as the land of بسكونس *Biscounes* belongs to the Christians, as likewise the territories of جالغان *Jalekan*. There are two boundaries to *Andalus*; one, the land of the Infidels (or Christians); the other, the sea: and all those towns which we have spoken of, as being situated on the sea-coast, are considerable places, and well-inhabited.

(24)

Andalus is now in the hands of the بني امیه *Beni Ommiah*, the Ommiades[*]; and the عباسیان *Abbassians*, the Abbassides, have not yet snatched it from them; nor has *Abdallah* yet obtained the superiority over them. At the time that the glory of the *Beni Ommiah* was declining, one of that family, who was at آبله *Abilah*, passed over to the جزیره جبل طارق *Jezireh Jibel-tarek*, Gibraltar, and subdued *Andalus*, which still remains in the possession of the *Ommiah* race.

These are the most remarkable cities of *Andalus*:—طلیطله *Toleitlah*, سدونه *Sedounah*, لارده *Lardah*, وادي الحجاره *Wadi al hejareh*, برخاله *Barkhalah*, بورنه *Bournah* حسان *Hesan*, مارده *Mardah*, ماحو *Mahou*, غافث *Ghafek*, لیله *Leilah*, فرمویه *Fermouiah* (or ترمویه *Karmouiah*), موروده *Mouroudah*, اسبیلیه *Asebiliah*. These are all considerable towns, and for the greater part their buildings are of stone.

بحانه *Behaneh* is situated in the vicinity of deserts. *Sirin*[†], on the coast of the ocean: there ambergris is found, but not in any place on the Mediterranean Sea. The author of this book says, "At the time when I was in شام *Syria*, on the coast of the

---

[*] The Ommiades retained their empire in Spain long after they had ceased to govern the other regions of Islam; where the Abbassides began to reign A. H. 132, (A. D. 748.) The Ommiades possessed Spain until the year of the Hegira 424, (A. D. 1032.)—*Ebn Shonah* in D'HERBELOT, Art. *Ommiah*.

[†] سرین Sometimes written نسرین *Nesrin* and بسرین *Basrin*.

(25)

" درياي روم *Mediterranean Sea*, something was thrown up,
" and I afterwards heard that at *Sirin* such was every year
" thrown on the shore: this is a certain *thing* which they call
" موهي *mouhi*, resembling fine beaver, or raw silk; *it rubs*
" *itself against the stones on the sea-shore, and its plumage, or*
" *down, comes off**, which the people come and gather, and
" weave into garments." The kings of *Andalus* are very fond of
this stuff, and will not allow it to be exported; and they have
garments of it which cost above a thousand dinars.

مالقه *Malaca* produces the سنغر *sanfar*†, of whose skin
they make the handles of swords.

جزيره طارق *Jezireh Tarek*, Aljezireh, was the first seat of
Islam in this country. The جبل طارق *Jebel-Tarek*, Gibraltar,
is a well-inhabited mountain, with villages or small towns on it:
it is the extreme point and last pass of *Andalus*.

طليطله *Toletilah* is a city situated on a lofty mountain: the
buildings are of marble, or hard stones, fastened with lead. About
this city there are seven hills, all cultivated and inhabited; and

---

* This *thing* چيزي seems here to be an animal. The original is as follows:

خويشتن را بآن سنگها كه در كنار درياست برمالد و پري از اوي جدا شود

† I must acknowledge my ignorance of this creature, and my suspicion that there is
an error in the writing of the word.

E

(26)

likewise a river equal to the دجله *Dejleh,* or Tigris: the name of that river is ناحیه *Naḥiah*; it proceeds from the town called سره *Sarrah,* and they call that district مدن بني سالم *Meden beni Salem.*

قده *Kedah* is a considerable district, the chief town of which is called ارحدوه *Arhadouh:* from this place came عمرو بن حفصو *Omru ben Hafsou.* فحص البلوط *Fahas-alilout* is a flourishing and considerable district, the capital of which is called غافت *Ghafek.* بورمه *Bourmah* was a large city, but has been ruined during a contest between two tribes or parties who were in the town, one of which called to their aid the جالقیان *Jalékians,* who came and plundered and destroyed the place.

In *Andalus* the *Beni Ommiah,* or family of the Ommiah sovereigns, are pre-eminent. The *Khutbah** is read in their name.

The cities of the *Jalékians* are, مارده *Mardah,* هره *Herah,* وادي الججار *Wadi al hejar,* طلیطله *Toletlah.* There is a country of the *Jalékians* bordering on *Andalus,* which they call استوره *Astourah*; and the king of the *Jalékians* resides in a city called ابنظ *Abnez,* which is far from the land of the Mussulmans.

But of all the tribes of Infidels (Christians) who border on An-

---

* خطبه A prayer for the reigning king, read every Friday in the principal mosques.

dalus, the most numerous are the فرنك Franks. Their king is called فاره Farah*. The Jalekians, though a considerable people, are not so numerous as these. The smallest tribe of all these Infidels are those whom they call اسكونس Askounes; but they are said to be one of the most brave and manly. There is a race also called عجلسكنس Ajilsekes, a tribe of very bad people, who live between Askounes and Frank.

Of the بربر Berbers, who inhabit Andalus and Magreb (Spain and Africa), there are two kinds; one called Berber, the other برانس Beranes. فيكره Feikerah, and مكيانه Mekianah, and هواده Houadah, and مديونه Mediounah, are of the Berbers in Andalus; and كنامه Kenamah, and ربايه Rebaiah, and مصموده Masmoudah, and بلبله Bilbilah, and طرياحيه Tehiahiah, are of the Beranes. The Rebaiah dwell in the districts of تاهوث Tahouth; and the Kenamah in the vicinity of شطيغـ Shateif. In Andalus are several mines of gold and silver. In the district of سره Sarrah and مرسغه Marsafah, near قرطبه Cortubah, there is a place called كولس Koules. Here, and at طليطله Tolitelah, are many sables or martins (سبور).

زويا له Zouialah† is a place which abounds in black slaves; but the inhabitants are of a brown complexion, though at a dis-

---

* Or قاره Karah.

† Here seems a sudden transition (not unfrequent in Oriental writings) from Spain to Africa.—This place is, probably, the زويله Zouileh before mentioned.

tance from the south. In the eastern parts they are darker, and have light-coloured eyes---some more remote, have fair comlexions, with blue eyes, and reddish hair: one race of them has black eyes, and black hair---these are said to be descended from the Arabs of the tribe of بني غساز *Ghusaz.* Between Magreb and the country of the Blacks, there are deserts, of which but a few places are accessible by any road. Between افريقيه *Afrikiah* and تاهوث *Tahouth,* there is a small tribe, called شراه *Sherah.*

The kings of Andalus are of the Beni Ommiah family, and the Abbassides have not yet had the *Khutbah** in their name. These kings of Andalus are descended from هشام بن عبدالملك *Hesham ben Abdalmolk,* and still have the Khutbah in their own name. Their kings, at this time, are *Abdarrahman Mohammed ben Abdallah ben Mohammed Abdarrahman†.*

* See Note, p. 26.

† عبد الرحمن محمدبن عبد الله بن محمد عبد الرحمن The original has پادشاهان, kings, in the plural. But it appears that our author alludes to *Abdarrahman,* the third of that name, who (according to D'Herbelot, art. *Abdalrahman*) reigned 60 years in Spain, and died in the year of the Hegira 350, (A. D. 961), after violent contests about the right of succession between the Ommiades and Abbassides

ذكر ديار مصر

Account of Egypt.

ONE of the boundaries of Egypt begins from the دَرِبايِ روم *Sea of Roum*, between اسكندريه *Iskanderiah* (Alexandria) and برقه *Barkah*, at the deserts behind واح *Wahh*; proceeding to the land of the Nubians, and to the land of بجه *Bajeh*, and back from اسوان *Asouan* to the Sea of Roum; and from Bajeh, to the دَرِبايِ قلزم *Sea of Kolzum* (the Red Sea), till it comes to the طور سينا *Tour Sina* (Mount Sinai), in the territories of the Children of Israel.

From the coast of the Sea of Roum to the land of the Nubians behind واح *Wahh*, is twenty-five merhileh. From the borders of Nubia you must go eight merhileh to the south; from قلزم *Kolzum*, on the coast of the Red Sea, to the تيه بني اسرايل *Tiah beni Israel*, or Desert of the Israelites, six merhileh; and from the sea to the borders of that Desert, or *Tiah*, where it is bounded by the Sea of Roum, eight merhileh; from اسوان *Asouan* to the Sea of Roum, twenty-five merhileh.

Now we present a map of this country.

The chief city of Egypt is called فسطاط *Fostat*,* situated on the bank of the River نيل *Nile* to the north. The Nile flows from the east; and all this city is situated on one side of it. Near to it are certain edifices, called جزيره *Jezireh*, or the Island, to which they pass from Fostat on a bridge; and from this Jezireh they have constructed a bridge to the other bank, where there is a place called جيره *Jeirah*. The extent of the city is about two thirds of a farsang: it is very well inhabited, and supplied with provisions; all their houses are seven or eight stories high. Near the town is a place called موتف *Mouekaf*, the soil of which is less marshy, and more firm and solid. It is said that *Fostat* was the name of a certain tribe.

حمرا *Hamra* is a town situated on the bank of the river Nile. It has two principal mosques; one in the middle of the town, built by عمرو بن عاص *Amru ben Aas*; and the other in the place called موتف *Mouekaf*, erected by لعهر بن طولون *Laaher ben Touloun*. Without the town is a certain place of above a mile in extent, which that Laaher Touloun caused to be built for his troops: this they call فطابع *Fetaia* or Ketaia. In like manner were the dwellings, called افاده *Afadeh*, of the آل اغلب *Al-i-Agleb* (or family of Agleb), situated without the town of قيروان *Kirouan*. In this place agriculture is much practised.

---

* *Fostat* is now, according to Mr. Browne (Travels, p. 80), " A long street, running parallel to the river, and occupying part of the space between Kahira (Cairo) and its bank." Of modern Cairo the foundation was laid A. D. 968.

There are great quantities of dates, and many corn fields, along the banks of the Nile, from that to near اسوان *Asouan,* and to the borders of اسكندريه *Eskanderiah.* When the weather becomes very warm, the water increases; and when it sinks, they sow their grain; after that, there is no necessity for water. In the land of Egypt there falls not either rain nor snow; nor is there in the whole country any running stream beside the river Nile.

فيوم *Fioum* is not a very considerable town. It is said that the prophet Joseph, on whom be the blessing of God! brought the water to that place, and called it لاهوت *Lahout:* And there is not any person who knows the fountains or source of the river Nile; on this account, because it issues from a cavern in the territories of زنكبار *Zingbar,* from a certain spot, which a man may very nearly approach, yet never can arrive at: after this, it runs through the inhabited and desert parts of the land of the Nubians to مصر *Misr* (Egypt); and there where it first becomes a river, it is equal to the دجله و فرات *Deljeh* and *Frat* (Tigris and Euphrates.) And the water of the River Nile is the most pure and delicious of all the waters on the face of the earth.

The Nile produces نهنك *crocodiles,* and the fish ماهي سقنقور *sekenkour:* and there is also a species of fish, called راعده *raadah,* which if any person take in his hand while it is alive, that person will be affected by a trembling of his body*; when dead, this fish resembles other fishes. The crocodile's head is very long, so long as to be one half of his whole form; and he has such teeth, that, if a lion were to come within their hold, he would be destroyed. It sometimes happens that the crocodile comes out of the water on the dry ground; but he has not then the same powers as when in the water. His skin is so hard that it resists the blows of all weapons when stricken on the back: they therefore wound him where the fore legs join the body (literally, *under the arm pits*), and between the thighs. The سقنقور *sekenkour* is a species of *that fish* (the crocodile), but the crocodile has *hands and feet*; and they use the sekenkour in medicinal and culinary preparations. This creature is not found any where but in the river Nile.

From اسوان *Asouan*, along the banks of the Nile, as far as the sea, the country is all inhabited and cultivated. On the southern side of the Nile there is a place called سعيد *Saied*, where are mines of زبرجد *zeberjed**, and emeralds (زمرد *zemrud*) far in the desert; and beside these there are not any mines of those precious stones. On the northern side of the river Nile,

---

* The original is very obscure: it may signify that the *fish*'s body is affected by an extraordinary tremulous motion while life remains.

† Chrysolite, kind of emerald, topaze, beryl, &c.

near Fostat, there is a certain hill, called معظم *Moazem*, in the vicinity of which is found the stone خماهن *khemahen*; and this hill extends to the land of the يونان *Iounans* (Greeks): And near that hill, in the district of Fostat, is a burying-place, where the tomb of Shafæi* is situated;---the Lord be merciful to him!

اسكندريه *Eskanderia*, Alexandria, is a considerable town, built on the sea-side: the houses, and other edifices, are of marble. And out in the sea there is a مناره *minareh*, or watch-tower, of hard stone, and very lofty; it contains about three hundred houses: No one without a guide can arrive there.

Of the buildings at Fostat, on the bank of the Nile, all that are above the city are called سعيد *Saied*, and all that are below the city are called زيف *Zeif*. At the distance of two farsang from Fostat, there are some ancient structures, called اهوام *Ahouam*; of which two are very lofty piles, and called هومان *Houman*: these are each, in height, four hundred گز *guz*†: And on the walls thereof are inscriptions written in the Greek language (يوناني); and this writing is said to signify, "*the building of Houman and Sertaier (was) in the sign Cancer*‡." These

---

* شافعي One of the chief Doctors of the Mussulmans, who was born at *Gaza*, A. H. 150, (A. D. 767,) and died A. H. 204, (A. D. 819.)

† See the Preface.

‡ بني الهومان و السرطاير في السرطان

F

edifices are quadrangular, and gradually diminish towards the summits, which are about large enough for a camel to stand on; within them there are passages in which a man cannot go without some difficulty. And in Houman is a cleft, or excavation, under the ground, supposed to have been, with some appearance of probability, the burial-place of the ancient sovereigns of this country.

The land of واحات *Wahat* was a pleasant and cultivated district, with trees, and water, and many inhabitants; but none at present remain. It abounded also in fruits. From the Egyptian Saied صعيد مصر *Saied Misr*, to the land of واح *Wahh*, in the south, is a journey of three days; and from that a small desert extends towards the land of the Blacks.

The sea which borders Egypt is bitter; but where the river Nile pours into it, and overcomes it, the waters of the sea are rendered sweet. Farther out, when the waters of the Nile are confounded with the sea, the bitterness again predominates. In this sea there are islands, to which one may pass over in boats or vessels. Of these islands are تنيس *Teneis* (or تينس *Teines*), and دمياط *Damiat*. In each of these agriculture is practised, and cattle are kept; and the kind of clothes called رفيع *refia*, (or رقيع *rekia*), comes from these places.

The waters of this sea are not very considerable, and vessels

(۳۵)

move on it by help of men*. It produces a certain fish مانند مشک like *meshk*†, which is called دلفین *delfin* (dolphin); and this is a fish of which if any person eat, he will be troubled with horrible dreams. From the borders of this sea, to those of the sea of شام *Syria,* it is all sand.

The town of اشمویین *Ashmouein* is small, but well-inhabited, and improved by agriculture; it produces dates: and opposite اشمویین *Ashmouein,* on the north of the river Nile, there is a little town called بوصیر *Bouseir,* where *Merwan ben Mohammed* was slain. It is said that the magicians of Pharaoh were from this بصیر *Beseir,* (or بوصیر *Bouseir,* as before written.)

اسوان *Asouan* is a place which produces dates. Agriculture is there much practised.

اخمیم *Akhmim* is situated amid the sands of the desert; but it is inhabited, and affords dates. It is said that *Dhu'l'Noun*‡, the Egyptian, was of this place.

فرما *Ferma* is situated on the sea-shore. It is a pleasant and cultivated spot. In it is the burial-place of جالینوس *Jalinous*

---

* وكشتي در و بمردي رود

† *Meshk,* or *mishk,* signifies *musk.*

‡ ذو النون Much celebrated among the Mussulmans for his piety, and founder of the religious sect called *Soufi,* died in Egypt. A. H. 245 (A. D. 859.)

(Galen) the Grecian. From Ferma to تنيس *Teneis* is a distance of two farsang by this sea.

Teneis is a vast pile or heap erected over the bodies of the dead, which were placed one above another until they formed a pile; which pile was called تركوم *Terkoum*: and this must have been done before the time of Moses, on whom be the peace and blessing of God!---for, in the time of Moses, according to the religion of the Egyptians, the dead were interred---a custom which was continued afterwards by the Christians, and is still practised by the Mussulmans. The author of this book says, that he himself had seen some of those bodies in their shrouds, or winding-sheets, with bones and skeletons of immense size.

There are some places on the river Nile which the crocodiles do not infest, near Fostat and Bouseir; and the عين الشمس *Aien-al-shems*, or Fountain of the Sun, lies to the south of Fostat. These two places are said to have been villas or pleasure-houses of Pharaoh. On the top of Mount معظم *Moazem* there is a place which they call the stove or furnace (تنور) of Pharaoh.

In the vicinity of Fostat, there grows a plant, called بلسم *balsam*, from which the oil is extracted. This is not to be found in any other part of the world.

The left side of the Nile is called خوف *Khouf*. In this division are situated تِباسه *Kiasah,* and جِرجیر *Jerjeir,* and قاتور *Kakour.* The opposite division, on the right side of the river Nile, they call زِبغ *Zeif.* These two places contain the chief villages of Egypt. The gold mines are in the land of بجه *Bajeh.* From اسوان *Asouan* to that place is a journey of fifteen farsang. The country where those mines are situated is sandy, and without any hills, fields, or tilled land: it furnishes slaves for Egypt. There are asses and mules, of considerable value, in Egypt: no other country produces such. The district of Asouan affords asses not larger than sheep, which will not live when brought out of that country; and in the land of سعید *Saied* there are Sclavonian asses, خران سقلابی *Kheran Siklabi.* The Egyptians say that the land of *Khefa,* or خفاقار *Khefakar,* was inhabited and cultivated in the time of Pharaoh.

ذِکر دیار شام

Description of Sham, or Syria.

THE western side of Syria is bounded by روم *Roum**; the eastern, by the desert from ایله *Aileh* to the فرات *Forat* (river Euphrates), and from the Euphrates to the borders of Roum. To

---

* Perhaps the word دریا (*Sea*) has been here omitted: The Sea of Roum, or Mediterranean.

the north of Syria lies the land of Roum; and to the south are the borders of Egypt, and the اسرايل بني تيه *Tiah beni Israel,* or Desert of the Children of Israel.

(Map of Syria.)

Of the cities and towns which are situated on the east and west of Syria, it is unnecessary here to make any mention, as we have already pointed them out in the map. Some places are called ثغورشام *Seghur Sham,* or frontiers of Syria: others are called جزيره *Seghur Jezireh,* or frontiers of Arabian Irak, or Mesopotamia, because all bordering on one half of the Euphrates belongs to Syria; and from ملطيه *Meltiah* to مرعش *Meraash* is called the Seghur of Jezireh, because people of Jezireh reside there, and it belongs to Syria.

The hills of كوه لكام *Lekam* extend for two hundred farsang into Roum; and the دار اسلام *Dar al'salam* (the mansion of salvation or peace) is between Meraash and هارونيه *Harouniah;* and the عين اربه *Aein Arbah,* or Fountain of Arbah. After having passed لدتيه *Ladikiah,* it is called كوه لكام *Mount Lekam.* From that, the continuation of this mountain is called سوخ *Soukh,* as far as حمص *Memehes;* and from that, throughout all Syria, it is called لبنان *Libnan* (Lebanon), till it comes near the Sea of Kolzum (Red Sea.) The borders of فلسطين *Palestine* are two days journey to the west, from the place called رمع *Remaa* to the borders of بحور *Behour*; and the breadth of the borders of Palestine, on the western side, is also, from that place to بلقا *Bilka*, two days journey; and the land of the tribe of Lot, قوم لوط (Sodom, &c.) and بحره *Baherah*, and Taberah, all that is situated between the two mountains, they call غور *Ghour*. It is lower down than the land of Syria; and part of it is reckoned as belonging to اردن *Arden,* and part to Palestine. The water of Palestine is rain water. Palestine is about one half of Syria; and the chief cities of it are رملة *Ramleh,* and the بيت المقدس *Beit-almokeds,* Holy House, or Jerusalèm, which is situated on a hill. Here is a mosque (مسجد), or temple, than which there is not, in all the land of the Mussulmans, one more large. Here also is the محراب *Mehrab,* the chief altar of David, on whom be peace!---a building of about fifty guz high, and thirty broad, of stone. On the top of this is the Mehrab of David; and this is the first object that presents itself as one comes from Ramleh.

At a distance of six miles from Jerusalem is a village called بيت اللحم *Beit Allehem* (Bethlehem or Bethlem.) Here عسي *Jesus,* on whom be peace! was born of his mother; and it is said that the date or palm tree, of whose fruit Mary ate, and which is celebrated by mention in the Koran*, has been placed in the dome or vault which is here, and held in high veneration and respect.

From Bethlehem, on the southern side, there is a small town, called the مسجد ابراهيم *Mesjed Ibrahim*, or Temple of Abraham: and in the mosque where they pray on the high feasts, are the burial places of Abraham, Isaac, and Jacob, (may peace be on them!) and those of their wives are opposite. Here are many hills and trees: all the hills of Palestine are covered with trees; and there is much fruit, olives, and figs.

نابلس *Nabolis* is a town of which the inhabitants are called سامريان *Samarian*; a people who have not any other residence.

In the extreme borders of Palestine, in the vicinity of Egypt, there is a city, called غزه *Ghazah*, which هاشم بن عبدالله *Hashem ben Abdallah* conquered, and in which شافعي *Shafæi* † was born.

جبال *Jebal*, and شراه *Sherah*, are two well inhabited and pleasant districts. The chief town of Jebal is called اذره *Ade-*

---

* Koran, chapter 19, سورت مريم Chapter of Mary.
† See Note, p. 33.

rah; of Sherah, *Rouad*. These have been conquered by the Arabians.

اردن *Arden*, the chief town of which is طبرثه *Tiberthah*, or Tiberiah, on the banks of the درياي كوچك *Small Sea*, or lake, whose waters are sweet, and its length twelve miles, and its breadth two or three farsang.---Here is a running stream of water, very warm, which goes on for about two farsang, and, when it reaches the town, is exceedingly hot.

In the district of غور *Ghour*, snow is almost unknown; but dates, and streams, and fountains, abound. It commences at the borders of اردن *Arden*; and when it passes them, it extends to the boundary of Palestine, and in like manner reaches to ايله *Aileh*.

صور *Sour* (Tyre) is a very strong town, situated on the sea-shore. It is the most ancient of all the cities on the coast; and all the Grecian philosophers حكمان يونان came from this place. اردن *Arden* was the dwelling-place of Jacob, to whom be peace!

دمشق *Demeshk* (Damascus) is a *chief city, the right hand of the cities of Syria.** It has ample territories among the

* شهري بزركوار است يعني شهرهاي شام

mountains; and is well watered by streams which flow around. The land about it produces trees, and is well cultivated by husbandmen. This tract is called غوطه *Ghouteh*. It extends about one merhileh by two. There is not, in all Syria, a more delightful place. There is a bridge in the midst of the city of Demeshk, by which a horseman may pass over the water, which goes on to the villages of Ghouteh, and runs amongst their inns, and hot-baths, and shops.

Here is one of the largest mosques in all the land of the Mussulmans, part of which was built in ancient times by the صابيان *Sabians*. Then it fell into the possession of the Greeks, and became a place of religious worship to them. After that, it fell into the hands of the Jews, and of certain princes who adored idols; and at that time they put to death Yahiah, the son of Zachariah, يحيي بن ذكريا to whom be peace! and fixed his head upon a pole, before the gate of this temple, at the place which they call باب جرون *Bab Jeroud* (probably جرون Jews'-gate.) It then passed into the hands of the Christians, who performed in it, likewise, their religious ceremonies, until, at length, it came into the possession of the True Believers (the Mussulmans), to whom it serves as a mosque. At the same spot where the head of Yahia ben Zachariah had been fixed, the head of Hosein, the son of Ali, to whom be peace! was also exposed. *Walid ben Abd-al-Molk,* وليد بن عبد الملك in his time, caused this building to be repaired, and beautified with pavements of marble, and also pillars of variegated marble, the tops of which were ornamented with gold, and studded with precious stones, and all the ceiling he caused to be covered with gold; and it is said that he expended the revenues of all Syria on this work.

Beyond the borders of Demeshk is بعلبك *Baalbek*, situated on an eminence. Here are the gates of palaces, sculptured in marble; and lofty columns, also of marble. In the whole region of Syria, there is not a more stupendous or considerable edifice than this.

طرابلس *Trabolis* (Tripolis) is a town on the shore of the Sea of Roum, well-inhabited, and abounding in dates. The chief town of this district is حمص *Hemes* (Emessa), a place well-supplied with provisions, and of excellent air. The inhabitants are celebrated as being handsome. Neither scorpions nor serpents are found here. It is copiously watered; the lands are cultivated, and there are many trees. There is also a church (كليسيه a Christian church, *Ecclesia*), to which there is not, in size, any church of Syria equal: one half of this building is a church; the other, a mosque. The streets here are paved with stone.

ازطرسوس *Aztarsous** is a castle or fortress, situated on the coast of the Sea of Roum. سلميسه *Selmisa* is a town on the

---

* The syllable از *Az* seems to have been prefixed through mistake or carelessness.

borders of the desert: most of the inhabitants are هاشمي *Hashemites*. The district of *Kanserin* كوره قنسرين is the pass between Irak and Syria. شبرز *Shebirz* and حما *Hema* are two small towns, agreeably situated, with good water, and many trees, and much cultivated land. مصرس *Mesres* is a town and district supplied with rain water. خناصره *Khenaserah* is a small town on the borders of the desert.

غراحلم *Gheraheln* is a district, of which the chief town is انطاكية *Antakiah*. After Demeshk, there is not any place more delightful. It has a fortification of stone, and abounds in plantations of palm and other trees, cultivated fields, water, and mills. Round the territories a horseman may go for two days. The water flows through the streets, and amidst the chief buildings. There is a place which they call the صخره موسي *Sekhreh Mousi*, or Rock of Moses, to whom be peace!

بالس *Balis* is a town on the banks of the river Euphrates. منج *Menje* is situated in the desert: rain-water is made use of there. صيحه *Saiheh* is a small town, where there is a bridge of stone, called the قنطره صيحة *Kentereh Saiheh*, than which, in all the land of Islam, there is not a more extraordinary bridge. سميساط *Samisat* is a town situated on the river Euphrates. حصن منصور *Hysn Mansour* is a small fortress, the land about which is watered with rain-water: here are oratories and mosques. حدث *Hedeth* and مرعش *Meraash* are two small towns, pleasantly situated, with trees and cultivated lands. زيطره *Zeitrah* is a considerable fortress in the vicinity of Roum (Natolia), and the Roumians have sacked and plundered it. هارونیه *Harouniah* is situated to the west of the كوه لكام *Mount Lekam*: it is a small castle, erected by order of Haroun Arrasheid.

اسكندرويه *Eskanderouiah* is a fortress situated on the coast of the Sea of Roum: it is small, but has some plantations of date trees. نثينان *Nethinan* is a fortress on the sea-coast: from this place they send into Egypt and Syria the wood of the fir-tree, (صنوبر). كبيسة *Keisah* is also a castle or fortress on the sea-shore. عين زريه *Aien-Zariah* is a place which produces dates and other fruits, and much corn.

مصيصه *Masisah* and كفرتوما *Kufertouma* are two towns situated on the banks of the river جيحان *Jihan*. Between these two towns there is a bridge of stone. The situation of these towns is so high, that if a person should look from the top of the mosque, he would see almost as far as the ocean. ادنه *Adneh* is a little town, about half the size of *Masisah*, on the banks of a small river called سيحان *Seihan*. The town is pleasant, and well-supplied. The river Seihan is less than the river Jihan: over it there is a very lofty bridge of stone. Both the Seihan and Jihan come from Roum.

طرسوس *Tarsous* is a considerable town, with a double wall of stone. The inhabitants are valiant men, horsemen, and fond of warlike achievements. It is a strong and pleasant place. From it to the borders of Roum are many hills and mountains of difficult ascent. They say that in Tarsous there are above a thousand horsemen; and in all the chief cities of Islam, such as Seiestan, and Kirman, and Pars, and Khuzistan, and Irak, and Hejaz, and Egypt, there are inns, or public places, appointed for the people of this town.

اولاس *Awlas* is a fortress situated on the sea-shore: the inhabitants are *a people who worship God**; and it is the extreme boundary of the Mussulman territories on the coast of the Sea of Roum. رقم *Rekem* is a town situated near بلقا *Bilka*: all the walls and houses are of stone, in such a manner that one would imagine they were all of one piece.

The land of the tribe of Lot (قوم لوط) is called ارض المقلوبه *Aredz Almokloubah*; that is, the land turned upside-down. Neither corn, nor herbage, nor cattle, are found here: the ground is black; and stones are seen scattered about, which one would imagine to be the stones showered down on that wicked race†.

* قومي خدا پرست

† See Koran, سورت الحجر *chapter of Hejr,* (so called from a district in the province of Hejaz.)

فاخذتهم الصيحت مشرقبن فجعلنا عاليها سا فلهاو امطرنا عليهم حجارت من سجيل
" Wherefore a terrible storm from Heaven assailed them at sun-rise, and we turned

معان *Moan* is a small town in possession of the (بني امية) Ommiades. بغراس *Bagheras* is a town in which there are publick inns, erected by زبيده *Zeibdeh*, or Zebideh; and in all Syria there are not any besides. سروت *Serout* is a pleasant town, in the district of Demeshk, on the borders of the Sea of Roum. *Auzai, the author of the Chronicles, dwelt there*.

مسافات شام و جزيره

Distances of Places in Sham and Jezireh.

THE length of the roads of Sham is taken from مليطيه *Melitiah* to رمح *Remah*. From Melitiah to منج *Menje* is four days journey; from Menje to حالب *Haleb*, Aleppo, two days journey; from Haleb to حمص *Hemess*, five days journey; and from Hemess to دمشق *Demeshk*, five days journey; from رمله *Ramlah*, to رمح *Remah*, two days journey: total, twenty-five days journey. Between اردن *Arden*, and حمص *Hemess*, and دمشق *Demeshk*, the extent is not more than a journey of

---

the city (Sodom) upside down, and rained on them stones of baked clay." The first passage is translated by Maracci, (Alcor. Vol. II. p. 383,) " Sustulit ergo eos clamor (Gabrielis) ad ortum solis pervenientes." I have offered some remarks on this passage in the Oriental Collections, Vol. II. p. 131.

* اوزاعي صاحب اخبار انجا مقام داشتي

three days; because that from Demeshk to طرابلس *Trabolis* is a journey of two days along the sea towards the west; from the extremity of غوطه *Ghoutah*, to that place where it joins the desert towards the east, is a journey of one day; from Hemess to سليميه *Selimiah*, in the desert, one day's journey to the east; from طبريه *Tiberiah* to صور *Sour*, in the water (در آب), one day's journey; from that to the borders of فيق *Feik*, in the territories of the بني فراره *Beni Farareh*, to the east, about the same distance.

Such are the length and breadth of Syria; and the distances from one place to another are these, beginning from Palestine, which is the chief part of Syria to the south, and its capital رمله *Ramlah*, from which to the town of بارما *Barmah* is half a merhileh; from Palestine to عسقلان *Ascalon*, is one merhileh, to عزه *Azzah*, one merhileh; from Ramlah to the بيت المقدس *Beit Almokeds*, or Holy House (Jerusalem), one day's journey; from Ramlah to قيساريه *Caisariah*, one day's journey; from Ramlah to نابلس *Nabolis*, one day's journey; from that to زعر *Zaar*, one day's journey; from that to the كوه شراه *Mount Sherah*, one day's journey; and from the Mount to the extremity of the country, three days journey.

The chief town of آر دن *Arden* (or *Orden*) is طبرثه *Tibertheh*, or *Tiberiah*; from which to صور *Sour* is a journey of two farsang; from that to بانياس *Banias,* two days easy journey; from that to عكبسه *Akebseh,* one day's journey. آرذن *Arden* is the smallest district of Syria.

دمشق *Demeshk* is the chief town of the district of that name. From that to بعلبك *Baalbek* is a journey of two days; and to Trabolis, two days; and to صيدا *Seida,* two days; and to اذرعا *Aderaa,* four days journey; and to the extreme boundary of Ghouteh, one day's journey; to هوران *Houran* and بنيه *Beniah,* two days journey.

The chief town of the district of تنسرين *Kanserin* bears the same name; but the governor's palace, the markets, great mosques, and public buildings, are at حلب *Haleb.* From Haleb to ثارب *Thareb* is one day's journey; from Haleb to قوس *Kous,* also one day's journey; and from Haleb to منبج *Menje,* two days journey.

انطاكيه *Antakiah* is the chief town of the district of غراصم *Gherasem.* From that to لاذقيه *Ladikiah* is a journey of three days: from that to بغراس *Bagheras* is one day's journey, and to ثارب *Thareb,* two days journey; and to Hemess, five merhileh: from that to مرعش *Meraash,* two days journey; and to حدث *Hedeth,* three days journey. This frontier has not any common capital; but each town is independent in itself.

منبج *Menje* is situated near this frontier. From Menje to the

Euphrates is one easy merhileh: from Menje to نوس *Kous*, two merhileh; and from Menje to ملطيه *Melitiah*, four days journey; and from Menje to سميساط *Samisat*, two days journey; and from Samísat to حصن منصور *Hysn Mansour*, one day's journey; from Hysn Mansour to Melitiah, two days journey; and from Hysn Mansour to نطيره *Netirah*, one day's journey; and from Hysn Mansour to حدث *Hedeth*, one day's journey; and from Hedeth to مرعش *Meraash*, a journey also of one day.

Those are the distances of the ثغور جزيره *Seghur Jezirah*.

Now we proceed to the distances of places in the ثغور شام *Seghur Sham*. From اسكندرويه *Eskanderouiah* to انباس *Anbas*, is one merhileh; from Anbas to مصيصه *Masisah*, as far as اذثه *Aditheh*, one day's journey; from Aditheh to طرسوس *Tarsous*, one day's journey; from Tarsous to حوران *Houran*, two days journey; and from Tarsous to اولاس *Aulas*, on the Sea of Roum, two farsang: from *Anbas*[*] to كنيسه *Kenisah*, and هارونيه *Harouniah*, one day's journey, or less; and from Harouniah to Meraash, which belongs to the Seghour, or frontiers of Jezireh, is a journey of one day.

---

[*] انباس *Anbas*, undoubtedly the same that was before written اولاس *Aulas*.

ذكر بحر روم

Description of the Sea of Roum, or Mediterranean.

THE Sea of Roum is a bay or gulph, proceeding from the great ocean at اندلس *Andalus*. Between بصيره *Basireh*, and between the land of طنجه *Tanjeh* and جزيره *Jezireh*, there is a certain mountain, which they call جبال الطارق *Jebal al Tarek*, situated on the point of the borders of Andalus. At that place the breadth of this sea is twelve farsang; and it becomes broader, and more considerable, as it extends to the coast of مغرب *Magreb*, on the eastern side (of Gibraltar), till it approaches the land of Egypt, and from that proceeds towards Syria, along those places which we have above described: it turns, and passes by the cities of Roum, as far as انطاكيه *Antakiah*; then it joins the sea which forms the bay of قسطنطنيه *Costantiniah*, Constantinople; then it proceeds along the coast of ايناس *Ainas**; then along the coast of روميه *Roumiah*; and then to فرنك *Frank*, France, along the shore to طرسوسه *Tarsousah*, on the sea of Andalus; and then, continuing along the coast of Andalus, it at last joins the ocean at Jebel al Tarek, opposite Basireh, and proceeds as far as بسرين *Besirin*, which is the extreme point of the land of Islam.

* Or انباس *Anbas*.

قلیبه *Kelimah,* or قلیبه *Kelmiah,* is a town which belonged to the روميان *Roumians*; and there is a gate at طرسوس *Tarsous,* which they call باب قلیبه *Bab Kelimah,* or the Gate of Kelimah. Kelimah is at a distance from the sea. About a merhileh's distance from that, there is a village on the sea-shore, called لامس *Lames*; from that village the country is Roum.

انطاکیه *Antakiah* is a very strong fortress, belonging to the Roumians, situated on the sea-shore. It is well-inhabited, and has many villages depending on it. The bay on which it is situated is of bitter or salt water; and they call it the Bay or Gulph of *Costantinah* خلیج قسطنطینه " A chain is (or may be) drawn across this gulph, to hinder any one from passing there from the sea or elsewhere;" * and this gulph falls into the Sea of Roum.

On the side of Roum there are shores which they call the coasts of *Asas* سواحل اساس and *Roumiah* رومیه These are two well-inhabited and considerable towns, with villages and tilled lands: they belong to the Christians, and are situated near the sea. Asas is the place from which came the یونان حکیمان Grecian Philosophers. Roumiah is one of the props of the kingdom of the Christians; they have one throne (کرسی) at Antakiah, one at اسکندریه *Eskanderouiah,* and one at Roumiah; and the throne which they have at بیت المقدس *Beit al Mokeds*

* برین خلیج سلسله کشیده باشد تاهیچکس انجا بگذرد از دریا و غیره

(Jerusalem) did not exist in the time of the Apostles (حواريان), but has been introduced for the greater honour and aggrandisement of that city. From those places the sea proceeds towards the coast of فرنك *Frank*, and, passing by سقاليه *Sikaliah* (Sicily), goes on to طرسوسه *Tarsousah*, belonging to the land of اندلس *Andalus*.

We have already spoken of the cities, towns, and coasts, of Magreb, and Egypt, and Syria, to the extremity of Islam: it is not necessary to say more on those subjects. In this Sea of Roum there are islands, great and small. سقاليه *Sikaliah* is the most considerable of them all. There are, besides, اقريطس *Akrites*, قبرس *Kibres*, and the mount called جبل القلال *Jebel al Kellal*.

Sikaliah is near Frank: it is an island of near nine merhileh in extent; and produces more corn and provisions, male slaves and female attendants, and cattle, than any other island belonging to the Mussulmans, in this sea. Akrites is a smaller island than Sikaliah: it is inhabited by the Mussulmans and غازيان *Ghazians*; and amongst them there is a tribe of Christians. The inhabitants of Kibres are all Christians. Akrites is a very strong island: at present the inhabitants are on terms of peace with the Mussulmans. They bring مصطكي *Mastiky* from Kibres to the countries of Islam.

The place called جبل القلال *Jebel al Kellal* has been ruined, but is now inhabited by Mussulmans; and it affords sufficient water and land. It is, in extent, two days journey, situated on the frontiers of Frank; but the Franks have not been able to get possession of it. There are not, any where, shores so delightfully interspersed with buildings on both sides, as the shores of this sea. Here the ships of Mussulmans and of Infidels sail about, and sometimes oppose each other in battle, to the number of an hundred ships on each side.

ذكر ديار جزيره

Description of Jezireh, or Mesopotamia.

THE tract of country called Jezireh is that which lies between the rivers دجله *Dejleh* (Tigris) and فرات *Forat* (Euphrates.) The Forat rises in Roum, at a distance of two days journey from ملطيه *Melitiah*, and then proceeds to سميساط *Samisat*. On the eastern side of the river Dejleh, and on the western side of the Forat, are various cities and towns, which are reckoned, on account of their vicinity, as belonging to Jezireh, although in fact not so.

Now we shall lay before the reader a map of this country, with the names of its several cities.

ذكر مسافات ديار جزيره

Distances of Places in Jezireh.

FROM the source of the Euphrates (فرات *Forat*) to the borders of Melitiah, to Samisat, two days journey: from Samisat to حسرمنج *Hasermenje*, four days journey; to رقه *Raccah*, two days journey: from Racca to انبار *Anbar*, twenty merhileh; from تكريث *Tacrith* to Anbar, two days journey; from Tacrith to موصل *Mousul*, six days journey; from Mousul to آمد *Amid*, four days journey; from Amid to Samisat, three days journey; from Samisat to Melitiah, three days journey; from Mousul to بلد *Beled*, one merhileh; and from Beled to نصيبين *Nisibin*, three merhileh; from Nisibin to راس العين *Ras-al-aien*, three merhileh; from Ras-al-aien to رقه *Racca*, a journey of four days.

ذكر شهرها و بقعها جزيره

Of the Towns and Districts of Jezireh.

نصيبين *Nisibin* is rendered, by its river and delightful verdure, one of the pleasantest places of Jezireh. It is a considerable town, situated on a level ground, watered by a stream which issues from a mountain called بالوصا *Balousa*, and thence proceeds among the gardens and corn-fields. کردان *Curdan* is a place inhabited by Christians. It produces deadly scorpions: And there is a very strong castle or fortress, which cannot be taken by force of arms; and the hill on which it is situated abounds in serpents, whose stings occasion death. In the vicinity of Nisibin there is a mountain called ماردین *Mardein*, which, from the bottom to the summit, measures two farsang; and on it is another impregnable castle. This mountain produces chrystal (بلور).

موصل *Mousul* is a city, the buildings of which are all of stone and mortar: it is a considerable place. بلد *Beled* is a small town on the banks of the river Dejleh (Tigris) to the west; and there is a stream running out of the Dejleh: it is planted with trees, and has some cultivated lands. سنجار *Senjar* is a town situated near a mountain, which produces date trees in great number; and in all the land of Jezireh there is not any other place that produces dates, except میلث *Meileth*, on the banks of the Euphrates.

انبار دارا *Anbar Dara* is a small town, with water and cultivated lands. کفرتوما *Kufertouma* is situated on a plain: it is larger than Dara (the Anbar Dara before mentioned); it has streams, and trees, and cultivated fields. راس العین *Ras-al-aien* is likewise situated on a level ground. Cotton grows here in great abundance. Near three hundred streams proceed from this spot: the water is so clear, that one may see whatever is at the bottom. Those streams are collected together, and are the source of the river خابوران *Khabouran*, on which, as far as ترتسبا *Karkesia*, there are about twenty hamlets and villages. Ras-al-aien is larger than Kufertouma, and has many trees, and much cultivated land.

آمد *Amid* is situated on the eastern side of the Dejleh (Tigris), and has strong walls, trees, and cultivated lands. جزيره ابن عمر *Jezireh Ebn Omar* is a small town, with some trees, on the western side of the river Dejleh. سميساط *Samisat* is the last town of Jezireh, situated on the east of the Dejleh and Forat. ملطيه *Melitiah*, and the تغور شام *Seghour Sham*, or frontiers of Syria, as we before mentioned, are reckoned as belonging to Jezireh, because the people of that province occasionally reside in those places. حديثه *Haditha* is situated on the banks of the Dejleh, to the east; it has many corn-fields, trees, and gardens. The river Dejleh runs by the skirts of the كوه بارما *Mount Barma*; and " on these hills there are springs or fountains that yield gold dust and bitumen*;" and these mountains extend through Jezireh towards the west†, till they come to the borders

---

* و درين كوه چشمهاي لعط و قير باشد

† سوي مغرب It certainly should be سوي شرقي towards the east.

of کرمان *Kirman* : and it is said that these are the mountains of *Masindan**.

ذکر دیار مُضر

Description of Diar Modhar.

رقه و رافقه *Rakka* and *Rafika* are two towns of this province, situated on the eastern side of the river Forat; they both have mosques, and are planted with trees: and on the western side of the Forat, between *Rakka* and بالس *Bales*, is the burial-place of عمرو بن یاسر *Omru-ben-Yaser*.

جدان *Jedan* is a town of middling size, inhabited by a race of people whom they call صابی *Sabians*. Their place of religious worship is on a lofty pile or heap (بر تلي بلند), which they ascribe to Abraham, on whom be the blessing of God! This place they hold in high veneration; esteeming it holy, and making pilgrimages to it from other quarters. There are but few trees and little water at *Jedan*.

زها *Zoha* is a place of nearly the same size. The Christians are

* ماسندان or Nasedan ناسدان But the word is so badly written, that the true reading may be quite different.

here predominant. In this town there are above three hundred churches or monasteries (سبصد دير زيادت). The land is well watered and cultivated; and there is here a Christian church (كليساي), than which in all Islam there is not any greater.

جسرمنج *Jasir Menje* and سميساط *Samisat*, are two towns, with gardens and cultivated lands, well-watered; both situated on the western side of the river Forat. قرقيسا *Karkisa* is on the banks of the river خابور *Khabour*: it abounds in fine prospects, cultivated lands, and gardens. رحبه مالك بن طوق *Rahabah Malek ben Tawk* is a town, well-watered, and planted with trees, situated on the eastern side of the river Forat. هيث *Heith* is on the western side of the Forat: it has a strong castle, and is opposite تكريت *Tacrith*. Tacrith is situated on the western side of the river Dejleh. انبار *Anbar* is a town of middling size. ابو العباس القايم بالله *Abou al Abbas al Kaiem Billah* resided there, and the remains of his palace are still visible. It is a pleasant place, producing excellent crops, and good provisions and dates. The territories of this place are extensive; and there is in Jezireh a race of people, from ربعيه *Rebaia* and مضر *Modhar*, who possess horses, and mules, and sheep. Some of these people dwell in the desert, and some in the villages on the borders of Jezireh.

زابين *Zabein* (the two Zabs) are considerable streams; each about half as great as the Dejleh. They rise among the mountains of آذر بایکان‎ *Azerbaigan.* Of these the larger is that which runs towards حديثة‎ *Haditheh.* These streams form part of the river Dejleh, and water the district of سامره‎ *Samerah.*

عانه‎ *Aaneh* is a small town, situated where the river Forat forms a bay or gulph. This place is called the حصن مسلمه‎ *Hysn Moselamah.* They say that it belonged to Moselamah ben Abdal Mulk. A branch of the Ommiades (بني اميه‎ *Beni-Ommiah*) is settled there. It is a pleasant place, and well-supplied with provisions. It belonged to عباس بن العبر الغنوي‎ *Abbas ben al Omar al Ghanoui.*

تل بني سيار‎ *Tel beni Seiar* (the heap or pile of the sons of Seiar) is a small town, inhabited by a tribe of Arabs of the بني غني‎ *Beni Ghunni.*

جودي‎ *Joudi* is a mountain near *Nisibin.* It is said that the Ark of Noah (to whom be peace!) rested on the summit of this mountain. At the foot of it there is a village called ثمابين‎ *Themabin;* and they say that the companions of Noah descended here from the ark, and built this village.

سروج‎ *Seruje* is a large town, abounding in fruit, at the distance of one merhileh from the town of جران‎ *Jeran.*

ذكر عراق عرب

Description of Irak Arabi.

THE length of Irak is taken from تكريت *Tacrith* to عبادان *Abadan*; and the breadth, from بغداد *Baghdad* to كوفه *Cufa*, to قدسيه *Cadesiah*, to حلوان *Holwan*; and from واسط *Waset*, to قلب *Kelb*, and ترتوب *Karkoub*; and from بصره *Basrah* to the borders of حي *Hey*; and from Tacrith to شهرزور *Shehrzour*, and the borders of Holwan and صيروان *Seirwan*, and صيمره *Seimereh*, and the borders of طيب *Teib*, and of سوس *Sus*; again to Hey, to the sea. From Tacrith to the sea there is, according to the line we have described, a considerable inflexion, or winding, towards the west, behind the سواد *souad** of Basrah in the desert; to the souad of Basrah, as far as بطايح *Betaiah*; to the souad of كوفه *Cufa*, to the river Forat, to انبار *Anbar*, to تكريت *Tacrith*, between the rivers Dejleh and Forat; and in this line of borders from the sea to Tacrith, there is likewise a winding or curve.

---

* The villages and small towns of Irak are, in general, called *souad*.

مسافات عراق

Distances of Places in Irak.

FROM Tacrith to the sea-shore, by the winding line on the eastern side, is a journey of one month; and from the sea to Tacrith, by the outline on the western side, is likewise a journey of one month. From Baghdad to سامره *Samereh* is a distance of three merhileh; and from Samereh to Tacrith, two merhileh: from Baghdad to Cufa, four merhileh; from Cufa to قادسيه *Cadesiah*, one merhileh: from Baghdad to واسط *Waset*, eight merhileh; and from Baghdad to حلوان *Holwan*, six merhileh: from the borders of صيمره *Seimereh* and صيروان *Seirwan*, the same distance. From Waset to بصره *Basrah* is a distance of eight merhileh; from Cufa to Waset, six merhileh; from Basrah to the sea, two merhileh; from Holwan to Cadesiah, eleven merhileh. The breadth, from سامره *Samereh*, on the banks of the river Dejleh, to the borders of شهرزور *Shehrzour** and آذربایجان *Azerbaijan*, is a distance of fifteen merhileh, or perhaps one merhileh more; and the breadth at Waset, four merhileh; and the

---

* Called, by the modern Turks, *Sheherzoul*. According to Persian Chronicles, Alexander the Great died at this place.—See the " *Epitome of the Ancient History of Persia*," page 26.

breadth of Basrah, from the city of Basrah to the borders of Hey, is one merhileh.

Such are the distances of places in Irak Arabi.

ذكر شهرهاي عراق عرب

Account of the Cities and Towns of Irak Arabi.

بصره *Basrah* is a considerable city, the foundation of which was laid in the time of عمر بن الخطاب *Omar ebn Alkhitab*---(may God reward him!)---and the building performed by عتبه ابن غزوان *Atbah ebn Ghazouan.* On the western side of Basrah the desert approaches, which is without water. "It is "said, that the rivers or streams of Basrah were reckoned in the "time of Belal ben Abi Bordeh, and amounted to the number of "one hundred and twenty thousand streams, on which boats were "employed. This anecdote astonished me: I went there, and be- "held, within the space of about an arrow's single flight, several "small streams, on which little boats were employed*."

* گویند که رودهاي بصره یشمردند در روزگار بلال بن ابي برده صد وبیست هزار رود برآمد که زورق در آن کارکردي و مرا این سخن شگفت آید آنجا رسیدم و دیدم که در مقداري یک تیر پرتاب بسیار رودهاي کوچک بوده که زورقها کوچک در آن کار میکردند

The extent of Basrah comprises about fifty farsang from سي *
Sey, to عبادان Abadan, which is the palm-plantation (نخلستان)
of Basrah. At Basrah is the tomb of طلحه بن عبدالله Tal-
hah ben Abdallah; may God reward him! And there are several
places, also, to which pilgrimages are made; such as the tomb of
الحرا بن سرير Al Hara ben Serir, and other learned men. The
river زهاد Zohad runs four farsang: it is so thickly interspersed
with villas and gardens, that you would imagine the whole place
was one garden. Many streams belong to this place, and palm-
trees are here in great number. When the water of the sea rises
or increases, the waters of those streams go back amongst the
gardens, and fields, and orchards; and when the water of the
sea sinks or diminishes, the river-waters return to their channels,
but are all brackish, or of a bitter taste. ابله Ableh is situated
on this river; and there is a dangerous place, called Hawer Ableh,
in it, against which vessels from the sea must be well guarded,
lest they should be sunk there. Ableh is a small town, but well
supplied with provisions, and pleasantly situated, one side being
towards the Dejleh. That river (above mentioned) comes from
the Dejleh, in a direct line to عبادان Abadan. The soil
or earth of Basrah is white. The towns of this district are,
Ableh, منتح Mentah, and مدار Medar; all small towns, situated on the river Dejleh. The chief of these is Ableh.

* Or حي Hey.

In the territories of Basrah are احما *Ahma* and بطايح *Betaiah.* Boats or vessels are moved here by the strength of men. Near this place are great gulphs or abysses: one would imagine that the land had been dry at some former time; and it is possible that the water, making its way from the rivers of Basrah, had settled wherever it found a deep furrow or pit.

واسط *Waset* is situated on the two banks of the Dejleh. It has been built since the introduction of Islam. The foundation was laid by حجاج يوسف *Hejaje Yusuf.* It is strongly built; and the castle of Hejaje is there, on the western side, with a few fields belonging to it. Waset is a populous town, and well supplied with provisions---of a purer air than Basrah: the vicinity of it is planted with gardens, and well cultivated.

كوفه *Cufa* is smaller than Basrah, but resembles it in some respects. The air and water of Cufa are better than those of Basrah. It is situated near the river Forat. The suburbs of Cufa were built by سعد بن وقاص *Saad ben Wakas.*

قادسيه *Cadesiah,* and حيره *Heirah,* and خورنق *Khawrnak,* are situated on the skirts of the desert, towards the west; the river (Euphrates) running by them on the east: they afford dates, and have some cultivated lands. From Cufa to these places is a distance of one merhileh. Heirah is an ancient city, and large; but when Cufa was built, Heirah was drained of its inhabitants.

Heirah enjoys a pure air, and is one farsang distant from Cufa. At Cufa is situated the tomb or *meshed* of the Commander of the Faithful, علي بن ابي طالب *Ali ben Abi Taleb*, on whom be peace! Some say it is in the cloister at the entrance of the chief mosque; and others say it is at a distance of two farsang. قادسيه *Cadesiah* is situated on the border of the desert: it has running water, and cultivated lands. From Cadesiah, on the confines of Irak, until you come to Medinah (مدينة السلام *Medinah Alssalam*, the city of Islam), there is not any running water.

بغداد *Baghdad* is a celebrated city, erected since the introduction of Islam. It was built by ابو جعفر منصور *Abou Jaffer Mansour**. At first the western quarter was built, and every one settled himself there in any manner he thought fit. Afterwards it became populous; and when مهدي *Mohdi* succeeded to the khalifat†, he encamped his troops on the eastern side. Buildings were then erected, and that quarter also became thickly inhabited. The villas and palaces extended for near two farsang from Baghdad to the river, and this city became the residence of the khalifs. The buildings were continued from the river to the district of واسط *Waset,* and from above the Dejleh to شماسيه

---

* This Khalif (of the House of *Abbas*) began to reign A. H. 136, (A. D. 754.) The foundation of Baghdad was laid in the year of the Hegira 145.

† He began to reign A. H. 158, (A. D. 775.)

Shemasiah, a distance of nearly five farsang. The eastern side they call باب الطاق رصافه *Bab al Tauk Resafeh*, and also عسكر المهدي *Asker al Mohdi*. It is said that the name *Bab al Tauk* is derived from a certain great dome, or cupola, in the principal bazar or market-place, called سوق العظيم *Souk al Azim*.

Resafeh is a considerable suburb, built by رشيد *Rashid*, near the مسجد جامع *Mesjed Jamia*: the western side is called كرخ *Korkh*. Here are three mosques; one, the Mesjed Jamia al Mansour; another, situated at the Bab al Tauk; and the other, at the دار الخلافه *Dar al Khalifah*, or palace of the Khalif: and the buildings continue as far as كلوازي *Kelwazi*, where there is a mosque. Over the river Dejleh a bridge has been constructed of boats; and from the دروازه خراسان *gate of Khorasan*, to the place called باب الياسرثه *Bab alia Sertheh*, the breadth of the city at both sides is about six miles.

Korkh is very well inhabited, and considerable commerce is there carried on; but the trees and streams are on the eastern side. The water they drink is of the river نهروان *Nehrwan*. On the western side there is a stream, called the نهرعسى *Nehr Isa*, or the river of Jesus---a branch of the Forat, which, passing by Baghdad, falls into the Dejleh.

Between Baghdad and كوفه *Cufa* there are many districts and villages, through which run streams from the river Forat. Here is situated the town of ضرصر *Sarsar,* on the stream called Sarsar, at a distance of three farsang from Baghdad. It is a pleasant town, with land well cultivated. After that, at a distance of two farsang, is the نهر الملک *Nehr al Molk* (or the King's river.) There is a bridge over it; and it is much more considerable than the river of Sarsar. The district of Nehr al Molk is better cultivated, and affords more corn and fruits, than Sarsar. From that one proceeds to قصر ابن هبیره *Kesr Ebn Hobeireh,* situated on the river Forat, and one of the most considerable places between Cufa and Baghdad. Here are several streams, so that the water is much augmented, and passes on to the town of سورا *Soura.* The great river Forat has not any branch more considerable than this. From Soura it proceeds to the *souad* (سواد) or villages in the neighbourhood of Cufa; and after that falls into the river of بطایح *Betaiah.*

کربلا *Kerbela* is situated on the west of the Forat, opposite to or near (برابر) *Kesr ebn Hobeireh.*

سامره *Samereh* is altogether situated to the east*. In this quarter there is not any running water, but the river *Al-katoul,* نهرلقاطول that runs at some distance from the town. Buildings, and streams, and trees, are opposite, on the western side, and

سامره جمله در شرقیست *

extend for near one merhileh. The first founder of this place was معتصم Motasem; and it has since fallen into the hands of متوکل Motawakel*, and is all in ruins, so much that within the space of a farsang there is not any building or cultivated land to be seen. The air and fruits of Samareh are better than those of Baghdad.

نهروان Nehrwan is situated at the distance of four farsang from Baghdad. A considerable stream flows there, and proceeds under the دار الخلافه Dar al Khalifah, in the *souad* of Baghdad, to the place which they call اسكاف بني حنيد Askaf beni Haneid, and other districts; and when one comes from Nehrwan to دسكره Deskereh, the waters are less, and the dates fewer: and from Deskereh to the borders of حلوان Holwan is a desert, without any buildings or inhabited places between it and Samereh, or between شهرزور Shehrzour and the borders of تكريت Tacrith.

مدائن Madaien is a little town, at the distance of one merhileh from Baghdad. In former times it was a very considerable city, and a favourite dwelling-place of kings. The ايوان كسري Aiwan Kesri† is situated there, built of stone and mortar. The

---

* *Motawakel* became Khalif in the year of the Hegira 232, (A. D. 847.) For anecdotes relative to the building of *Catoul* and *Samareh* by the Khalif Motassem, see D'Herbelot's *Bibliot. Orient.* Art. Motassem.

† Called also the طاق كسري *Tawk-i-Kesri*, or palace of the Persian monarchs, styled *Khosrus*, or *Kesris*. It was built by *Nushirvan*, in the middle of the sixth century of the Christian æra.

Kesris had not any edifices greater than this; and Madaien was larger than any place, except Baghdad, which we have before described.

*بابل *Babel* is a small village, but the most ancient spot in all Irak. The whole region is denominated Babel, from this place. The kings of كنعان *Canaan* resided there, and ruins of great edifices still remain. I am of opinion, that, in former times, it was a very considerable place. They say that Babel was founded by ضحاک پیوراسپ *Zohak Piurasp* †; and there was Abraham (to whom be peace!) thrown into the fire. There are two heaps, one of which is in a place called كودي طريق *Koudi Tereik*, the other, *Koudi Derbar* دربار: in this the ashes still remain; and they say that it was the آتش نمرود *fire of Nimrod* into which Abraham was cast; may peace be on him!

مداين *Madaien* is situated on the east of the river Dejleh; and they reckon it one merhileh from Baghdad to that place. It is said that ذولقرنين *Zhu l'Kernein* (Alexander the Great) found at that place the divine mandate, (*i. e.* died there); but I suspect that this tradition is not true, because he was poisoned at the time of his returning from Cheen, and his coffin was taken to

---

* Of this passage, as far as the word *littleness* on the opposite page, I have given the original Persian in the Appendix.

† Fifth king of the Peishdadian, or first dynasty of the Persian sovereigns, supposed to have reigned about 780 years before Christ.—See the "*Epitome of the Ancient History of Persia*," p. 6 and 8.

Alexandria to his mother. It is also said, that there has been a bridge at Madaien, on the river Dejleh; but I did not see any vestiges of it.

عكبرا *Akbera*, and بردان *Berdan*, and نعمانيه *Neamaniah*, and جرجرايا *Deir-alaakoul*, and دجيل *Dejeil*, and دير العاتول *Jerjeraya**, and فم الصلح *Fomas'salah*, and نهر سايس *Nehr Saies*, and other places on the banks of the river Dejleh, which we have mentioned, are situated one near another, and are nearly equal in *greatness and littleness*.

حلوان *Holwan* is a well-inhabited and pleasant town. After Cufa, and Basrah, and Waset, and Baghdad, and Samereh, and Hobeireh, there is not any city more considerable in Irak. Snow falls there; and on the mountains in its vicinity there is at all times snow.

دسكره *Deskereh* is a populous and pleasant place, with a strong castle, and corn fields. It is said that a king† from time to time resided there, on which account it was styled دسكره الملك *Deskereh al Molk*. From Deskereh to above Samereh,

---

* In the Eton MS. this name is written جرحرانا *Jerherana*.

† According to the Persian manuscript, intituled لب التواريخ *Leb-al-Towarikh*, this castle of *Deskereh* was built by *Hormuz*, the son of *Shapour*, third king of the Sassanian or fourth dynasty, who began to reign A. D. 272. See " *Epitome of the Ancient History of Persia,*" p. 42.

till one comes near عايث *Aayeth* in this line, and likewise to the borders of the district of Waset, from the borders of Irak to the borders of كوه *Kouh**, the buildings are few, and the greater part is pasture land of the Arabs. Thus, to the west of Tacrith, to Anbar, between the rivers Dejleh and Forat, there are not any buildings, unless those opposite (or near) Samereh: almost all the rest is the bare and barren desert.

It were unnecessary to dwell longer on the account of Irak, as it is a country so famous and so well known amongst men.

ذكر ديار خوزستان

Description of the Province of Khuzistan.

THE eastern boundaries of Khuzistan are the borders of پارس *Pars* and سپاهان *Spahaun*†. Between the borders of Pars and of Spahaun, there is a certain river called نهر طاب *Nehr Tab*, in the vicinity of ماهي رويان *Mahi-rooyan*: from that, the boundary is between دورق *Dourek* and Mahi-rooyan towards

---

* كوه signifies a mountain, in general; but here, perhaps, is the name of a fortress situated on the mountains of Merdin, mentioned by PETIS de la CROIX, in his *Hist. of Timur*, Vol. I. ch. 39.

† *Ispahan, Sfahan*, or *Isfahan*---The name is variously written in the course of this work, as in most other MSS.

the sea-side. On the western side, the boundaries of Khuzistan are the territories of Waset, and that place which they call دورابواستي *Durabouasty*. On the north it has the borders of صيمره *Seimereh*, and كرخه *Kurkheh*, and لور *Lour*, as far as the borders of جبال *Jebal*, adjoining the territories of Spahaun. It is said that Lour was once reckoned as belonging to Khuzistan; but at present it is comprehended within Jebal.

The boundaries of Khuzistan towards Pars and صغاهان *Sfahan*, and the borders of Jebal and Waset, are straight lines on the four sides: But on the southern side, from عبادان *Abadan*, to the villages about Waset, the boundary is an irregular line; and from Abadan to the sea, and the borders of Pars: then this southern boundary proceeds along the sea shore; then to the Dejleh, and passes from بارما *Barma*: thence winds from above مفتح *Meftah* and مدار *Medar*, among the villages of Waset, there whence we first set out.

صورت ديار خوزستان
(Map of Khuzistan.)

هرمز شهر *Hormuz Shehr*. كوره' اهواز *Koureh Ahwaz* is also called The other places of Khuzistan are the شهر لشكر *Shehr Leshkur*, which they also call عسكر مكرم *Asker Mokrem*; سوس *Sus*; جندي شاپور *Jondi Shapour*; شوشتر *Shushter*; رام هرمز *Ram Hormuz*; and بازار *Bazar*: all these are the names of cities, but Bazar, which they call سوق Souk, and its town دورق Dourek; ایذح Aidah, نهر تیری Neher Tiri, خایزان Khaizan, حومه النط Houmah al net, حومه السان Houmeh al San, سوق اسنبیل Souk asunbeil, مبادر الکبری Mebader al Kebri, مبادر الصغری Mebadar al Sagheri, حي Hei, طب Teb, کلیوان Keliwan, are all towns of this district. حصن Bosi, ارم Arem, سوق الاربعا Souk al Arbaa, بصّي سلیمانان Hysn Mohdi, باسان Basan, سلسان Selsan, مهدي Solymanan, ترقوب Carcoub, بردون Berdoun, and کرخه Karkheh.

The land of Khuzistan is level. It has many running streams, the chief of which is the river of Shushter: and King Shapour[*] caused to be constructed on this river a wall (or mound) called شادروان Shadervan; by means of which the town of Shushter, situated on an eminence, might be supplied with water. This river comes from لشکر Leshkur (or Asker Mokrem) to اهواز Ahwaz, and falls into the river Sedreh, رود سدره and goes on to the Hysn Mohdi, on the sea side. Another river of Khuzistan is called نهر المشرتان Nehr al Mushirkan, on which, at Leshkur, a great bridge has been erected; and by this river one may go from Leshkur to Ahwaz, a distance of eight farsang: but

---

[*] *Shapour Zhulectaf*, who began to reign A. D. 309. He was the eighth king of the fourth or *Sassanian* dynasty. (See " *Epitome of the Ancient History of Persia,*" p. 46, &c.) The *Tarikh Gozideh*, and other MSS. speak of this *Shadervan*, in passages which shall be given at length in a future work on Asiatick Geography.

when one has gone six farsang, all the water is drained off, for various purposes of husbandry and agriculture; and for two farsang the bed of the river is altogether dry. In the land of Khuzistan there is not any place more populous or cultivated than Musherkan.

The streams of Khuzistan, from Ahwaz, and Dourek, and Shushter, and all that rise in this quarter, are collected together at Hysn Mohdi, and there, forming one great river, fall into the sea. There is not any of the sea in Khuzistan, except a little of the دریای پارس *Persian Sea*, from رویان ماهی *Mahi rooyan*, to near سلیمانان *Solymanan*, opposite عبادان *Abadan*: nor is there in all Khuzistan, any mountain, nor sand, except at Shushter, and جندی شاپور *Jondi Shapour*, and ایذج *Aidej*, as far as the borders of صغاهان *Sfahan*: all the rest is soft clay and level ground: And in any of the cities of Khuzistan I know not that they drink well-water: and the land of this province is more dry, in proportion as it is distant from the river Dejleh: that part nearer the Dejleh is like the soil of Basrah, and that region.

Throughout Khuzistan there is not either ice or snow; nor is there any part of it which does not afford dates. It is a very unhealthy country. All kinds of fruit are to be found in Khuzistan, except walnuts (کردکان), and the fruit of trees peculiar to a cold climate.

For the greater part, Arabick and Persian are spoken in this province: there is also a particular dialect in Khuzistan. The fashion of the people, in their dress, resembles that of the inhabitants of Irak. They are in general of bad dispositions; and mostly of a yellow complexion, with scanty beards; and of the معتزلي *Motazelite* sect (Mahommedan schismaticks.)

Among the wonders of Khuzistan, is the *Shadervan* of *Shapour* (before mentioned) at Shushter. It is said to be a mile in length, constructed of stone and mortar, for the purpose of conducting water to Shushter.

In the city of سوس *Sus*, there is a river; and I have heard, that, in the time of ابو موسي اشعري *Abou Mousa Ashoari*, a coffin was found there: and it is said the bones of Daniel the Prophet (to whom be peace!) were in that coffin. These the people held in great veneration; and in time of distress, or famine from droughts, they brought them out, and prayed for rain. Abou Mousa Ashoara ordered this coffin to be brought, and three coverings or cases to be made for it; the first, or outside one, of which was of boards, exceedingly strong; and caused it to be buried, so that it could not be viewed. A bay or gulf of the river came over this grave, which may be seen by any one who dives to the bottom of the water.

There is also, in the district of سنبيل *Sumbeil,* near the borders of Pars, a mountain, from which fire issues at all times. At night this fire gives light; and smoke comes forth in the day-time: and the general opinion is, that there is here a fountain of نفت *Naphta,* or of pitch (زفت), which has taken fire. There is also a species of scorpion (كژدم) which they call كزوره *kezoureh:* they are like the leaves of انجدان *anjedan* (the herb laserpitium or pellitory), and are more destructive than serpents.

Very rich garments of brocade are manufactured at Shushter. At Sus there is a species of orange, which they call پنج انكشت *penj-angusht,* (or five fingers,) said to be exceedingly fragrant. In this district there is a place called بصي *Bosi,* where they weave beautiful tapestry; as also at كليوان *Keliwan,* and at بردون *Berdoun.*

جندي شاپور *Jondi Shapour,* or كُندي شاپور *Gondi Shapour,* is a considerable city, populous and pleasant, abounding in dates and the produce of agriculture; يعقوب بن ليث *Iacoub ben Leith,* of the Soffarian Dynasty*, resided in this city; and his tomb is there. نهر تيري *Neher Tiri* is a town in which they manufacture garments like those of Baghdad. حي *Hey* is a town with territories dependent on it, and cultivated lands,

---

* *Iacoub ben Leith,* founder of the Soffarian Dynasty, died in the year of the Hegira 265, (A, D. 878.)

with date trees in abundance: the imam of the Motezalah sect ابوعلي *Abu Aly*, was of this place. At زاويه *Zawieh*, near حصن مهدي *Hysn Mohdi*, on the sea-side, a great many streams are collected into one body of water, affected by tides, flux and reflux. طيب *Teib* is remarkable for its manufactory of شلوار بند *shelwar bend*, or fastenings for breeches and drawers; they are like those made in Roum: and none are found equal to them in any place except Armenia.

لور *Lour* is a pleasant and well-inhabited place; the mountain air prevails there: it was formerly reckoned as belonging to Khuzistan: but now they comprehend it within the territories of كوهستان *Kouhestan*. سنبيل *Sumbeil* is a district, which, in the time of محمد بن واصل *Mohammed ben Wasel*, was reckoned among the territories of Pars; at present it belongs to the province of Khuzistan. نط *Nat* and خايزان *Khaizan* are situated on a river. اسل *Asel* has a small plantation of date trees: there was a battle at this place, in which, it is said, forty men of شراه *Sherah* defeated a thousand men of the army of Baghdad. ارغان *Arghan* is a town where دوشاب *doushab** is made, and sent to all parts of the world. مبادر الكبرى *Mebader al Kebri*, and مبادر الصغرى *Mebader al Sagheri* (the greater and lesser), are two well-inhabited and pleasant places, abounding in dates.

* A particular kind of syrup, of a thick consistence, used in the composition of sherbet, &c.

ذكر مسافات خوزستان

Distances of Places in Khuzistan.

From Pars to Irak there are two roads; one by the way of Basrah, the other by way of Waset. The Basrah road is this: From ارغان *Arghan* to اسل *Asel*, two easy merhileh; from that to a village called ديدان *Deidan*, one merhileh; from Deidan to دورق *Dourek*, and from that to ساسان *Sasan*, a pleasant town, through which a river flows: from Sasan to حصن مهدي *Hysn Mohdi*, is a journey of two merhileh: from these two places one must go by water: and from Hysn Mohdi to بنات *Benat*, two merhileh; and they go from Dourek to باسان *Basan* by water, it being much easier than going by land. This is the extreme boundary of Khuzistan. Benat is situated on the banks of the river Dejleh; and, if one chooses he may go by water to Ablah, or by land, crossing over when he comes opposite Ablah.

The road from Pars to Irak, by way of Waset, is from Arghan to بازار *Bazar*, one merhileh; from that to رامز *Ramuz* (probably for رام هرمز *Ram Hormuz*), two merhileh; from Ramuz to لشكر *Leshkur*, or Asker Mokrem, three merhileh; from that to شوشتر *Shushter*, one merhileh: from Shushter to جندي شاپور

Jondi Shapour, one merhileh ; and from Jondi Shapour to سوس *Sus,* one merhileh ; and from that to ترتوب *Corcoub,* one merhileh. From Shushter to Jondi Shapour, is one merhileh ; from that to طيب *Teib,* one merhileh ; this place borders on the territories of Waset. From Leshkur to اهواز *Ahwaz,* is one merhileh ; from Ahwaz to دورق *Dourak,* three merhileh ; and this is a shorter way from Leshkur to Waset than that which passes by Shushter. From Leshkur to ايدج *Aidej* is four merhileh ; from Ahwaz to Ramuz, three merhileh, " because Ahwaz and Leshkur are situated on the same line, and Ramuz forms a triangle with them*." From Leshkur to بازار *Bazar,* one merhileh ; and from Bazar to Hysn Mohdi, one merhileh ; from Ahwaz to نهر تيري *Neher Tiri,* one day's journey ; and from Sus to بصي *Bosi,* not so much as one merhileh ; and from Sus to بردون *Bardoun,* one merhileh ; and from Sus to متنوت *Matout*†, one merhileh.

Those are the whole of the distances, and stages in the province of Khuzistan.

* زيرا كه اهواز و لشكر بريك قبـت نهاده‌اند رامز برمثلثه آن است

† Or متوب *Matoub,* according to the Eton MS.

ذکر دیار پارس

Description of the Province of Pars,
(or Farsistan---Persia Proper.)

THE eastern side of Pars is bounded by the province of کرمان *Kirman:* the western side by خوزستان *Khuzistan* and اصفهان *Isfahan.* On the the north, it has the deserts of خراسان *Khorasan,* and part of the territories of Isfahan: and it is bounded on the south by the Persian Sea, دریای پارس

We shall describe the whole face of this country, except the smaller villages and hills, which are too numerous and diversified for particular mention.

(Blank page for the Map of Pars.)

(82)

ذكر كورههاي فارس

Account of the Kourehs, or Districts, in the Province of Fars, or Pars.

THERE are five Kourehs in this province, the most considerable of which is the كوره ٔ اصطخر *Koureh of Istakhar:* اردشير دره *Ardeshir Dereh,* in which are the cities of شيراز *Shiraz* and سيراف *Siraf.* جور *Jawr* also belongs to this district of Ardeshir, because it was built by him, and was his capital. ارغان *Arghan* is also a large city. The كوره شاپور *Koureh Shapour* is the smallest of these districts of Pars: the town is called after Shapour, who built it, in the vicinity of كازرون *Cazeroun.*

But there are five places in Pars, which they call زم *Zem* *. The signification of this word is, a tribe, or race (Arab. قبيله). One of these is more considerable than the others---the زم حيلويه *Zem Heilouieh:* this is called زم سنجان *Zem Senjan.* The second is the زم احمد بن الليث *Zem of Ahmed ben Leith:* it is called *Zem*† * * * * *. The third is called احمد بن صالح

---

* In the Eton MS. there is a title in red ink prefixed to this passage—زمومهايفارس " The *Zemoums of Fars*;" an extraordinary plural of *Zem*. As this section, and that which follows, afford some curious matter, they are given in the original Persian, at the end of this volume.

† The word following *Zem* in my MS. is rendered illegible by a blot of ink; and in

Zem Ahmed ben Saleh. The fourth is the زم شهريار *Zem Shehryar*, which they call زم بادنجان *Zem Badenjan*. The fifth is the زم احمد بن الحسين *Zem Ahmed ben Alhosein*, called زم كارما *Zem Karma*; and this is the زم اردشير *Zem Ardeshir*.

ذكر جومهاي كردان

Account of the Joums of the Curds *.

THE Joums of the Curds are more than can be exactly numbered; but it is said that in Pars there are above five hundred thousand houses (خانه or families), which, during winter and summer, remain on the pasture-lands. Some of these Curds maintain two hundred persons, such as shepherds, and labourers, and grooms, and boys or servants, and such like. Their number cannot be ascertained.

---

the Eton MS. (like too many other proper names) it is written without any diacritical points, thus نوادحار—and consequently capable of various readings.

* If the word *Joum* had not been too plainly written in this place, and the following passage, I would have altered it to قوم *Koum*, tribe, people, family, &c.—Captain FRANCKLIN, in his *Tour to Persia* (London edition, 1790, octavo, p. 199), mentions "some hundreds of wandering Curds and Turkomans," whom his party met in the vicinity of Persepolis. They were then removing, with their families, flocks, and herds, to the southward of Shiraz; and resembled, in their sun-burnt, tawny complexions, the Gypsies of Europe.

ذكر رودهاي پارس

Account of the Rivers of Pars.

THE Rivers of Pars, which are navigable for boats, are the رود شاكان Nehr Tab, نهر شيرين Nehr Shirin, نهر طاب Rood Shakan, رود درجند Rood Derjend, رود جويدان Rood Jouidan, رود روييـن Rood Rouyin, رود سكان Rood Sekan, رود خشبو Rood Koshbù, رود خشين Rood Kushein, رود فرواب Rood Kas, رود کس Rood Foruab, and the رود هرده Rood Herdeh.

ذكر درياي‌ها فارس

Of the Lakes of Fars.

THE chief Lakes are the درياي بختنكان Derayi Bakhtegan, the درياي دشت Deryai Desht, the بحيرة الثو Beheiret (lake) Alsour, and the بحيرة الحربايان Beheiret al Hurbaian.

ذكر آتشكده‌هاي فارس

Of the Fire-Temples of Fars.

THERE is not any district, nor any town of Fars, without a Fire-Temple. These are held in high veneration. We shall, hereafter, more minutely describe them. Also, throughout Fars, there are castles in every quarter, *one stronger than another*, (يكي از ديكر استوارتر). The greater number of them are situated in the district of سيف بني الصغار *Seif beni al Seghar*. All these we shall describe in the course of this work, so that they shall be known. " And there are many considerable districts, which possess essential importance, yet have not been much celebrated or spoken of; but we shall notice all these places, and give a concise description of them, in this work*."

* و بسيار ناحيت بزرك هست كه در ذات خويش عظمي دارد و نام و ذكر بسيار ندا يـ‌د و ما جمله اين مواضع را ياد كنيم و بيان شافي بكويم درين رساله

ذَكَرَ نَوَاحِي كُورَهِ اصطخر

Account of the Districts of the Koureh of Istakhar.

THE district of يزد *Yezd* is the most considerable division of the Koureh of Istakhar. There are in it three places with mosques, كته *Kattah*, and ميبد *Meibed*, and ماهين *Mahein*. Part of this district was formerly reckoned as belonging to the province of كرمان *Kirman*, but now is included in the territories of Fars.

The extent of the district of Istakhar is about sixty farsang. ابرقوه *Aberkouh* is one of the cities. اقليد *Aklid* and سرمق *Surmek*, are two towns which, in Persian, are written كليد *Kelid* and سرمه *Surmeh*. حوباقان *Houbakan* they call مشكان *Meshkan*. ازجهان *Azhaman* is a town. جارين *Jarin*, and قوين *Kouin*, and طرخينسان *Tarkhinsan*, have not any oratories or pulpits (منبر). آباده *Abadeh* is the village of Abdar'-rahman عبدالرحمن. دهيه *Mehruian*, مهرويان and Sahel al Kebri, صاهل الكبري have not oratories or pulpits; neither have مروسف *Marousef*, nor فانك *Fanek*, هراه رودكان *Harah Rudgan*, كلس *Keles*, دحيره *Deheireh*, ارکان *Arkan*, سرشك *Sershek*, رادان *Radan*, بيضا *Beiza*, هران *Heran*, ماهين *Mahein*, nor رامجرد *Ramjerd*.

Of the district, or طسوج *Tesouje*, the principal towns are حومه *Hhoumah*, سرواب *Sirouab*, مكي *Meki*, رادن *Radan*, Se‑ سرادسين *Seradsin*, اللون *Lawen*, ذكورث *Zakoureth*, كلار *Kellar*, اسدان *Asedan*, سردن *Serden*, لوردكان *Lourdegan*, خمارد كان *Khemardegan*, بامان *Baman*, اسلان *Aselan*, سغلي *Sefli*.

ذكر نواحي اردشير كوره

Account of the Districts of Ardeshir Koureh.

شيراز *Shiraz* is the centre for the عاملان *Aumilans* (Intendants or Collectors of the Revenue) of Pars. There are twelve طسوج *Tesoujes* (portions or tracts of land.) In each of these is a district with buildings. Each Tesouje is an عاملي *Aumily* (or certain tract under one Aumil or Collector of Revenues.) These twelve Tesoujes are, the Tesouje كفره العليا *Kafrah-al-aalia*, the Tesouje كفره السغلي *Kaffrah al Sefli*, the Tesouje كبير *Kabir*, the Tesouje حديم *Hedim*, the Tesouje ديركان *Deirgan*, the Tesouje تيبول الكاويان *Taiboul al Kawian*, the Tesouje انباربانان *Anbarbanan*, the Tesouje ابنديان *Abendian*, the Tesouje شاهرنك *Shahrung*, the Tesouje شهرستان *Shehristan*, the Tesouje طبرار *Tirar*, and the Tesouje طسوج خان *Khan*.

ذكر نواحي اردشير خره

Account of the Districts of Ardeshir Khereh.

جور *Jawr* and ممید *Memeid.* The principal places of these are مانین *Manein,* ممکان *Memkan,* and شهران *Shehran,* and صمکان *Samgan:* these have not any oratories or pulpits; neither فرخان *Farkhan,* nor خنیفان *Khanifan.* نادوان *Nadouan,* حمرس *Hamres,* خورسان *Khoorsan,* دریجان *Derijan,* همید *Hemeid,* هرمز *Hormuz,* سکانات *Sekanat,* سیف بنی الصغار *Seif beni al Seghar,* هیجان *Haijan,* کومکان *Koumgan,* کسری *Kesri,* حسکان *Heskan,* سیف الابی *Seif al Abi,* دهیر سیف عمارة *Deheir Seif Omareh:* these places have not pulpits or oratories; but سیراف *Siraf* has three. بجیرم *Bajirem,* عسدجان *Asdejan,* خم *Khem,* دشت *Desht,* وازین *Wazin,* دستیغان *Destikan;* the chief town is سفاره *Sefareh:* نوح خریک *Noah Kherik,* the chief town of الغرستان *Lagheristan;* شکیر *Shekeir,* کارزین *Karzein,* امدن *Ameden,* سمیران *Semiran,* کوان *Kouan;* کهرجان *Keherjan,* a large island.

ذكر نواحي داراب كرد

Account of the Territories of Darabgird.

THE district of كوم *Koum* has two principal towns, اماده *Amadeh* and كرد *Gird*; تصريسا *Keserisa*, طبيسان *Tebisan*, مسيجان *Behouleh*, كردمان *Kirdman*, حببير *Hembeir*, بحوله *Mesihan*, ركان *Rekan*, اريراه *Arirah*, سان *San*, جويم *Jouim*, ماروان *Marouan*, هرين *Herin*, اصطهفايان *Astehefaian*, هيج *Hije*, روستاي رشاق *Roustai Rouiah*, رويج *Rouiah*, حسوا *Hesoua*, مدح *Reshak*, مساكنات *Medah*, بازم *Bazem*, مساكنات *Mesakenat*, تنطره *Kantereh*, سوانجان *Souanjan*, شق الرشاق *Shuk al reshak*, شق الماسانان *Shuk al rud*, تالت *Talat*, شق الماسانان *Shuk al masanan*, زم شهرازو *Zem Shehrazu.*

ذكر حدود كوره شاپور

Account of the Borders or Territories of the Koureh Shapour.

باسان *Basan*, حجار *Hejar*, كازرون *Kazeroun*, شاپور *Shapour*, خشت *Khisht*, خواج *Khouaje*, درتك *Dertek*, حفيه *Hafieh*, كياوم *Khisht*, كياوم *Keiawem*, حدىجان شاپور *Hedijan Shapour,*

(90)

تیرمردان *Tîr Merdan :* except Shapour and Kazeroun, all these towns are without pulpits or oratories. نوبندكان *Nubendgan,* منبر شعب *Member Shaab,* بينول *Beinoul,* بوان *Bouan,* البور *Almour,* درنجان *Derenjan,* درجند *Derjend,* ملغان کنبذ *Kumbuz Malghan,* انبوران *Ambouran,* اسل *Asel,* فرطاست *Fertast,* شکيره *Shekireh,* بهلوق *Bahalouk,* بهلسكان *Bahelsegan,* كام فيروز *Kam Firouz;* this place has five villages belonging to it: ارزو *Arzu,* نادر *Nader,* استادان *Astadan,* كاكان *Kakan,* آتشكاه مسيحان *Ateshgah Mesihan* (or the Fire-temple of Mesihan), سجان *Sejan,* مدر *Meder,* هياز *Heyaz,* خمايكان *Khemaigan,* بالايين *Balaien,* سيسكان *Seisekan,* نبوليس *Nebulis,* صوردادي *Sourdadi,* ارجان *Arjan,* بسميل *Besmeil,* اسلجار *Aseljar,* ديدالوت *Deidalout,* ديرعمر *Deir Omr,* فردک *Fardek,* مهرويان *Mehruian,* جنابه *Jenabah,* صوار الخس *Souar al Khess,* سيس *Seis.*

ذكر نواحي كوره ارغان

Account of the Territories of the Koureh Arghan.

To every زم *Zem* there is a town and territory, in which resides a chief (ريسي), who collects the tolls and tributes; and in his charge are the guides (بدرتهراهها) upon the roads.

The زم حيلويه *Zem Heilouieh* is also called سنجان *Senjan:*

it lies near Isfahan ; and one side of it borders the Koureh Istakhar, another the Koureh Shapour, and another the كوره ارجان *Koureh Arjan*. Besides these, it has a boundary (حدود) near بيضا *Beiza*, another near Isfahan, and a third near Khuzistan; one also near the borders of Shapour: and the towns and villages of these different quarters are all reckoned as belonging to this Zem.

The زم دلوان *Zem Delouan* belonged to بن صالح *Ebn Saleh*: it partly borders on the Koureh Shapour: one border of it lies next Ardeshir, and three boundaries of it turn back on the Koureh Shapour. The Zem بادانجان *Badenjan* belonged to احمد بن ليث *Amed ben Leith*: it is of the Koureh Ardeshir; one border on the sea, and three on اردشير دره *Ardeshir Dereh*. The Zem كاريان *Karian* has one border on the سيف الصغار *Seif al Seghar*, and one on the Zem Badenjan; three on the confines of Kirman, and another on the Ardeshir Dereh.

ذكر زموم انجا

Account of (other) Zems* in that Country.

زم بروحی *Kirmanian,* درمانیان *Dermanian,* كرمانیان
Zem Berouhi, محمد بن بشر *Mohammed ben Besher*; the
قبیله محمد بن اسحق *Kabilah Mohammed ben Ishak,*
ادركانیان *Sebahian,* اسحاقیان *Ishakian,* صباحیان *Ader-*
ganian, شهركبار *Sheher Kobar,* طهاریان *Taharian,* ربادیان
Rebadian, شهروبان *Sheheruban,* خرویان *Khoruian,* زنكیان
Zingian, صغریان *Seferian,* شهماریان *Shehmarian,* مطلسان
Mutlesan, ممالیان *Memalian,* سماكامان *Semakaman,* خلیلیان
Khalilian. These are what we know of them: but if any person
wishes to be informed of all, he must recollect that we have before
mentioned (see p. 83), that this people (طایفه) amount to near five
hundred thousand families; and one† tribe (قبیله) of them goes
forth two thousand horsemen; and there is not any tribe of less
than an hundred horsemen. Summer and winter they pass on
the feeding or pasture lands. A few of their people dwell on the

---

* It would seem, that in using the word *Zem* here, and *Joum* in the chapter where these people are before mentioned, some confusion or mistake has occurred, which I am not at present able to correct, as the Eton MS. agrees with my own.

† That the reader may satisfy himself, on the subject of this extraordinary people, I have given the original Persian of the whole passage, in the Appendix.

borders of صرور Sarour and جرور Jarour, and depart not from those places. Their weapons and accoutrements, their numbers, war-horses, and troops, are such that they are able to contend with kings; and it is said that their race is originally Arabian. They have sheep, and mares (or مادیان *she asses*), and camels, but not so many: and I have heard that this people consist of above one hundred tribes; but I only know between thirty and forty* of the tribes.

ذکر حصنهای پارس

Of the Fortresses and Castles of Pars.

THERE are certain cities surrounded with strong walls; and others, in which there are citadels with strong outworks; and there are some castles, exceedingly strong, situated on hills and mountains. Among the cities which have citadels, is اصطخر *Istakhar*, round the castle of which are strong fortifications. بیضا *Beiza* has a citadel with fortifications; also سرمه *Sermeh*, and کلید *Keleid*: ترنه الاس *Kurnah allas*, in Persian called دهیه مورد *Dhey Moured*, has an ancient دژ *dez*, or castle; and the fortifications of شیراز *Shiraz* have a کهندز *kohendez*;

---

* The word انل *and*, according to that most excellent Dictionary, the *Ferhung Barhan Kattee*, signifies *some*, *a few*, any number *from three to nine*, &c.

or an ancient castle. جور *Jour* has a citadel, but no outworks. كازرون *Kazeroun*, has a kohendez also, with fortifications. فسا *Fesa*, has a kohendez, with fortifications. دارابجرد *Darab-jerd* has a castle and walls. And I have heard, that in the province of Pars there are more than five celebrated castles, situated in towns and on hills, which no king has ever been able to take. One of them is the castle of *Ebn Omareh*, قلعه ابن عماره which they call قلعه دانبان *Kelaa Danban*. There the family of Omareh used to seize upon every tenth ship. The castle of كادبان *Kadban* is situated on a mountain: neither محمد بن واصل *Mohammed ben Wasel*, with his army, nor احمد بن الحسين *Ahmed ben Allosein*, were able to take it.

The castle of سعيد آباد *Saied Abad* (the residence of Good Fortune) is one farsang from the Koureh of Istakhar. It was originally called the Castle of اسفنديار *Asfendiar*. In the time of the Commander of the Faithful, the Prince of the Saints of God, علي بن ابيطالب *Ali ben Abitaleb*, to whom be peace! this castle was the residence of زياد بن اميه *Zeyad ben Ommiah*, and from that circumstance was called after him. In the time of the بني اميه *Beni Ommiah*, منصور بن محمد بن جعفر *Mansour ben Mohammed ben Jaffer* was Governor of Pars, and resided in this castle, which then received its name from him. Some time after that, it was ruined; and soon again repaired by محمد بن واصل *Mohammed ben Wasel*, who was Governor of Pars. When it was taken by يعقوب بن ليث *Yacoub ben*

Leith, he caused it to be once more demolished; it was, however, again repaired, and they used it as a prison.

The castle of اسکنون *Asknoun* is supplied with water by a stream flowing from the heights of مانين *Manein*, and it is very difficult of access. The castle of خودرث *Khouderth* is situated on the borders of Kam Firouz: it is strong, and difficult of access. The castle of ارجان *Arjan* is exceedingly strong; and it is impossible for me to describe all the castles which cannot be taken either by force or stratagem.

ذکر آتشکدها پارس

Account of the Fire-Temples of Pars.

THERE is not any district of this province, nor any village, without a Fire-temple. One, near Shapour, they call *Kunbud Kaush* * کنبد کاوش. At کازرون *Kazeroun* there is a Fire-temple, called خیفه *Kheifeh*: and another, called کلادن *Kul-laden* and مسوبان *Mesouban*: And in the religion of the *Guebres* it is thus ordained, that " omnis fœmina quæ tem-" pore graviditatis aut tempore menstruorum, fornicationem seu

---

* So written both in the Eton MS. and my own; but it should, probably, have been کاوس *Kaus*, the name of an ancient king of Persia.

" adulterium fecerit, pura non erit, donec ad Pyræum (seu tem-
" plum Ignicolarum) accesserit (et) coram *Heirbed* (Sacerdote)
" nuda fuerit et urinâ vaccæ se laverit*.

ذكر رودهاي پارس

Account of the Rivers of Pars.

The river *Tab* رود طاب issues from the mountains of Isfahan, near برج *Berje*; and, being joined by another stream from the same quarter, at the village of مس *Mes*, proceeds to ارجان *Arjan*, and passes under the bridge called دكان *Dekan*, and affords water to Pars, and Khuzistan, and روستاي زم *Roustai-Zem*, and falls into the sea.

The river *Shadgan* رود شادكان comes from بارزيك *Barzik*; and, passing under the bridge *Mereh* مره پول waters the villages of ديرابر *Deir Aber*, and مانين *Manein*, and كهرگان *Kehergan*: and, bordering the دشت رشتقال *Desht-Reshtikal*, falls into the bitter or salt lake.

The river *Doujend* رود دوجند comes from جوبندان *Jou-*

---

* This is the literal translation of a passage which the reader will find in the original Persian, among the articles of the Appendix.

l̤endan; and, proceeding to هوران *Houran* and جلادان *Jeladan*, falls into the sea. The river رمین *Remin*, runs from خیمایکان *Khaimaigan* to لاهین *Lahein*, and falls into the river of *Shapour*, رود شاپور, and thence proceeds to موج مایها *Mouje Maiha*, and falls into the sea.

The river *Khashein* رود خشین issues from the mountains of دادین *Dadein*; and when it reaches حیغان *Heifan*, it falls into the river *Mouje* رود موج.

The river *Sekan* رود سکان flows from the village of دیحان *Deihan*, from the place called شادافزای *Shadafzai*, and watering the meadows and fields there, proceeds to کوره *Koureh*, and to the territories of جمکان *Jemgan*, and کازرون *Kazeroun*, and falls into the sea.

The river حرستک *Harestek* issues from the village of ماسرم *Maserm*; and, proceeding to the village of مسیحار *Mesihar*, runs under the bridge of مسول *Mesoul*, which is an ancient structure of stone; and from that goes on to the village of حره *Hareh*, and at the village of کارزین *Karzein* joins the river خشین *Khashein*.

The river کردانه *Curdaneh* comes from کردان *Curdan*, from the borders of ارد *Aurd**, or *Ord*, and derives its name from Cur-

---

* The wandering Curds or Turcomans, whom Captain FRANCKLIN met in the

dan: it waters the territories of کام فیروز *Kam Firouz*; and, going by کاسکان *Kasegan* and طسوخ *Tesoukh*, falls into a lake called عمرو *Omru*; it is said that this water runs subterraneously into the sea.

The فرواب *Foruab* comes from the place of the same name, and runs under the پول خراسان *Khorasan bridge*, near the gates of اصطخر *Istakhar*. But the rivers are very numerous in this province, and cannot be all described here.

ذکر دریاهای پارس

Of the Lakes of Pars.

THE Persian Sea is a bay of that great ocean which extends as far as چین *China*, along the coast of Hindoostan. In Persian it is called the Sea of Pars, or of کرمان *Kirman*, because that none of the countries situated on it are more populous, cultivated, or delightful, and because, in ancient times, the kings of Pars were the most powerful and illustrious; and even at this present time the people of Pars are famous in all quarters.

One of the lakes is called بختگان *Bakhtegan*, into which falls

vicinity of Persepolis, informed him, that the name of their tribe was *Ort*.—*Tour to Persia*, &c. octavo edition, p. 199.

the river کر *Kar,* and it reaches to the borders of Kirman. It is in length about twenty farsang, and its waters are salt. This lake is in the Koureh of Istakhar. There is a small lake in the Koureh of Shapour, at the Desht دشت (or waste) of ارزن *Arzen,* the length of which is ten farsang: its waters are sweet and pleasant; they were at one time dried up; no water remained in this place: all the small sturgeon (ماهي شير) are taken here. There is another small lake in the Koureh of Shapour, near کارزین *Karzein,* the length of which is about ten farsang. Near مور *Mour* the water is bitter, or saltish; and there is much fishing in it.

The lake حيكان *Heikan* is of bitter water: it is twelve farsang in length. Salt is collected on its banks. It is part of اردشیر کوره *Ardeshir Koureh,* and they say belongs to اردشیر خره *Ardeshir Khereh.* Its beginning is at the distance of two farsang from Shiraz, and it ends near the borders of Khuzistan. The lake of سفهویه *Sefhouiah* is near eight farsang in length: it affords much fishing: On its banks are thick forests, and reeds or canes in great abundance: it belongs to the borders of Istakhar.

ذكر شهرهاي بزرک و بناهاي معروف

Description of the great Cities and remarkable Edifices.

اصطخر *Istakhar** is a city neither small nor great, more ancient than any city whatsoever of Pars. The extent of it is about one mile; and the sovereigns of Pars had their dwellings there, and Ardeshir resided in that place; and there is a tradition that Solomon, the Prophet (the blessing of God be on him!) used to set out from تبرثه *Tabertha*† in the morning, and at night arrive at Istakhar. There is in Istakhar a mosque, which they call the Mosque of Solomon, the son of David: and some people affirm that جم *Jem*, who reigned before ضحاک *Zohak*, was Solomon; but that opinion is erroneous. In ancient times Istakhar was well inhabited; and the bridge called *Pool-i-Khorasan* پول خراسان or the Khorasan bridge, is without the city.

بشادور *Beshadour* was built by King Shapour. It has strong ramparts, and a ditch with water, in which weeds and thorns grow as high as the waist of a man, so thickly entangled, that one cannot, without considerable difficulty, be extricated

---

* The reader will find the original Persian of this passage in my "*Epitome of the Ancient History of Persia,*" Appendix, p. 91.

† Ot *Tiberiah*.

from them. This place has four gates; and in the midst of it is a singular hill, or eminence, like a tower or dome. The buildings are of clay.

جور *Jawr* was built by Ardeshir. It is said that this place was formerly a small lake, and that Ardeshir, having there obtained a victory over his enemy, desired to build a city on the spot, and ordered the water to be drained away. The walls are of clay. There are four gates: One is called the باب مهر *Bab Mihr*; it leads to the east: another is the باب بهرام *Bab Behram*, leading to the west. On the right hand is situated the دروازه هرمز *Derwazeh Hormuz*, or Gate of Hormuz; and on the left the gate of *Ardeshir* دروازه اردشیر This gate was erected by Ardeshir; and from it there is a view of all the districts and territories. Opposite to this is a hill, from which water gushes with great force, and falls into an aqueduct, which was formed of stone and mortar, but is now fallen to ruin. The city is well supplied with running water; and in the vicinity of each gate there is about a farsang laid out in gardens and pleasure-grounds.

شیراز *Shiraz* is a modern city, built by محمد بن القاسم عقایل *Mohammed ben alcassem Okail*, uncle (or cousin-german) of حجاج بن یوسف *Hejaje ben Yousuf*. The productions of every city are brought to Shiraz, and are not taken from that to any place. This was chosen as the station of the army of Islam,

(102)

on account of its vicinity to Istakhar, during the war*. The city was at that time built: it extends about one farsang, and has not any walls. Here is a ديوان *Divan* (Court of Revenue, Tribunal, &c.) and the Collectors of the Revenue go there.

كارزين *Karzein* is a small town, about the size of Istakhar, and the best in that Koureh. The town called مكه *Mekeh* † is situated near the borders of يزد *Yezd* and ابرقوه *Aberkouh*, and near the territories of Kirman; and هريه *Herieh* goes between from the شقّ كرمان *Shek* of *Kirman* and the borders of Isfahan ‡. Mekeh is situated on the skirt of the desert: it is a pleasant town, and well supplied with provisions. There is a town with a castle and two iron gates; one called باب ابرو *Bab Abrou*; the other باب المسجد *Bab al Mesjed*. Here is a mosque; and they drink water conveyed in trenches or canals; and there is a stream also which flows from the castle. In this village there is great abundance of fruit, and many trees and edifices.

ابرقوه *Aberkouh* is a plentiful town, about the same size as

---

* The war which gave the Mussulmans possession of the Persian empire, in the middle of the seventh century of the Christian æra.

† Probably for كته *Katta*.

‡ The reader must recollect, that I have only undertaken, in the present volume, a mere translation. The numerous obscurities of the text, I shall endeavour to illustrate in a future work, of which I have given an outline in the Preface.

Istakhar: it has not any trees. رودان *Rudan* resembles Aberkouh in every respect, but that it produces more fruit, and is better supplied with provisions. سرور *Serour* is a small town; but plentifully supplied. بیضا *Beiza* is one of the largest towns in the Koureh of Istakhar: it is a pleasant and well-inhabited place: its walls are white; and it was the station of the Mussulman army at the time of the conquest of Istakhar. From this place they send corn to Shiraz.

ذکر کوره شاپور

Of the Koureh of Shapour.

ONE of the chief cities in the Koureh Shapour, is کازرون *Cazeroun*. It is about the size of نوبندجان *Nubendjan*; but Cazeroun is more populous, and stronger, and of better air: the air of Cazeroun is the purest of all Pars. They drink there, well-water; and have abundance of fruits and crops. Cazeroun and Nubendjan are the most plentiful places of all the Koureh of Shapour.

ذكر كوره دارابجرد

Of the Koureh of Darabjerd.

THE largest town in the Koureh of Darabjerd is بسا *Besa*. It is of the same size as Shiraz; and the air of Besa is better than that of Shiraz. In their buildings they use cypress wood. It is an ancient city, with a castle, and walls and ditches. All the productions of a warm and cold climate are to be found there; dates, oranges, &c. All the towns of Darabjerd are near each other.

Of the towns of اردشیر دره *Ardeshir Dereh* we have already mentioned Shiraz. After that is سیراف *Siraf*, about as large as Shiraz. Here are very wealthy men, such as merchants, and others, who expend thirty thousand dinars on the building of their houses. There are not any trees immediately about Siraf. There is a mountain on the east of the city which they call جم *Jem*; this affords fruits and water for the town. Siraf enjoys a warmer climate than any of those other towns.

ارجان *Arjan* is a considerable city, producing dates and olives in great plenty. From Arjan to the sea is a distance of one merhileh: so that it partakes of the land and sea, of the mountainous and level country.

The greatest cities of Pars are Shiraz, and سیراف *Siraf*, and ارغان *Arghan*.

نوبندجان *Nubendjan* enjoys a warm climate: it has a few date trees. شعب بوان *Shaab bouan* is within two farsang of Nubendjan: it consists of several villages, with running water, and so many trees that the sun with difficulty shines upon the ground. جنابه *Jenabah,* and سنیر *Sinir,* and ماهي رویان *Mahirooyan,* are of very warm air, situated on the sea coast, and abounding in the fruits of a warm climate.

ذکر مسافات فارس

The Distances of Places in Fars.

From Shiraz to Siraf, five farsang; from Shiraz to کفر *Kefer,* five farsang; from Kefer to بحر *Beher,* five farsang; from Beher to بنجهان *Benjeman,* five farsang; from Benjeman to کوار *Kouar,* six farsang; from Kouar to دشت شوراب *Desht Shourab* (the waste or desert of bitter water), five farsang; from that to خان داود *Khan Daoud* (David's Inn), from which there is a desert for about three farsang; from the خان بادیه *Khan*

Badyeh, six farsang; from that to دبهه مي *Dhey Mei,* six farsang; and from Dhey Mei to سرعقبه *Serakiah,* six farsang; and from بادرکان *Badergan* to ترکا *Terka,* to the خان *Khan,* four farsang; from that to سیراف *Siraf,* seven farsang; and from دوبین *Doubein* to Serakiah: In all, is a distance of sixty-eight farsang.

راه از شیراز تا جنابه

Road from Shiraz to Jenabah.

FROM Shiraz to خان‌شیر *Khan-Sheir,* on the river سکان *Sekan,* six farsang; from دوبین *Doubein* to سرعقبه *Serakiah,* four farsang; from سیرکوه *Sir Kouh,* to the town of توج *Touje,* twenty-four farsang; from Touje to Jenabah, twelve farsang: In all forty-four farsang *.

---

* In this, as in the *Nozehat al Coloub,* and most other Asiatick Works on Geography, the reader must calculate the distances himself, if he wishes for an accurate *total.*

مسافات از شیراز بسرکان

Route from Shiraz to Sirgan.

FROM Shiraz to Istakhar, twelve farsang; to the *Reseid Gah Kelouder,* رصید گاه کلودر eight farsang; from Reseid Gah to زیادآباد *Zyad-Abad,* which has been reckoned as part of خورستان *Khuristan,* five farsang; from Zyad-Abad to the village of حربایان *Herbaian*,* where there is a small lake, six farsang: from Herbaian to the دیه عبدالرحمن *Dhey Abdarrahman,* three farsang; from Abdarrahman to دیه مورد *Dhey Moured,* where is a town called بودنجان *Boudenjan,* six farsang; from Dhey Moured to ساحل الکبری *Sahel al Kebri,* eight farsang; and from Sahel al Kebri to the رباط سرمغان *Rebat Sirmkan,* eight farsang; from Sirmkan to Rebat پشت خم *Posht Khem,* nine farsang; and from Rebat Sirmkan to سیرکان *Sirgan,* of Kirman, nine farsang; the Rebat Sirmkan belongs to the borders of Kirman.

* I must acknowledge, that in this name I have supplied by conjecture the diacritical points of the *ya,* as in my MS. the word is thus written, حربابان—I had hopes that the Eton MS. might enable me to ascertain the true reading; but I found it in this as in most similar cases, still more unsatisfactory and equivocal than my own, the points being altogether omitted, and the word appearing thus, حربابان—I have noticed in the Preface the various pronunciations of such a character, according to the application of points.

P 2

راه از شیراز تا کته

Road from Shiraz to Kattah.*

THIS is the road of Khorasan: From Shiraz to دوتاق *Dukak,* six farsang; from Dukak to اصطخر *Istakhar,* six farsang; from Istakhar to پیر قریه *Pir Kurieh,* four farsang; from Pir Kurieh to کهندز *Kohendiz,* six farsang; from Kohendiz to دیهه بند *Dhey Bend,* eight farsang; from Dhey Bend to Aberkouh, ابرقوه twelve farsang; from Aberkouh to دیهه شیر *Dhey Shir,* thirteen farsang; from Dhey Shir to حور *Hawr,* six farsang; from Hawr to the قلعه مجوس *Kelaa-Majious* (or the Castle of the Magi), which is now in ruins, six farsang; and from the Kelaa Majious to the town of کته *Kattah,* five farsang; from یزد *Yezd* to هره *Hereh,* six farsang; and from Hereh to Katta, seven farsang. This is the extreme point of the territories of Fars. The total, eighty-seven farsang.

---

* This section has been given in the "*Epitome of the Ancient History of Persia,*" p. 91, Appendix.

ذکر راه از شیراز باصغهان

Account of the Road from Shiraz to Isfahan.

FROM Shiraz to هزار *Hezar*, nineteen farsang; from Hezar to مانیین *Manein*, six farsang; from Manein to رکیسا *Rekisa*, which is the صیدکاه *Reseid Gah* (the place of watching)*, six farsang; from Rekisa to کمار *Kumar*, four farsang; from Kumar to *Kesr Aaien*, قصر اعین seven farsang; to اصطخران *Istakharan*, which is a village, seven farsang; from Istakharan to خان اویس *Khan Aweis*, seven farsang; from Khan Aweis to دیهه کوز *Dhey Gouz*, seven farsang; from Dhey Gouz to کره *Kereh*, eight farsang; from Kereh to خان لنجان *Khan Lenjan*, seven farsang; and from Khan Lenjan to Isfahan, nine farsang. The borders of Pars extend to the Khan; and from Shiraz to that, is forty-three farsang; and from Shiraz to Isfahan, seventy-two farsang; from Shiraz to کهرکان *Kehrgan*, seven farsang; and from that to خورستان *Khurestan*, a small town, nine farsang; from Khurestan to a رباط *rebat*, four farsang; from the rebat to کروم *Keroum*, four farsang; from Keroum to بسا *Besa*, five farsang; from Besa to the town of طبیسان *Te-*

---

* صیدکاه without the ر would signify " the place of the chace, the hunting-ground," &c.

misan, four farsang; from Temisan to جومه مسیحان *Joumeh Mesehan*, six farsang; from مرزند خان *Merzend Khan* to سان *San*, four farsang; from San to the village of دارابکرد *Darabgird*, to زم مهدي *Zem Mohdi*, five farsang; from روستا *Rousta* (the village) to فرخ *Firkh*, eight farsang; from Firkh to بازم *Bazem*, fourteen farsang. The total from Shiraz, eighty-two farsang.

راه از شیراز بارجان

Road from Shiraz to Arjan.

From Shiraz to the town of جوین *Jouein*, five farsang; from that to ده خلان *Deh Khellan*, four farsang; from Khellan to خواره *Khouareh*, five farsang; from Khouareh to کرکان *Gurkan*, five farsang; from Gurkan to نوبنجان *Nubenjan*, six farsang; from that to حورروان *Hhourwan*, four farsang; from Hhourwan to درچند *Derchend*, four farsang; from Derchend to خان خماد *Khan Khammad*, four farsang: from Khan Khammad to بندل *Bendil*, eight farsang; from Bendil to دیه عقارب *Dhey Akareb*, (the village of scorpions) called also هیر *Heir*, four farsang; from Heir to راسین *Rasein*, four farsang; from Rasein to ارجان *Arjan*, the end of the journey: In all, from Shiraz to Arjan, sixty farsang.

ذکر مسافات فارس میان شهرها بزرگ

Account of the Stages and Distances between the principal Towns of Fars.

FROM کازرون *Cazeroun* to Shiraz, fifty farsang; from بسا *Besa* to جهرم *Jehrem*, ten farsang; from Shiraz to Istakhar, twelve farsang; from Shiraz to کوان *Kouan*, ten farsang; from Shiraz to بیضا *Beiza*, eight farsang; from Shiraz to دارآبکرد *Darabgerd*, fifty farsang; from Shiraz to جور *Jawr*, twenty farsang; from Shiraz to سیراف *Siraf*, sixty farsang; from Shiraz to نوبنجان *Nubenjan*, twenty-five farsang; from Shiraz to یزد *Yezd*, seventy-four farsang; from Shiraz to Aberkouh, ابرقوه thirty-two farsang; from Shiraz to جنابه *Jenabah*, fifty-two farsang; from Shiraz to حومه *Houmah*, fourteen farsang; from Shiraz to جهرم *Jehrem*, thirty farsang; from جور *Jawr* to کازرون *Cazeroun*, sixteen farsang; from سیراف *Siraf* to بجیرم *Bejirem*, twelve farsang; from ماهي روبان *Mahi Rooian* to حصن ابن عماره *Hesn ebn Omareh*, which is the extent of Pars, one hundred and sixty farsang.

From Kirman to the borders of Isfahan: From رودان *Roudan* to انار *Anar*, eighteen farsang; from انار مهرج *Anar Meherje* to کته *Kattah*, five farsang; from Kattah to میبد *Meimed*, ten farsang; from Meimed to عقده Akdeh, ten farsang; from Akdeh to مانين Manein, fifteen farsang; from Manein to Isfahan, forty-five farsang; from Roudan to Manein, eighty-three farsang.

ذکر آب و هوا و خاک فارس

Of the Water, and Climate, and Soil of Fars*.

THE land of Fars is divided into the warm region, lying to the south, as far as کارزین Karzin, and زم Zem, and دارابکرد Darabgird, to فرخ Firkh and هرج Hereje. The northern division is cold.

In the warm region are comprised ارغان Arghan, and نوبندجان Nubendjan, and مهرویان Mahrooian, and سنیر Sinir, and جنابه Jenabah, and توج T'ouje, and دشت رشاک Deshti Reshak, and حره Hereh, and دارین Darein, and جور Jawr, and کازرون Cazeroun, and مارین Marein, and هرمزکران Hormuz Keran, and خمایکان Khemaigan, and سبیران Semiran, and سیراف Siraf, and بجرم Bijerem, and حصن ابن عماره Hesn ebn Omareh, and other places; but these are the principal.

* The title of this section is given from the Eton MS.—In mine a blank space is left for it.

To the colder region belong اصطخر *Istakhar*, and بيضا *Beiza*, and مانين *Manein*, ايدج *Aideje* and كام فيروز *Kam Firouz*, and كورد *Goured*, and كلار *Kellar*, and سرسير *Sersir*, and اولنجان *Awlenjan*, and يزد *Yezd*, and روز *Rouz*, and جران *Jeran*, and بازريك *Bazrik*, and سردر *Serder*, and حومه *Houmah*, and جهره *Jehreh*, and ستودر *Setouder*, and مشكانات *Meshkanath*, and اصطهاجان *Astehajan*, and برم *Berm*, and رهبان *Rahban*, and لوار *Louar*, and طرجنسان *Tarjensan*. اقليد *Akleid*, سرمغ *Sermek*, and many other places, all belong to this cold part of Fars. But Jawr, and Besa, and Shiraz, and بشادور *Beshadour*, and Cazeroun, are nearly alike in climate. The cold region is that in which fruits do not arrive at perfection, and where corn only is produced, such as Yezd, and كورد *Goured*, and روستاق *Roustak*, and Istakhar, and Rahban.

In the warm places, during the summer season, no bird remains on account of the excessive heat. In some parts of it, flesh, if laid upon the stones, in summer time, will be roasted. The climate of the cold region is very healthy: that of the warm parts is not so good, especially of Darabgird. Arghan enjoys a better air, such as Siraf and Jenabah. Shiraz, and Besa, and Cazeroun, and Jawr, are of a more temperate and salubrious climate. The water at Darabgird is bad.

ذكر صورت اهل فارس

Of the Persons (also of the Manners, Languages, Religions, and Chief Families) of the People of Fars.

THE inhabitants of the warm parts of this province are of slender make, and brown complexions*, with little hair. In the colder region they are fatter, and have more hair, and their complexions are fairer. And they have three languages: The *Parsi* (زبان پارسی), which they use in speaking, one to another; though there may be some variations of dialects in different districts, yet it is in fact all the same, and they all understand the language of each other, and none of their expressions or words are unintelligible: The *Pehlavi* language, زبان پهلوي which was formerly used in writings; this language now requires a commentary تفسیر or explanatory treatise, and the *Arabick* language, زبان تازي which at present is used in the Divans, or Royal Courts of Justice, Revenue, &c.

The dress and ornaments of the princes are, short coats, or tunicks, open before; and large cloaks, or outer garments; small sashes wrapped round the turbans, and swords hung by belts,

* Literally *wheat-coloured* کندم کون

with tight boots. The Cazis (or magistrates) wear on their heads caps (کلاه), so that their ears are covered, the end hanging on their shoulders. Their shirts are of a fine texture; but they do not wear boots, nor the outer cloak. The secretaries, or writers (دبیران) of Pars, wear the cloak and boots, and their habits resemble those of the Arabians.

As to the manners of the people in Pars, those who are the chief men, and who occupy the higher offices in the service of the sovereign, are polite and courteous: they have fine palaces, and are very hospitable. The people, in general, are kind and civil in their manners. The merchants are remarkably covetous, and desirous of wealth. I have heard that there was a certain man of Siraf who had passed forty years at sea, never leaving his ship during that time: whenever he came to a port, he sent some of his people on shore to transact his commercial affairs; and when that business was finished, he sailed on to some other place. The inhabitants of Siraf devote their whole time to commerce and merchandize. The Author of the book says, " I myself saw at this place several persons who possessed *four thousand thousand* dinars; and there were some who had still more; and their clothes were like those of hired labourers." But the people of Cazeroun and Besa traffick on shore; and they derive their fortunes from this kind of commerce: they are persevering and patient in the acquiring of riches; and the men of Pars, wheresoever they go, are powerful and wealthy.

As to the different religious sects of the people of Pars, those who inhabit the sea-shore are of the same sect as the people of Basrah. From Siraf to Mahi-rooyan, and to ارغان *Arghan*, are nearly all the same. The inhabitants of جهرم *Jehrem* are of the Moatazelite heresy: Those who dwell in the warm region are of seven different sects: and those of the cold region, of Shiraz, and Istakhar, and Besa, are believers in the Sonna (or traditions of Mahommed); and some are like the people of Baghdad, and have the Fetwa, according to the rules of those who follow the Hadith, or holy traditions.

In Pars there are Fire-worshippers, or Guebres (کبران), and Christians (ترسایان), and some Jews (جهودان); " and the books of the Guebres, their fire temples, and their customs or ceremonies of Guebrism, or Magism, still continue among the people of Pars; and there are not in any country of Islam so many Guebres as in the land of Pars, which has been their capital or chief residence*."

In the books of the Persians (پارسیان) it is recorded that several of their kings were of Pars, such as Zohak, and Jem, and Feridoun, and others, till the time that Feridoun divided the earth among his sons; and they were the kings of the earth till the time that Zhu'l'karnein (Alexander the Great) came, and slew

---

* See the original of this passage in the Appendix.

Dara, the son of Darab; and the empire declined until the time of Ardeshir. After him there were kings, such as Shapour, and Baharam, and Kobad, and Firouz, and Hormuz*, and others; most of whom were of Pars, or of Arabia: their dominion extended to the borders of روم Roum. But when an Arabian race conquered the whole world, Pars became as a considerable province to them, and the seat of empire was removed to Irak. The kings of Pars have been highly celebrated; their history is so well known, that it were unnecessary to say more of it in this place.

Since the introduction of the true faith (Islam), there have been many illustrious men from this province, (Pars.) One of these was هرمز Hormuz, a Guebre, who, in the time of Omar ebn Alkhitab, may God reward him! was taken by Abdallah ben Omar, and put to death.

سلمان فارسی Selman Farsi (Selman the Persian) also was one of those illustrious men: his piety is celebrated throughout the world: he sought the truth of religion in all quarters, until he found it at Medina, with the prophet, the peace and blessing of God be on him! in consequence of which, Selman became a true believer†.

---

* See the series of all these kings in the "*Epitome of the Ancient History of Persia.*"
† *Vide* D'HERBELOT *Bibl. Orient.* Art. *Selman.*

The race of *Omareh* آل عماره also called آل جلندي *Je-lendi* formerly possessed extensive territories and wide dominions in this country, on the sea-coast, in the vicinity of Kirman. It is said that their empire existed before the time of Moses, on whom be the blessing of God! and that it is to some princes of this family the Koran alludes in that passage,

و كان وراءهم ملك ياخذ كل سفينة غصبا

" And there was behind them a king, who forcibly seized on every (sound) ship*." And to this very time they have soldiers, and plunder on the sea, and pay not tribute to any king: and it was with عبدالله بن احمد الجلندي *Abdallah ben Ahmed al Jelendi* that عمرو بن الليث *Omru ben Leith* made war for two years; and he did not conquer him until he had called to his assistance two of the family of Omru.

The بني الصغار *Beni Alseghar* are also of the race of *Jelendi* آل جلندي It is said that سيف الصغار *Seif al-Seghar* is called after them. Those we have mentioned are the more ancient kings of Pars.

سامه بن بوي *Abu Zeheir* was of the family of ابو زهير *Sameh ben Boui.* سيف بني زهير *Seif beni Zeheir* was

---

* This king is before mentioned, p. 12.

called after him. ابو سارة *Abu Sareh,* who seized upon Pars, was of this family: he retained possession of Pars until the Khalif مامون *Mamoun* sent محمد بن الاشعث *Mohammed ben alashaath* against him, when, in the desert of Shiraz, his army was defeated, and himself slain. To جعفر بن ابي زهير *Jaffer ben abi Zoheir,* هارون الرشيد *Haroun Arrashid* gave the viziership. مظفر بن جعفر رشاق *Muzuffer ben Jaffer Reshak* has it, and is Lord of the Scymetar خداوند شمشیر and from the border of حى *Hei* to بحرم *Bejerm,* belongs to him.

The race of *Khanteleh,* آل خنظله the sons of *Temim:* بني تميم They are of the family of عروه بن ادیه *Arweh ben Adyeh,* who crossed over from بحرين *Bahrein* to Pars, in the time of the Ommiades (بني اميه). After the death of Arweh, they settled in Istakhar, where they accumulated great riches, and lived in splendour. One of them, called عمرو *Omru,* was so wealthy that he purchased a book * (مصحف) at the price of one thousand dinars, and bequeathed sums of money for religious purposes, and alms, throughout all the cities and provinces of Islam; and the income and taxes of their estates were *ten thousand thousand* direms.

عمرو بن ابراهيم *Omru ben Ibrahim* received from the Khalif

---
* More particularly the Koran.

Mamoun the sovereignty of the sea. After him, مرداس بن عمرو *Merdas ben Omru*, who was called بویلان *Bouyellan*, possessed such estates, that every year his taxes amounted to three thousand direms. His son, محمد بن واصل *Mohammed ben Wasel*, was equally rich. The chief of this tribe was عمرو بن عیسه *Omru ben Aiseh*. At the time the Turks assumed the Khalifat, they desired to remove them from court; and the province of Fars was divided among forty nobles of the Turks, the chief of whom was مولد *Mouled*: Having reproved them for their tyrannical conduct and wickedness, they all conspired against him, and sought to kill him: he applied for protection to Merdas, who saved him from those nobles, and sent him to Baghdad. The Turks then gave the command to ابراهیم بن سیمارا *Ibrahim ben Simara*; and عبدالله بن یحیی *Abdallah ben Yahia* sent a letter, desiring that those nobles might be seized, and put to death. Ibrahim ben Simara took four of them, and slew them; and pardoned the others. From that time forth he was chief of the Turks (ریس و مقدم ترکان) in Pars.

محمد بن واصل *Mohammed ben Wasel* was in possession of Pars; and عبدالرحمن بن مفلح *Abdar'rahman ben Moflah* was sent from Baghdad with a great army, and a general, named طاشم *Tashem*. In a battle with Mohammed ben Wasel, this Tashem was slain; and Abdar'rahman, being taken prisoner, was put to death. Pars continued in his possession until his kinsman Merdas invited Yacoub ben Leith, who came into Pars, and defeated Mohammed ben Wasel, who fled from بیضا Beiza to مرو Merou. At the time that Mohammed ben Wasel returned from battle with Abdarrahman ben Moflah, Yacoub ben Leith defeated Mohammed, who went to sea (or fell into the sea, بدریا افتاد), and was brought from that to Yacoub: he was confined for some years in a castle; but, whilst Yacoub was absent, having gone to the borders of نیشاپور Nishapour, Mohammed, with a band of the prisoners, got possession of the castle, and Yacoub sent people to put them to death.

The race of Saman آل سامان (the Samanides) are descended from بهرام Bahram, and Bahram was of خیر Kheir in ارد شیرجرد Ardeshirgerd: there he resided, and went from that to هرات Herat, and conquered the army of the Turks ترکان, and was so successful that the army of کسری Kesri (the Persian monarch) was terrified at his exploits *. But the story is very long. The family of Saman is descended from him; and for many years the government of ماور النهر Maweral'nahr and بلخ Balkh and the countries bordering on the جیحون Jihoun, or river Oxus, was in their hands.

اسمعیل بن احمد بن اسد Ismael ben Ahmed ben Asad possessed so extensive an empire, that Khorasan, and Mawarlnahr, and Tabaristan, and کرکان Gurkan, and کومش Koumesh, and

---

* See D'Herbelot Bibl. Orient. Art. Saman and Baharam Giubin.

ري *Rey*, and تزوين *Casvin*, and ابهر *Ebher*, and رنكان *Rengan*, were all under his dominion; at no other time were all these countries or places in the possession of an individual: and he raised himself to such glory and power, that the kings of Cheen and Turkestan were stricken with terror; and he was as renowned in those countries as in the land of Islam. To him succeeded نصر بن احمد *Nasser ben Ahmed*. In his time nobody could oppose or controul his sway.

علي بن الحسين بن بشر *Ali ben Alhosein ben Bashr* was of the tribe of ازد *Azd*, which dwelt at بخارا *Bokharah*. He entered Pars, and acquired power, until Yacoub ben Leith opposed him in battle, and overcame him at قنطره *Kantereh*, a place near Shiraz. He was taken prisoner, and for some time confined, and after that put to death.

The kings of the Zems پادشاهان زمهاي: These kings had in their courts not less than a thousand horsemen. The زم مسجان *Zem Mesejan*, which was called the *Zem* of *Jelouiah al mehrjan ben Ruzbah* زم جيلويه المهرجان بن روزبه. Jelouiah went to this Zem from حمايكان سغلي *Hemaigan Sefly* of the Koureh of Istakhar, and served سله *Seleh*. When Seleh died (فرمان يافت) Jelouiah took possession of the Zem, which from that time was called after him. His success continued, and arrived at such a degree that he attacked the family of *Budolph* ال بودلف, and slew معقل بن عيسي *Maakel ben Isa*, the brother of Budolf. Then Budolf came and slew him, and cut off his head; and the family of Budolf, as long as they existed, considered this head as lucky, and productive of good fortune to them. For some time they put it on a spear, and bore it about in front of the army. The skull was set in silver, and continued till the time that عمرو بن ليث *Omru ben Leith* defeated احمد بن عبد العزيز *Ahmed ben abdalaziz*, when that curiosity having fallen into his hands, he ordered it to be broken. The government of this Zem is still in the hands of the family of Jelouiah.

The زم ديوان *Zem Divan:* The chief of this was *Azad Murd* of *Kouhestan* آزاد مرد كوهستاني The government of this still continues in his family; and it was محمد بن ابرهيم *Mohammed ben Ibrahim* who drew forth an army against Azad Murd, until at last he fled before him.

The زم كاريان *Zem Karian* is in possession of the race of *Soffar* (آل صغار). Their chief is حجر بن احمد بن الحسن *Hajer ben Ahmed ben Alhassan.*

The زم بادنجان *Zem Badenjan:* the chief of this was شهريار *Shehriar.* Now it has passed to موسي ابرهيم *Musa Ibrahim.* Some of this tribe have removed from Pars to Isfahan: their estates in Pars are very considerable, and the government is still in their family.

Of the Debiran (دبیران Writers or Secretaries) of Pars, who were illustrious there, was عبد الحميد بن يحيى *Abd al Humeid ben Yahia*: he was of the Ommiah family, and his story is well known.

عبدالله بن المقفع *Abdallah ben al Mefakaa* was of Pars: he dwelt in Basrah; and was slain there in the time of منصور *Mansour*. The occasion of this was as follows: he had given a passport, or letter of security, for عبدالله بن علي بن منصور *Abdallah ben Ali ben Mansour*; and in it was written "If this "promise of protection should not be observed, or if violence "should be offered to him, Mussulmans shall nevertheless be free "from any blame." Mansour, enraged at this, sent an order to the Aumil (or Chief Collector of Revenue) at Basrah, that he should privately destroy Abdallah ben al Mefakaa.

يهويه *Yahouiah*, the Grammarian and Scribe, was originally of Istakhar: he resided at Basrah, and died at Shiraz, where his tomb is. He composed a Treatise on Grammar.

A great many officers of the Khalif's Divans (or Courts of Justice, Revenue, &c.) were of Pars; some viziers, such as the برامكه *Barmeks* (Barmecides). At all times the offices of state were filled by men from Pars, who are peculiarly qualified for those situations, because they are rendered so expert in business, by the multiplicity and various forms of their Courts and Tribunals, that one person will discharge the functions of several difficult offices. I have not seen any others who were so universally acquainted with business, except two or three: معلي بن النصر *Maali ben al Nasser*, who was secretary to حسن رجا *Hassan Reja*; he came from Irak, and was killed at Shiraz. Hassan Reja, who managed the war department, caused a tomb to be erected for him at Shiraz.

بدار هداف بن ضرار المازني *Bedar Hedaf ben Zerar al Mazeni* was fifty years employed in the Divans, and lived six years after he became blind. هامان بن بهرام *Haman ben Behram* was of Shiraz, and belonged to the Divan of *Ali ben al hosein ben Basher*: علي بن الحسين بن بشر he was afterwards transferred to the Divan of محمد بن واصل *Mohammed ben Wasel*, and superintended every Divan except that of Ambassadors.

حسين بن عبدالله *Hosein ben Abdallah*, who was surnamed ابو سعيد *Abu Saied*; his proper name was *Abdallah ben Almerzian* عبدالله بن المرزبان He was originally of بسا *Besa*, and dwelt at Shiraz, and traced his descent, by the mother's side, from the race of مروان *Merwan*: he was introduced into the Divans of Pars, and resided at بخارا *Bokhara*.

There is a race or family in Pars, called the اهل بيوت *Ahil Biout*, to whom the business of the Divans belongs by hereditary right. The family of حبيب مدرك *Habib Medrek*, and the family of *Fazl*, the son of that *Habib*, are of this tribe, which is originally of کام فیروز *Kam Firouz*. They settled at Shiraz, and managed important matters, and became great; and the Khalif Mamoun invited مدرک بن حبیب *Medrek ben Habib* to Baghdad, and held him in high esteem. His death happened in Baghdad, in the time of معتصم *Motazem*. It is said that یحیی اکثم *Yahia Aksem* hired some person to murder him privately.

The race of the *Beni Sefar* آل بنی صغار are of the tribe of بامله *Bamlah*. یحیی *Yahia*, and عبدالرحمن *Abdarrahman*, and عبدالله *Abdallah*, of the children of *Mohammed ben Ismael* محمد بن اسمعیل, resided in Pars during the reign of Mamoun, and filled the offices of the Divan. The family of مرزبان بن زاویه *Merzban ben Zawieh* of Shiraz. حسن مرزبان هندار بن محمد واصل *Hassan Merzban hindar ben Mohammed Wasel*. After him was یعقوب بن لیث *Iacoub ben Leith*. جعفر بن سهیل بن البرزبان *Jaffer ben Soheil ben al Merzban* was secretary of حارث فریعون *Hareth Feriaoun*. There was not any family more ancient or more great than the race of مرزبان بن فراسداد *Merzban ben Ferasdad*.

ابو سعید بن الحسن بن عبدالله نصر بن منصور بن البرزبان احمد بن حداد *Abu Saied al Hassan, ben Abdallah Nasser ben Mansour, ben al merzban Ahmed ben Hedad*, at this time conducts the business of the Divan; and *Merdshad ben ali*

Merdshad مرڈشان مرڈشان بن علي and the sons of Hassan, حسين و احمد *Hosein and Ahmed*, are Aumils of the Divan. (عمال ديوان) Many other men of Pars have arrived at high religious dignity in various places.

حسين بن منصور الحلاج *Hosein ben Mansour al Hellah* was of Beiza. He was a man of probity, and virtue, and wisdom; and arrived at considerable eminence. He said, "Whosoever "honestly strives with all his heart, and, separating himself from "the allurements of pleasure, shall hold fast the bridle of sensual "desire, and patiently wait, shall ascend to the court of honours "by the steps of uprightness, and gradually be purified from the "infirmities of human nature; or if human nature should occa- "sionally shew itself in him, it will be such as was imparted to "Mary the Virgin, by the power of the spirit of Almighty God, "the fruit of which was Jesus, on whom be peace! All that "such a man shall utter, will be, as it were, the voice of the "Lord; and all his actions, as it were, divine; and all his com- "mands like those of Heaven." In this manner spoke Hosein ben Mansour, and preached to all the people about him, till many of the viziers and officers of the Divan began to imitate him; and he gained influence over the nobles and princes of Irak, and Jezireh, and Jebal, and Rei. He would not return to Pars; and meditating on his own business, he went to Baghdad, and was in the palace of the Khalif, and had attendants, porters, and slaves, till at length he was hanged alive.

حسن *Hassan,* surnamed ابو سعيد *Abu Saied,* was of low origin. He introduced the heresy of the ترمسطيان *Karmestians.* Having gone to Bahrein on mercantile business, he preached to the people of Arabia, and great numbers followed him; and he acquired such power that he defeated armies, and took a castle from the people of عمان *Oman,* and seized some towns of Arabia; but was at last slain.

سلمان بن حسن *Selman ben Hassan* was a man who went into the road of the hadjes, or pilgrims going to Mecca, and robbed and slew them: and at last proceeded to such lengths, that he plundered the treasures of the Kaaba, and killed the pious men who devoted themselves there to incessant prayer. In consequence of this, حجاج *Hejaje* ordered his kinsmen to be seized, and brought to Shiraz: they were kept a while in confinement; but, being men of good character, were not made responsible for his offences.

ذكر بناهاي غرايب پارس.

Account of the most extraordinary Edifices in Pars, (and other Curiosities.)

In the territory of اصطخر *Istakhar* is a great building, with statues carved in stone; and there, also, are inscriptions, and paintings. It is said that this was a temple of Solomon, to whom be peace! and that it was built by the Dives, or Demons: similar edifices are in Syria, and Baalbeck, and Egypt.

In the territory of Istakhar, also, there is a kind of apple, half of which is sweet, and half sour. Merdas ben Omru mentioned this circumstance to Hassan Reja: he denied the possibility of it, and Merdas sent and caused one to be brought, and shewed it to him*.

At the village of *Abdar'rahman* ديه عبدالرحمن there is a certain great pit, the bottom of which is dry all the year, except at the season for watering the fields, when water issues from it, and serves for the purposes of agriculture and for drinking. When it is not any longer necessary for the husbandman's use, the water disappears.

In the territory of شاپور *Shapour*, there is a mountain; and in that mountain are the statues of all the kings, and generals, and high priests (موبد *Moubed*), and illustrious men, who have existed in Pars: " And in that place are some persons who have representations of them, and the stories of them written †;" and this tribe belongs to the territory of ارغان *Arghan*, at *Hysn Mohdi* حسن مهدي.

* See the Persian of this and the preceding passage in the Appendix.
† انجا كساني هستند كه صورتها و قصها ايشان نبشته دارند

At the city of جور *Jawr*, near the northern gate, is a pond, or pool of water, in which a brazen vessel is so placed, that, from a hole in it, the water issues with great violence.

In the vicinity of ابرقوه *Aberkouh* are considerable heaps of ashes. The common people say, that here was the fire of Nimrod (into which he caused Abraham to be thrown.) But this is not true: the fact is, that Nimrod, and the kings of Canaan, dwelt in the land of Babylon.

In the Koureh of Arghan, at the village called ساحل العرب *Sahil al Areb*, there is a well, from which proceeds water enough to turn a mill, and water the fields. The people here say, that they have made various efforts to ascertain the depth of this well, but have not ever been able to reach the bottom.

In the Koureh of رستاق الرستاق *Rostak ar'rostak*, there is a place between two hills, from which smoke constantly issues; and it is said, that if a bird should fly near that place, it would drop down.

In the دشت وارين *Desht-Varein*, there is a village called خسروهين *Khosruhein*, in which there is not any tree. Here is a family, of whose sorceries and magick I have heard such an anecdote as cannot be repeated.

In اردشیر دره *Ardeshir Dereh,* near the gate of Shiraz, is a fountain, of which they drink the water as a purgative: one cup full operates once upon the body; two cups full, twice: if one drinks many, it occasions vomitings, and excessive evacuations.

Near Arghan, on the borders of Khuzistan, is a remarkable pile, or heap, called the تل دیلمي *Tel Deilemi,* with a vault or recess, two hundred paces broad, and so high that a man, mounted on a mule, with a standard in his hand, cannot reach the top.

In the territory of کوان *Kouan,* there is a certain flower, which they eat green, like the leaves of the چغندر *Chukender.*

In the territory of Shiraz there is a plant, or herb, which they call سوسن نرکس *Susen Nergus,* (the Lily Narcissus.)

Near وارین *Varein* there is a river, called نهر چین *Nehr-Cheen,* the water of which is pleasant to the taste, and is used for the purposes of agriculture; but when clothes are washed in it, it becomes green.

ذکر آنچه از ولایت فارس بر آید از متاعهای

Account of the Commodities and Productions of Fars

THE rose-water of Shiraz is most remarkably excellent, and highly esteemed in all parts of the world. It is chiefly made at جور *Jawr*, and sent by sea to حجاز *Hejaz*, and یمن *Yemen*: it is also sent to Syria, and Egypt, and Magreb or Africa, and Khorasan. Here also is made oil, better than that of any other place, except the oil of *Kheiri* روغن خیری, and that of کوفه *Cufah*.

At سینیر *Sinir*, and جنابا *Jenabah*, and کازرون *Kazeroun*, and توج *Tooje*, linen (کتان) garments are manufactured; and the embroidery and clothes made at بسا *Besa* are esteemed by the princes in all countries, and sent into all parts of the world. The gold brocade worn by the princes is made at Besa. This embroidery is performed with a needle: and here they also weave cloth of gold, and fine garments, and hangings, and silk, and camel's hair.

At یزد *Yezd* and ابرقوه *Aberkouh* they manufacture clothes of silk and cotton; at جهرم *Jehrem*, fine carpets. At عبدجان *Abdejan*, which is a town of the دشت وارین *Desht-i-Varein*, they make beautiful tapestry and carpets. Besa is remarkable for needle-work; and they excel there, in respect to that art, the people of ترتوب *Corcoub*.

At سيراف *Siraf* they abound in marine productions, and commodities brought by sea; such as aloes, ambergris, camphire, pearls, canes, ivory, and ebony: pepper, sandal, and various kinds of drugs and medicines, are sent from that place to all quarters of the world; and in this city there are such wealthy merchants, that several of them possess fortunes of sixty thousand thousand direms; *and I have seen them.*

At ارغان *Arghan*, in the village called افارسك *Afaresk*, they make such excellent دوشاب *doushab* (syrup), that no other place can equal it in that respect, except سيلان *Seilan*.

At كازرون *Kazeroun* there is a certain species of date, called خيلان *kheilan*, which they send into Irak and Isfahan. At دارابكرد *Darabgird*, in the ditches which surround the town, there is a certain fish extremely pleasing to the taste, without any bone.

In the vicinity of Darabgird, *mummy* موميباي is found. Once every year they open the place where it is produced, and a certain quantity of it is taken for the king's use, in presence of confidential persons, who then seal up the place. And in the territory of Darabgird there are hills of salt, white, black, yellow and green.

In the land of Pars there are mines of silver, and iron, and lead, and sulphur, and naphta. The silver is scarce, and found in the cold region called مانين *Manein*. Iron is brought from the mountains of Istakhar, and from the place called Darabgird.

The striped stuffs of Shiraz are well known; and in the Koureh of Istakhar they manufacture fine linen.

ذكر نغود اهل فارس

Of the Money, the Weights, and Measures, of the People of Fars.

In buying and selling, they use direms and dinars: but since the time of the Kesris*, to the present day, there has not been any coinage of direms in Pars, unless in the name of the *Emir al Moumenin* امير البومنين Commander of the Faithful.

* The fourth Dynasty of Persian kings, or the *Sassanides* are called the *Akasreh* or *Kesris*; of these *Noushirvan* was peculiarly styled *Kesri*: in his reign Mohammed was born. The last of this Dynasty was *Yezdegerd*, who died Anno Hegiræ 32, (A. D. 652.)

In Pars the weight of the direm is two مثقال *methkals*. The stone (سنک) is of two kinds, great and small: the great stone is *one mun* (من) *a thousand and forty direms*, like the stone of *Ardebil* سنک اردبیل; the small stone is the stone of Baghdad and the stone of بیضا *Beiza, one mun eight hundred direms.* At Istakhar four hundred direms make the stone. At بحره *Behreh,* two hundred and eighty direms; at Shapour, three hundred direms; and at اردشیر خره *Ardeshir Khereh,* two hundred and forty direms.

The جریب *Jereib* of Shiraz contains ten تغیز *kefiz*; and a kefiz, sixteen رطل *rotels,* a little more or less. The jereib is one hundred and thirty rotels; and that is divided into half, third, and quarter. The jereib of Istakhar is half the jereib of Shiraz. The measure or weight (کیل) of Beiza is more than that of Istakhar by about a tenth and half a tenth; and the measure of Kam Firouz is greater than that of Beiza, by about one tenth. The measure of Arghan exceeds that of Shiraz by a fourth: and the measure of Kazeroun and of Shapour is a sixteenth more.

ذكر ابواب المال

Account of the GATES OF WEALTH, *or the manner of raising the Revenue.*

THE *gates of wealth,* or those by which money is supplied in the Divans, are the taxes or tribute: a tenth on ships; a fifth on the mines, on corn, fodder, the mint, the roads, the canals, fruits, iced waters, salt, &c.

The tribute of lands is of three kinds: by division, and by regulations and statutes. All the proportions are exactly ascertained, and admit not of any diminution. Whether the ground be tilled, or not tilled, the measurements and divisions take place: if the ground is cultivated, it pays tribute; if not cultivated, it is so much lost.

The greater part of the country is subject to measurement, as far as the *Zems* are. The taxes of Shiraz are more considerable, in proportion as their jereib is the great jereib for such things as wheat and barley. The jereib is two hundred and thirty-seven direms. The *garden jereib* is one thousand four hundred and twenty-five direms. The small jereib is sixty كَز *guz,* of the king's cubit or yard (ذراع الملك); and the king's cubit is nine

(137)

قبضة *kebsets*, or handfuls. The great tax is the tax of Shiraz, because جعفر بن ابي زهير *Jaffer ben Abi Zoheir* spoke to Haroun Ar'rasheid on the subject, and he ordered that a third and a fourth should be paid. The tribute of Istakhar is not so considerable as that of Shiraz.

The tax of division is of two kinds. The better is that of the Emir al Moumenin Omar, (may God reward him!) and the other khalifs, which divides into tens, threes, and fours. These are taxes paid on the products of agriculture, and various other duties and tributes, nearly the same as in other countries.

In all Pars there is not any mint, except at Shiraz. The land belongs to the sovereign: he lets it out to farm at certain rents. There was not any tax in Pars on shops, or work-houses, or gardens, or trees. علي بن عيسي *Ali ben Isa* laid a tax on them in the year 302 *.

* A. D. 914—most probably our author's own time.

ذكر بلاد كرمان

Of the Province of Kirman.

To the east of Kirman lie the land of مكران *Makran*, and the deserts of that country, and بحرين *Bahrein* (the two seas), on the borders of بلوج *Bolouje*. To the west of Kirman lies the land of Pars, which we have before described. On the north are the deserts of Khorasan and Sejestan; and on the south the Persian sea and سيركان *Seirgan*; and, in a corner, a part of Pars.

In the region of Kirman the climate is both warm and cold. The fruits are of all kinds; chiefly those of the warm climates. Part of Kirman is bordered by the sea. Here are their harbours and ports, which are subject to excessive heat, such as هرموز *Hormuz*, and جرون *Jaroun*, and some others; and the air in general is not pure.

Now we proceed to describe the cities and mountains of Kirman, and to lay before the reader a map of that province, such as we have seen it.

(Page left blank for a map of Kirman.)

هرمز Hormuz, بم Bam, جيرفت Jireft, سيركان Sirgan, دوهين Douhin: these cities are, by some, reckoned as belonging to Pars; by others to Kirman. جيروقان Jiroukan, مزرقان Mezerkan, سورقان Sourkan, الاس Allas, كري Keri, معون Maaun.

Between سيركان Sirgan and the desert of يزد Yezd are the towns of جرده Jirdeh, زرند Zerend, فردين Ferdin, ماهان Mahan, and خبيص Khebis; and on the side of the desert, near Bam, is برماسير Bermasir. مهرج Mehreje, سنج Sinje, situated in the midst of the desert, and remote from Kirman, though reckoned as some of its territories. خواس Khouas, the boundary of Kirman, is said, by some, to be a territory of Sejestan.

The mountains of دهر حومه Deher Houmah, قارن Karen: ايقان Aikan, are by some assigned to كوهستان ابو غانم Kouhestan abou Ghanem. Between Hormuz and Jireft are the towns of منوجان Menujan, مرزنكان Merzingan, كومين Koumin. On the sea-coast are the mountains or hills of Kefes, بارن Baren and the mountains of the silver mines. جبال تغص

In Kirman there is not any lake or great river: there is that bay, or gulph, called the Persian Sea, which comes from the ocean near Hormuz; the water is salt, and ships pass on it to and fro. In parts of Kirman there are several mines.

ذکر کوههای کرمان

Of the Mountains of Kirman, (the Inhabitants, and Chief Cities.)

THE mountains of تفص *Kefes* lie on the southern border, near the sea. To the north, near the borders of Jireft, are رودان *Rudan* and the Kouhestan, or hilly country of ابوغانم *Abu-ghanem*. On the east is خواس *Khouas*, and the desert extending towards Kefes, and the province of Makran. On the south of that is بلوج *Bolouje*, or *Bolouche*, and the borders of میرجان *Mirjan*.

In the mountains near Hormuz, it is said, there is much cultivated land, and cattle, and many strong places. On every mountain there is a chief: and they have an allowance from the Sultan or Sovereign; yet they infest the roads of Kirman, and as far as the borders of Fars and of Sejestan: they commit their robberies on foot; and it is said that their race is of Arabian origin, and that they have accumulated vast wealth. " The بلوج *Boloujes*, are " in the desert of *Mount Kefes* کوه تفص and Kefes in the " Parsi language is کوج *Kouje*; and they call these two people " Koujes and Boloujes. The Boloujes are people who *dwell*

" *in the desert* * : they infest the roads, and have not respect for
" any person."

The mountains of مارن *Maren* belong to the cold region of Kirman: they are fertile and strong; snow falls on them: and in the time of the Guebres, or Fire-worshippers, they used to come down from these mountains and rob; but in the reign of the Abbassides they became converts to the true religion, and have kept their hands from evil actions. These mountains afford mines of iron. The mountains of the silver mines are near the borders of Jireft, and extend to the pass of دربان *Derban*; from that to the silver mountains is a journey of two merhileh. There are pleasant and fertile valleys, with small towns, and many delightful villas.

The warm part of Kirman is more extensive than the cold; insomuch that there is not above one-fourth of the province liable to the cold, from the borders of سیرکان *Sirgan* to the desert, in the vicinity of بم *Bam*. The warm region extends from the borders of Hormuz to Makran, and to the confines of Pars, and of Sirgan, throughout Hormuz, and میبوکان *Miougan*, and Jireft,

* The epithet *Sehra Nishin* (See Appendix) is sometimes used to express a solitary retired man, a hermit, &c. The *Ferhung Borhan Kattea* informs us, that بلوچ *Bolouche* is the name of a *people inhabiting the desert* (قومي صحرائي); also the name of a country of Iran or Persia. I write the name *Bolouche*, on the authority of this excellent dictionary, which accents the first syllable with *damma*, and describes the last letter *chim Farsi*.

and the hills of كوج *Kouje,* and the دشت ويران *desht viran,* or " the dreary waste;" also throughout Bam and the desert, and to the borders of Kirman, and to خيص *Kheis.*

The inhabitants of Kirman are lean and slender, with brown complexions*. Towards the west of Jireft, snow falls. Among the hills of silver, and as far as Derban to Jireft, and likewise from before the hill of بارم *Barem* to near Jireft, and the place called مسيحان *Mesihan* and درمان *Derman,* there runs a considerable river, with such a rapid stream, that it is not to be crossed without difficulty: it turns about twenty mills.

هرموز *Hormuz* is the emporium of the merchants in Kirman, and their chief sea-port: it has mosques and market places, and the merchants reside in the suburbs.

جيرفت *Jireft* is in extent nearly two miles; it is situated near the sea: here they enjoy at once all the productions of both warm and cold climates.

بم *Bam* is a considerable town, with extensive suburbs. Prayers are said on the chief festivals, in three different great mosques, and there is a small one in the market-place. Some of the people are of the Sonnite sect. In the castle of the city there is another mosque, with a publick treasury, and other offices.

* Literally *wheat-coloured* كندم كون.

The town of سیرکان *Sirgan* is watered by subterraneous trenches or aqueducts: in the suburbs they raise water from wells. This is the largest of all the cities in Kirman. The inhabitants are observers of the Hadith, (or holy traditions.) The people of رودبار *Rudbar*, قهستان *Kohestan*, بو غانم *Bou Ghanem*, and بلوج *Bolouje*, are all of the Shiah sect: and from the borders of معون *Maaoun*, and لشکرد *Lashgird*, to the territories of Hormuz, the people are industrious and honest; they cultivate sugar, and eat bread made of millet (ارزن). They give one tenth of their dates to the king, like the people of Basrah: and whatever dates are shaken from the trees by the wind, they do not touch, but leave them for those who have not any, or for travellers: and it happened one year, that half the dates were thus blown off the trees, yet the owner did not take one of them.

The territory of رویست *Rouiest* is a dry soil. The people are, for the greater part, robbers and plunderers. There are a town and a village on the sea-coast, where they catch fish. It is a stage on the road to Pars.

The language of the inhabitants of Kirman is the Persian; but the Kouches have another language, and also the Bolouches.

Fine linen and striped stuffs are manufactured at زرید *Zareid*, and are sent into Pars and Irak.

The خواس *Khouas* are a tribe of the desert: they have camels, and date trees; and their houses are made of reeds.

ذكر مسافات كرمان

The Distances of Places in Kirman.

FROM سيركان *Sirgan* to كاهون *Kahoun*, two merhileh; from Kahoun to حسنابان *Husnabad*, two farsang; from Husnabad to رشاق *Reshak*, two merhileh: from Sirgan to *Roudan Hemed* رودان هید, four farsang; from Hemed to كردكان *Kirdgan*, two farsang; from Kirdgan to اباس *Abaus*, one merhileh: from that to Roudan, one merhileh: from Sirgan to رباط شرقان *Rebat Shirkan*, two long merhileh.

On the road of بم *Bam*, one goes from Sirgan to سیهاب *Simab*, one merhileh; from that to بهار *Behar*, one merhileh; and to حباب *Hebab*, one merhileh: to غیرا *Ghira*, one merhileh: to كرعون *Keraoun*, one farsang; to رابین *Rabein*, one merhileh. One goes to a town on the Bam road; and, from that turning back on the right hand, one comes to the village of كوز *Kouz*, one merhileh; from that to جیرفت *Jireft*, one merhileh; from Jireft to the *Silver-hills*, one merhileh; from them to ازرباي *Azerbai*, one merhileh; from that to Jireft, one merhileh; from Sirgan to زرید *Zareid*, and from تركان *Terkan* to بردسیر *Ber-*

dasir, two merhileh; from Berdasir, that is, واشیر *Vashir*, to خبرود *Khemrud*, one long merhileh; and from Khemrud to Zareid, one merhileh; and from Zareid to the desert, one long merhileh.

On the road from Sirgan to خبص *Khebes*, one first goes to برماشیر *Bermashir*, one merhileh: from Bermashir to برج *Beherje*, one merhileh; this is on the skirts of the desert: from Bam to Jireft, one merhileh.

The road of Jireft to Pars is, from Jireft to معون *Maaoun*, two merhileh; to کاشکرد *Kashgird*, one merhileh; from Kashgird to سوردان *Sourdan* to موروان *Mourouan*, one merhileh; from Mourouan to جیروان *Jirouan*, one farsang; from Jirouan to کسیسان *Kesisan*, one; to روبین *Roubin*, one merhileh; to بارم *Barem*, one merhileh.

The distances on the road from Jireft to Hormuz are these: From Jireft to Kashgird, and from that, going on the left hand, to کونین *Kounein*, one merhileh; from Kounein to بهرنکان *Beherrengan*, one merhileh; from that to منونجان *Menunjan*, one; from that to Hormuz, one merhileh; from Hormuz to the city (شهر *Shehr*) and the sea-side, one merhileh.

These are all the roads and distances of Kirman. After this, we shall proceed to speak of the Land of سند *Sind*, and part of هند *Hind*, if God permit.

ذكر بلاد هند و بعضي از هند

Of the Country of Sind, and part of Hind.

WE proceed to describe the land of Sind, and some part of Hind, and the country of مكران *Makran*, and طوران *Touran*, and ندهه *Nedeheh*, and the bordering territories which belong to the possessors of Islam.

The eastern boundary of these regions is the Persian Sea. On the western side lie Kirman, and the deserts of Sejestan, and some territories of that province. On the north is the land of Hind, and its territories. The southern boundaries are the deserts of Makran, and the territory of the Bolouches; and a part of this borders on the Persian Sea, which is winding and curved on these confines.

Now we shall lay before the reader a map of those parts of Hind and Sind, and describe the curious and extraordinary places of them. Some parts belong to Guebres (كبران), and a greater portion of this country to كافران *Kafers* (Infidels) and Idolaters

(بت پرستان); a minute description of these places would, therefore, be unnecessary and unprofitable.

(Blank page for a Map of Sind and Hind.)

ذكر شهرهاكه در اين اقليم افتاده است

Of the Cities and Towns situated in these Countries.

راسك Rasek, الس Alis, كسر Kusr, فرمون Fermoun, درك Derek, مسكي Meski, قلعهره Kelaahereh, تصربند Kesrbend, ميل Meil, ارمايل Armaiel. Of طوران Touran the towns are, محالي Mehali, كبركامان Kibrkaman, سوره Sureh, قندابيل Kandabil. The other cities of Sind are, منصوره Mansourah, which they call سنديه Sindiah, دنبل Danbul, بلوي Baloui, ايري Airi, مانوي Manoui, مروي Meroui, مسحاري Mesouahi, بهرج Beherje, ماسه Maseh, مسواهي Meshari, سدوسان Sedusan.

There are سيدان Seidan, ميمون Meimoun, ملتان Multan, حيدور Heidour; names of cities in Sind and part of Hind. These, for the greater part, are inhabited by Infidels: but there are, in this country, some Mussulmans, who have mosques, and on stated days read the Khutbah: and the Indian sovereign who dwells here has a very extensive empire.

The city of Mansourah is about a mile in breadth, and as much in length; and a bay or arm of the river مهران *Mihran* passes by it, and renders it like an island. The inhabitants of Mansoureh are of the descendants of هبار ابن الاسود *Hebar ebn Alasoud.* He took the place, and it continues till this time in the possession of his family. It enjoys a warm climate, and produces dates, apples, and pears, and a fruit resembling the peach: it is a place abounding in provisions. Their coins are the تاهري *Kaheri,* every direm of which is equivalent to (or weighs) fifty direms; and another of silver, which they call طاطوي *Tautooi,* one direm of which is fifty direms; they also use gold in their commercial intercourse. Their dress and habits resemble those of the people of Irak; but their kings affect the appearance of Indian kings, and wear pendants in their ears.

The city of مولتان *Moultan* is about half the size of Mansoureh. It is called the "Golden House;" for there is in the city a certain idol, to which the Indians of the country come as on a religious pilgrimage, every year, and bring great riches with them; and those who pray in the temple of this idol must pay a tribute. This temple is situated in the centre of Moultan; and in the middle of the temple there is a great cupola or dome. All round this building are various houses, in which the servants and attendants of the idol reside. Moultan is not reckoned as belonging to Hindoostan; but there is in it a race of idolaters who worship in this temple. The idol is made in the form of a man, with the feet on a bench, formed of tiles, or bricks and mortar: it is clothed in a red garment, resembling Morocco leather (سختیان), and no part of the body is to be seen except the two eyes. Some people say the body is made of wood; but they do not permit any one to see more of it than the eyes, which are composed of precious stones. On the head is a diadem of gold. It sits upon a square throne, the hands resting on the knees.

All the riches which are brought to this idol from Hindoostan, are taken by the امیر *Emir* of Moultan, who distributes a portion among the servants of the temple. When the Indians come there in a hostile manner, and endeavour to carry off the idol from them, the people of Moultan take it forth, and seem to make preparations for breaking and burning it; when the Indians perceive that, they desist from fighting, and return back. If it were not for this circumstance, the Indians would destroy Moultan. There is here a castle, or citadel; but Mansoureh is more populous and improved.

Moultan was styled the بیت الزهب *Beit Alzahab*, or Golden House, because the Mussulmans were in great distress when they seized on this town, and found in it vast quantities of gold, and acquired power. About half a farsang from the town is a villa, in which resides the Emir of Moultan—on the appointed festivals he goes into the town—he is a قریشی *Coreishi* of the children of Sam the son of Noah, who conquered Moultan;

and he is called the Emir of that place. He has not any power over Mansourah; but the Khutbah is read in the name of the Khalif.

بسميد *Besmeid* is a small town. Besmeid, and Moultan, and چندوار *Chendvar*, are situated on the eastern side of the river of Moultan, each at the distance of one farsang from the bank of the river. The water used in these towns is well-water.

دنبل *Danbul* is situated on the eastern side of the river مهران *Mihran*, on the sea coast; it is the port of this country. In the cultivation of their lands, the inhabitants do not use water. It is a barren place; but people dwell there for the convenience of transacting mercantile business.

بيلرون *Bileroun* is a town between Dambul and Mansoureh, on the west of the river Mihran; and بهرج *Beherje*, and مسواي *Mesouai*, and سدوسان *Sedousan*, and هلبه *Helbeh*, are situated on the western side of the river Mihran. اندي *Andi* and دالوي *Daloui* are both on the eastern side of it, at a distance from the river, in going from Mansoureh to Moultan.

Baloui is situated on the banks of the river Mihran, near a bay, formed by that river behind Mansoureh. فامهل *Famhel* is a town on the first borders of Hindoostan.

مانه *Manah* is a small town, built by عبدالعزيز هباره *Abdalaziz Hebareh*, the ancestor of that race which took Mansourah.

ندهه *Nedeheh* is a tract of flat land between طوران *Touran*, and Mekran, and Moultan, and the towns of Mansoureh. This territory lies on the west of the river Mihran. It is a place remarkable for camels. The chief town of this district is a place of much commerce; it is called قندابيل *Kandabil*. The men of this town resemble those of the desert; they have houses constructed of reeds, along the banks of the river Mihran, as far as the borders of Moultan, and to the sea side; and between Mihran and Famhel they have pasture lands and meadows. They are a numerous tribe. Famhel, and Sedousan, and ميمون *Meimoun*, and كنيابه *Keniabeh*; all four have mosques, in which the religious ceremonies of Islam are publickly performed: there are great quantities of the Indian wall-nut (كوزهندي), and of the fruit called موز *Mouz*, with various kinds of herbs, and much honey.

راهوق *Rahouk* and كلوان *Kelwan* are two districts between ارمايل *Armaiel* and كير *Kair*: both these are without water: they abound in cattle.

طوران *Touran* is a little district, with many small villages and hamlets belonging to it. احمد بن معبر *Ahmed ben Maamr* possesses them, and the Khutbah is read in the Khalif's name. The town in which he resides is a considerable place, well supplied with provisions, and abounding in fruits; it is never subject to cold weather. Between مانيه *Maniah* and Famhel there is a desert; also between Famhel and كنيابه *Keniabah*.

تاصيمون *Tasimoun* is a populous district, in which the Mussulmans and Indians are intermixed. In this place the only garment they wear is the ازار *azar*, or sash round the middle, as the heat renders all others unnecessary: it is also the custom at Moultan. In the province of Makran they speak the Persian and Makrani languages. The merchants wear the cloak and turban.

Makran is an extensive country, but liable to scarcity and want of provisions. حسين بن عسي بن معدان *Hosein ben Isa ben Maadan* took possession of the district called مهرا *Mihra*, and dwelt in the town of كير *Kair*, which is as large as Moultan, and a good harbour: it has many date trees: in the territory of it is a well called the "Well of Makran." It is the largest town in Makran.

There is a district called خروج *Kherouje*, the capital of which is راسك *Rasek*, and there is a village belonging to it called حرمان *Herman*: these places belong to ظفر بن رجا *Zefer ben Reja*, and the Khutbah is read in the name of the Khalif. His territory extends near three merhileh; it affords some hundred of date trees, and furnishes فانید *Faneid* (a kind of sweet paste or candied cakes), to all quarters; its villages border on those of the province of Kirman, at the place called مسکنی *Meskeni*.

رساسل *Resasil* and تنتلی *Kanteli* are two large towns within two menzils: from Resasil to the sea is half a farsang.

تندابیل *Kandabil* is a considerable city situated in the desert. کیرکانان *Kirkanan* is another large town in the desert.

In the district of ازند *Azend* the Mussulmans and infidels are all intermixed. Here they have cattle and gardens. The name of a man who took this place was نایل *Naiel* (or نابل *Nabul*), and it is called after him.

ذکر مسافات دیار سند

Distances of Places in Sind.

FROM بین *Bein* to کبر *Kebr*, five merhileh; from Kebr to فتریون *Fetrioun*, two merhileh; and if one goes from the road of Fetrioun, by the road of Makran, it is the same distance: from Fetrioun to درک *Derek*, three merhileh; from that to اصفقه *Asofkah*, two merhileh; from that to مد *Med*, one merhileh; from Med to تصر *Kesr*, one merhileh; from کبر *Kebr*

to ارمايل *Armaiel*, six merhileh; from Mansoureh to طوران
Touran, fifteen merhileh; from تصدان *Kesdan* to Moultan,
twenty merhileh. Kesdan is the chief town of Touran. From
Mansourah to the borders of ندهه *Nedeheh*, five merhileh; and
from Kebr, which is the residence of Isa ben Maadan, to ندہ
Nedeh, ten merhileh; from Nedeh to بین *Bein*, fifteen merhileh; from Bein to Kesdan, twelve merhileh; from ندهه مولتان
Nedeheh of *Moultan*, to the extremity of the borders of تتار
Tetar, which they call بالس *Bales*, ten merhileh; and when
one goes from Mansourah towards Nedeheh, to سدوسان *Sedusan*, the way is by the bank of the river Mihran. From Kandabil to مسبح *Mesbah*, in the territory of Bein, four merhileh;
from Kesdan to Kandabil, five farsang; from Kandabil to Mansourah, about eight merhileh; and from Kandabil to Moultan,
ten merhileh of desert; from Mansourah to Famhel, twenty
merhileh; from Famhel to کینابه *Keinabah* four merhileh.

سوربه *Sourbah* is near the sea: from سندان *Sindan* to
Sourbah, is five merhileh; from Moultan to بسمید *Besmeid*,
two merhileh; from Besmeid to رود *Rud* (or the River), three
merhileh; from that to ابري *Aberi*, four merhileh; from Abari
to فلدي *Feldi*, four merhileh; from Feldi to Mansoureh, one
merhileh; from Danbul to پیروز *Pirouz*, four merhileh; from
Pirouz to محابري *Mehaberi*, two merhileh; from فالوي *Faloui*
to بلدان *Beldan*, four farsang.

ذکر رودهای این اقلیم

Of the Rivers in this Country.

OF the مهران Mihran it is said that the source is the river جیحون Jihoun; it comes out at Moultan, and passes on to the borders of Besmeid, and by Mansourah, and falls into the sea on the east of Dambul. The waters of the river Mihran are pleasant and wholesome; and they say it is liable to tides, or flux and reflux, like the Nile, and that it is infested by crocodiles. The سند رود Sind Rud, at three merhileh from Moultan, is of pleasant water, and joins the river Mihran. Water is very scarce throughout the land of Makran; there is some near Mansoureh. Many of the inhabitants of Makran resemble the Arabs; they eat fowl and fish: others of them are like the Curds. Here is the extreme boundary of the land of Islam in this direction.

Now we shall turn back, and begin to describe ارمنیه Armenia, and اران Aran, and اذربایکان Azerbaigan.

ذکر ارمنیه و اران و اذربایکان

Description of Armenia, and Aran, and Azerbaijan.

ALL the boundaries of these countries, کوهستان *Kouhestan* on the east, and the banks of the Caspian Sea, and the provinces adjacent to ارمن *Armen*, and الان *Alan*, and اران *Aran*, and the mountains of قپچاق *Kipchak**, and the borders of Irak and Jezireh, on the south; all these boundaries we lay before the reader in the annexed map.

صورت ارمنیه واران واذربایکان
(Blank page for a Map.)

اردبیل *Ardebil* is the most considerable city of Azerbaijan: it is about half a farsang in length and breadth, and contains the Governor's palace: it has walls, and four gates, and is a pleasant town, and well supplied with provisions. It has extensive suburbs; and within two farsang of it there is a mountain called سبلان *Seilan*, which is never free from snow either in winter or summer.

---

* قبشاق *Kibshak*, according to the Arabian mode of expressing the Persian or Turkish letters *Ba* and *Chim*.

مراغه *Meraghah* is nearly of the same size as Ardebil; in former times it was the seat of government: it has villages, and suburbs, orchards, and gardens, and land improved by agriculture. The town had walls: but ابي السّاح *Abi al Sah* demolished them.

Armenia is an extensive and fertile region, bounded by the sea, and full of delightful situations: the towns are مسان *Misan*, خونه *Khounah*, بروانان *Bervanan*, خوي *Khoui*, سلماس *Selmas*, نشوي *Neshoui*, مرند *Marend*, تبريز *Tabriz*, برزند *Bezerend*, دربان *Derban*, موقان *Moukan*, and خابران *Khaberan*; and several smaller towns.

برذع *Berdaa* is a populous and flourishing city, with cultivated lands and much fruit. After Rey and Isfahan, there is not in Irak or Khorasan a city more large, more beautiful, or pleasant, than Berdaa. At the distance of one farsang from Berdaa, between كريه *Kerieh*, and لصوت *Lesout*, and near بقطان *Bektan*, there is a well called اندراب *Anderab*; and for one day's journey the whole country is laid out in gardens and orchards. The fruits are excellent; their filberds (ندقت) are better than those of Samarcand, and their chesnuts (شاه بلوط) superior to the chesnuts of Syria; and the figs of Berdaa are more delicious than those of any other place. There are also mulberries; and silk is sent from that to Khuzistan, and to Irak.

In the river *Kur* رود کر they take fish of two kinds, رافن
Rafen and عشر *Aasher*, which are better than any other fish.
At the *Curd's Gate* (دروازه کردان) there is a market-place, or
bazar, called کرکی *Gurki* : every Sunday the people assemble
there: it is about a farsang square. Men from Khorasan and
from Irak meet there. The Revenue Office is in the great mosque,
and the bazars on the ramparts.

دربند *Derbend* is a city built on the shore of the sea, on two
banks of a bay, with two walls constructed so as to render the
navigation of ships more convenient and safe; and a chain is
drawn across the entrance, that ships may not enter or sail out
without permission; and these two walls are formed of stone and
lead: and this town of Derbend is situated on the coast of the
sea of طبرستان *Taberistan*. It is larger than Ardebil, with
many fields, and meadows, and cultivated lands. It does not produce much fruit; but the people supply that from other quarters.
A wall of stone extends from the city to the mountain; and
another of clay, to hinder the کافران *Cafres* (Infidels) from
coming into the town. Part of this wall projects a little way into
the sea, so that ships may not come too near the ramparts. This
wall is a strong building, and was the work of نوشیروان عادل
Noushirvan Aadel (the Just.)

This city of Derbend is very large, and remarkable: it is surrounded by enemies, who have different languages. On one side of Derbend is a great mountain called اديب *Adeib*; on this they assemble every year, and make many fires, that they may confound and disperse their enemies from the borders of Azerbaijan, and Armenia, and Arran: they are as numerous as the waves of the sea that come up to the walls of the city. It is said that this mountain, which is close to Derbend, contains above seventy different tribes, who have each a peculiar dialect, and understand not one the language of another.

The sovereigns of Persia have considered the possession of this city as a matter of great importance, and have established a race of people to guard it, called طبربران *Tairberan*; and there is another tribe called حيلابشار *Heilabshar*, and another called لكزان *Lekzan*: there are also two other tribes, the لنيران *Leniran* and سروان *Servan*: the foot soldiers are mostly of these tribes; they have few horsemen. Derbend is the port-town for خزر *Khozr*, and سرير *Serir*, and كركان *Gurkan*, and طبرستان *Taberistan*, and كرج *Kurge*, and قبچاق *Kapchak*; and from it they send linen clothes to all parts of Aran and Azerbaijan. Here they also weave tapestry, or carpets, and cultivate saffron.

On the coast of this sea (the Caspian) is another town called شابران *Shaberan*; it is a small place, but pleasant and well supplied with provisions: it has many villages belonging to it. Above those is the village of جسمدان *Jesmeden,* as far as the borders of شروان *Shirvan,* and باكوه *Baku,* and دريتك *Derituk,* and لكز *Lekez;* and in this village is a castle so very extensive that all the cattle in the country may be secured in it, without any guards or centinels left to watch them.

تغليس *Teflis* is a smaller city than Derbend: it is a pleasant place, and abounds in provisions: it has two walls of clay, and produces much fruit, and agriculture is practised in its territories. It has hot baths, in which, as at طبريه *Tiberiah,* the water is warm without fire. In all Aran there are not any cities more considerable than Berdaa, Derbend, and Teflis.

As for بيلغان *Bilkan,* and ريان *Reyan,* and برزنج *Berzenje,* and شماخي *Shamakhy,* and شابران *Shaberan,* and شروان *Shirvan,* and الأنجان *Alenjan,* and قبله *Kablah,* and كنجه *Kaujah,* and شمكور *Shemkour,* and شروسند *Sherousend;* they are small towns, but pleasant and plentiful.

دينل *Deinel* is a larger city than Ardebil, and the chief town of Armenia; the palace of the governor is there, as at Berdaa, the capital of Aran. It has very wide and extraordinary ramparts. There are great numbers of Christians and Jews here; and the churches are interspersed among the mosques. Here they manufacture fine hangings, and carpets, and make the beautiful colour called قرمز kermez. I have heard that this kermez is a certain worm*.

This place has heretofore been in the hands of شنباط بن اشوط Shenbat ben Ashout, and at all times has belonged to Christian princes; the greater number of the people of Armenia are Christians. Armenia is bordered on one side by Berdaa; on another by the confines of Jezireh; on another by Azerbaijan, and Jebal, and Dilem, and Rey: the south side is bordered by the Seghour of Roum (ثغور روم).

طرابزون Trabzoun is situated on the extreme confines of Roum; it is much frequented by merchants. میافارقین Miafarekin and سروج Serouah are small but pleasant towns.

ذکر رودها و دریاهای این دیار

Of the Rivers and Lakes of this Country (and other Matters).

THE most considerable rivers are the کر Kur, the آرس Aras, and the اسغندرود Asfendrud, which is between Ardebil and

---

* The Persian Dictionary, intituled *Ferhang-Borhan-Kattea,* informs us; that *Kermez* is the name of a substance with which they tinge or dye; and that it is said to be an insect gathered from certain shrubs, and afterwards dried; and that the Arabians style it دود الصباغین *Dud-al-Sebaghein,* " the Dyer's Worm."

زمکان Zemgan. The waters of the river Kur are sweet and wholesome; it comes from the mountain of اوهله Auhileh, and goes on to the borders of کنجه Kenjah, and passes by شمکور Shemkour, and through the midst of تغليس Teflis, and to the land of the Infidels. The river Aras has also pleasant waters; it comes from Armenia, and, falling into the river Kur, at the borders of موقان Moukan, near محمود اباد Mahmoud abad, falls into the sea.

There is a lake in Azerbaijan called the Lake of *Armia* (دریای ارمیه): the water is salt or bitter, and contains not any living creature. All round this lake are villages and buildings: from the lake to مراغه *Meraghah* is a distance of three farsang; to ارمی *Armi* two farsang. The length of this lake is five days journey, by land; and by water, with a fair wind, a person may traverse it in the space of one night.

In Armenia there is a lake near ارجیس *Arjeis*; in it are great numbers of the fish طرع *Teraa*, which they send to all quarters. The Sea of Khozr is also on this border. Derbend and Baku are situated on it. Naphta is found at Baku. A small part of the river Tigris (دجله *Dejleh*) runs on the confines of Armenia. The borders of Azerbaijan extend from تارم *Tarem* to زنکان *Zingán*, to دینل *Deinel*, and حلوان *Holwan*, and to شهرزور *Shehrzour*, to the river Dejleh, and back to the borders of Armenia. All the necessaries of life are very cheap in this country:

in it are places where they sell sheep for two direms, and a munn of corn for one direm.

There are powerful princes in this region: such as شروان شاه *Shirvan Shah,* and others. All this country belongs to the cold climate.

The stone of Ardebil weighs twelve hundred direms. Throughout this country the Persian and Arabian languages are understood. The inhabitants of Ardebil use also the Armenian tongue; in the mountainous country belonging to Berdaa, the people use a different dialect.

In Azerbaijan, and Aran, and Armenia, gold and silver coins are current.

ذكر مسافات اين ديار

Of the Distances of Places in this Country.

From Berdaa to ورنان *Vernan,* seven farsang; from that to بيلقان *Bilkan,* seven farsang; from برزند *Berzend* to Ardebil, fifteen farsang; from Berdaa to Berzend, eighteen farsang; from that one passes the river *Kur* رود كر, to شماخي *Shamakhy,* fourteen farsang; from Shamakhy to شروان *Shirvan,* three farsang; from Shirvan to لانجان Lanjan, two days journey; from Lanjan to the پول میمون Poul-i-meimoun (Bridge of Meimoun), twelve farsang; from the Poul-i-meimoun to Derbend, twenty farsang; from کنجه Kanjah to شمکور Shemkour, four farsang; from Shemkour to حبان Heban, eleven farsang; from Heban to the Castle of Aber Kendman قلعه ابر کندمان, ten farsang; from that to تغلیس Teflis, twelve farsang.

The road between Berdaa and دینل Deinel: from Berdaa to قلقاطرین Kelkaterin, twelve farsang; from that to میرس Mires, to دومیش Doumish, twelve farsang; from Doumish to Kelilgoun کلیلکون, sixteen farsang; from that to Deinel, sixteen farsang; all this space belongs to سنباط بن اشوط Senbat ben Ashout.

From Ardebil to رود Rud, or the river, two merhileh; from that to خونه Khouneh, two days journey; from Khouneh to توت سواران Tawet Souaren, one day's journey; from that to زنکان Zengen, one day's journey.

From Ardebil to مراغه Meraghah, the road is this: from Ardebil to میانه Mianeh, twenty farsang; from Mianeh to خونه Khouneh, eight farsang: from Meraghah to دیر خرقان Deir Kherkan, two merhileh; from that to تبریز Tabriz, two merhileh; from Tabriz to مرند Merend, two merhileh; from Merend to سلماس Selmas, two merhileh; from Selmas to خوی

Khoui, eight farsang; from Khoui to برکري *Berkeri*, thirty farsang; from Berkeri to ارجیش *Arjeish*, two days' journey; from Arjeish to خلاط *Khullat*, three days journey; from Khullat to بدلیس *Bedlis*, three days journey; from Bedlis to *Miafarekein* میافارقین, three days journey; and from Miafarekein to آمد *Amed*, four days journey.

The distance from Maraghah to دینور *Deinour*, is thirty farsang; from ارمي *Armi* to Selmas, fourteen farsang; from Selmas to Khoui, eight farsang; from Khoui to نخجوان *Nakhjevan*, three merhileh; from Nakhjevan to Deinel, four merhileh: from Maraghah to Deinour, sixty farsang.

ذکر کوهستان یعني عراق عجم

Description of Kouhestan, that is, Irak Agemi.

ON the east of Kouhestan are the deserts of Khorasan, and part of Fars, and Isfahan, and the eastern side of Khuzistan. On the west of Kouhestan lies the province of Azerbaijan. On the north is دیلمان *Deilman*, and قزوین *Cazvin*, and ري *Rey*, and ماردین *Mardein*. These towns, Rey, and Cazvin, and ابهر *Abher*, and زنکان *Zengan*, we have not placed in the map as belonging to Kouhestan; we rather assign them to the province of Deilman, because it winds irregularly along Kouhestan. The southern boundaries of Kouhestan are Irak, and part of Khuzistan.

There are many great and celebrated cities in the province of Kouhestan; such as همدان *Hamadan*, and دینور *Deinour*, اصفاهان *Isfahan*, and قم *Kom*: the smaller cities are کاشان *Kashan*, and نهاوند *Nehavend*, and لور *Lour*, and جربادقان *Jerbadcan*.

صورت عراق عجم

(Page left blank for a Map of Irak Agemi.)

ذکر مسافات این دیار

Distances of Places in this Province.

FROM همدان *Hamadan* to اسدآباد *Asedebad*, nine farsang; from Asedebad to قصر دزدان *Keser Duzdan*, seven farsang; from that to قنطره النعبان *Kantereh al Naaman*, seven farsang: from Kantereh al Naaman to دهیه ابو ایوب *Dehieh abou Ayoub*, four farsang; from thence to بیستون *Bisutoun*, two farsang; from Bisutoun to کرمان شاهان *Kirman Shahan*, eight farsang; from Kirman Shahan to زیبدیه *Zeibedieh*, eight farsang; thence to مرح *Merah*, which is a castle (قلعه), nine farsang; from Merah to حلوان *Hulwan,* ten farsang; from Hulwan to ساوه *Saveh,* thirty farsang; from Saveh to ري *Rey,* thirty farsang; from Hamdan to Azerbaijan, to بار *Bar* or *Yar,* thirteen farsang; from مارسين *Marsin* to اود *Aoud,* eight farsang; from Aoud to نزوين *Cazvin,* two days journey; and between Hamadan and Cazvin there is not any town; and from Cazvin to اوهر *Auher,* or *Avhar,* twelve farsang; from Auher to راكان *Rakan,* fifteen farsang; and one may go to Rakan from Hamadan by the road of شهرورد *Sherwerd.*

از همدان تا دينور

From Hamadan to Deinour.

FROM Hamadan to مادران رود *Maderan Roud,* and thence to صحنه *Seheneh,* four farsang; from Seheneh to دينور *Deinour,* four farsang; from that to روكرد *Rugird,* or وردكرد *Wirdgird,* eleven farsang; from Wirdgird to كره *Kurreh,* fifteen farsang; from Kurreh to برج *Berah,* twelve farsang; from Berah to خومنجان *Khoumenjan,* ten farsang; from Khoumenjan to سپاهان *Spahan,* thirty farsang; desert from Hamadan to the رود راور *Rud Rawer,* seven farsang; from the Rud Rawer to نهاوند *Nehavend,* nine farsang; from Nehavend to لاشتر *Lashter,* ten farsang; from Lashter to شابر خواست *Shaber Khuast,* twelve farsang; from Shaber Khuast to لور* *Lour*, or بور *Bour*, thirty farsang of an uninhabited dreary country; from لور *Lour* to اندمش *Andemesh*, two farsang; from پول اندامش *Pul Andemesh* to جندي شاپور *Jondi Shapour*, two farsang; from Hamadan to ساوه *Saveh*, thirty farsang: from Saveh to قم *Kom*, twelve farsang; from Kom to قاشان *Cashan*, twelve farsang; from ري *Rey* to قزوین *Cazvin*, twenty-seven farsang; from Hamadan to Dinour, between twenty and thirty farsang; from Dinour to شهر زور *Shehrzour*, four merhileh; from Sherzour to Holwan, four merhileh; from Dinour to صبیره *Semireh*, five merhileh; and from Dinour to Shehrzour, four merhileh; from Dinour to سیروان *Sirvan*, four farsang; from Sirvan to صیمره *Simreh*, one day's journey; and from the دهیم لور *Dehieh Lour* to كره *Kurreh*, six merhileh; and from سپاهان *Spahan* to كاشان *Cashan* (before spelt قاشان) three merhileh.

ذكر اسامي شهرهاي عراق عجم

Names of Cities and Towns in Irak Agemi.

HAMADAN, ورد کرد *Werdgerd*, رودراور *Rud Rawer*, رامر *Ramer*, لاسبین, سابر خاست *Saber Khast*, فراونده *Feravendeh*,

---

* I have already taken occasion to remark the indistinctness of my manuscript, and of the copy at Eton, in the writing of proper names.

Lausin, دينور *Kesri Duzdan,* تصر دزبان *Asedabad,* اسدآباد *Dinour,* طرزحومه *Merah,* مرج *Kirman Shahan,* كرمان شاهان *Turezhumeh,* شهرود *Shehrud,* ابهر *Abeher,* سمنان *Semnan,* *Kom,* قم *Kashan,* قاشان *Rudeh,* روده *Kurreh,* كره *Berd,* برد *Gerbadcan,* كرباد كان *Semireh* (spelt before صميره), *Sirvan,* سروان *Dur,* دور *Rasi,* راسي *Bordan,* بردان سپاهان *Spahan,* *Jehudistan,* جهودستان *Khan Lekhan,* خان لخان *Kesralberadin,* تصرالبرادين *Casvin,* قزوين *Takaun,* طاقان *Renjan.* رنجان

Hamadan is a considerable city, of about one farsang in length and breadth. It has four iron gates: the buildings are of clay. It abounds in gardens and orchards. دينور *Deinour* is not quite so large as Hamadan. Both places have mosques.

اسپهان *Ispahan* is the most flourishing of all the cities in كوهستان *Kouhestan,* and possesses more riches than all the other places; and it is the pass between Kouhestan, and Pars, and Khorasan, and Khuzistan. The garments of silk (ابرشيم), and fine linen (كرپاس), of this place, are carried to all parts of the empire, as well as the fruits.

كره *Kurreh* is a town of scattered houses: it is called *Kurreh* of *Budulph* كره بودلف his children resided there till the time that they ceased to govern; but the ruins of their villas and palaces still remain. This place abounds in cattle; and the land about it is well cultivated. Fruit is brought to it from Werdgird. It is a long town, about one farsang in length. It has two bazars; one near the gate of the chief mosque. Between the two bazars the distance is considerable.

ورد‌کرد *Werdgird* is an extensive and flourishing city: its length is two farsang. Saffron is cultivated here.

نهاوند *Nehavend* is situated on a hill. It has many pleasant gardens and orchards, with excellent fruits, and two mosques; one modern, the other ancient. Saffron also comes from Nehavend.

رود راور *Rud Rawer* is a village, and there is a small town which they call کره رود راور *Kurreh Rud Rawer*. It is a well-inhabited, plentiful, and pleasant place, where saffron is cultivated in greater quantities, and of a better kind, than anywhere else: it is therefore sent from this place to all parts.

هلوان *Hulwan* is a town of these mountains. All its walls are of clay and stone. Its air is warm; and here are many fig-trees.

صبیره *Semireh*, and سروان *Sirvan*, have both a hot and cold temperature; and running water flows among the houses of these places.

شهرزور *Shehrzour* is a small town, which the Curds have seized on; also the town شهروړد *Shehrwerd*: these two places are in the hands of the Curds.

Shehrwerd is a place of which the inhabitants are mostly Curds (اكراد), and notorious robbers and plunderers. Saul (طالوت), the king of the Children of Israel, was of this place.

قزوين *Casvin* is a great city, with walls and a castle, and running water just enough for the people to drink; but the gardens, and meadows, and orchards, are well watered. This place affords much almonds, and the fruit called موز *Mawz*; and here they weave excellent camelot, or stuffs made of the under or woolly hair of goats.

قم *Kom* has not any walls, and the inhabitants drink well-water. In spring and summer a great river runs by the gate of this city. In all Irak, date trees are not to be found, except at Semirah, and سيروان *Sirvan*, and سابر خواست *Saber Khast*, where there are a few: and the people of Kom and Kashan are all of the Shiah sect, and originally from Arabia.

قاشان *Kashan* is a small town. Here are great numbers of black scorpions, who kill, and another species called حيراره *heirarah*.

In all كوستان Kouhistan there is not any sea, or great lake: it is all a hilly country, except from Hamadan to Rey, or Kom, where the hills are fewer, and less considerable.

From Shehrzour to Hulwan, to صيمره Semireh, to سيروان Sirvan, to لور Lour, to the vicinity of اصفهان Isfahan, and the borders of Saber Khast, and from that in the direction of Kashan and Hamadan, to Shehrzour and the borders of Azerbaijan, it is all a mountainous country, and there is not any spot from which the hills may not be seen.

Rey, which we have mentioned, on the confines of *Deilman* ولايت ديلمان, is equally belonging to جبال *Jebal* and Khorassan; and after Baghdad, there is not any city of the east larger or more flourishing than it, except نيشاپور *Nishapour*.

Among the mountains of this country, the principal is *Damavend* كوه دماوند, from which one can see fifty farsang around, and I have never heard that any man ever ascended to its summit; and, in the romances of the Persians (درخرافات پارسيان), it is said that Zohak is confined in chains within this mountain. And the mountain of بيستون *Bisetoun* is likewise very lofty and difficult of ascent; the face of the mountain you would suppose to be carved, or hewn out; and they say there was a certain king who wished to make a summer house, or palace, of this moun-

(173)

tain, in order to display his power to the people *. " And at the back of this mountain, on the side of the road, there is a cavern, or grotto, from which a fountain of water issues forth; and there they have carved the statue of a horse, and the figure of a giant sitting on its back †."

The mountain of سيلان *Seilan* is greater than that of Damavend; and here is a race of people who practise a kind of magism, or fire-worship (كبري).

It is said that the mountain of جرث *Jerth* is called in Persian ماست كوه *Maset Kouh*, and is larger than all the others.

I have not heard that there are in Kouhestan any mines of gold or silver. Antimony is found at Isfahan. This country abounds in sheep.

---

* Rather to gratify the whim of a favourite mistress, according to the Persian romances.—See the story of *Khofru* and *Shireen*, in the Oriental Collections, Vol. I. p. 218, &c.

† و بر پشت این کوه بر کنار راه غاريهست و چشمه اب از بى غاريرون مي امد و در ان جايگاه صورت اسپي نکاشته اند و صورت کبري بر پشت ان نشسته

Perhaps كبري, which I have translated *Giant*, may signify here an illustrious personage, or (in its most obvious sense) a *Guebre*, a Pagan, or ancient Persian.

ذکر دیلمان و طبرستان

Of the Provinces of Deilman and Taberistan.

THE southern borders of Deilman are قزوین Cazvin, and طارم Tarem, and part of Azerbaijan, and part of ری Rey. On the north it has the Caspian Sea (دریای خزر), or Sea of Khozr. On the west, part of Azerbaijan, and the towns of that country. On the east are the mountains of Rey, and the hills of قارن Karen, and کرکان Gurkan, and the Caspian sea. The region of Deilman is partly mountainous, and partly flat; the level tract is that of کیلان Gilan, on the borders of the Caspian sea, under the mountains of Deilman. The sovereign (پادشاه) of Deilman resides at رودبار Rudbar. This territory is covered for the greater part with forests and woods.

طبرستان Taberistan is a flat country, and well cultivated: here they breed much cattle; and they have a peculiar dialect, neither Arabick nor Persian; and in many parts of Deilman their language is not understood. Until the time of حیر بن زید Hair ben Zeid (may God reward him!), the inhabitants of Taberistan, and of Deilman were Infidels (کافر): then many of them became Mussulmans; but it is said that in the mountains of Deilman some of them still continue to practise the rites of Paganism.

The mountains of قارن *Karen* are difficult of access, and very strong: in every hill there is a chief. Here are lofty trees, and forests, and streams, but no towns except شهمار *Shehmar*. To ساربن *Sarein** (or ساري *Sari*) one merhileh. This was the residence of قارن *Karen*, who was their king (كه پادشاه ايشان بود); and the seat of government, and the place where the treasures were deposited. From the mountains of *Bardestan* جبال باردستان to Sari, is one merhileh.

From the borders of Deilman, and the coast of the sea, to استراباد *Asterabad*, is one day's journey; it is not more. The district of ري *Rey* is adjoining to Cazvin. ابهر *Ebher*, and رنكان *Rengan*, and طالقان *Talekan*, and قصر الرادين *Kesr al radein*, are in these territories; and قومس *Koumes*, and سمنان *Semnan*, and دامغان *Damghan*, and بستام *Bustam*, are all connected one with another.

And امل *Amol*, and مليل *Melil*, and سالوس *Salous*, and كلار *Kellar*, and روبان *Rouban*, and مسله *Mesleh*, and *Aien alhem* عين الهم, and مهطر *Memta*, and ساري *Sari*, and مهروان *Mehrwan*, and البراسك *Almerasek*, and بيشه *Bemisheh*, are reckoned as belonging to Taberistan.

---

* I have before remarked the extreme obscurity and inaccuracy of several passages in this work. I shall endeavour, in a future publication, to illustrate and correct them.

ابسكون Abis- استراباد Asterabad, and طبرسير Temseir, and
goun, and دهستان Dehestan, to كركان Gurkan; and in the
mountains I know not of any towns, besides سمنان Semnan,
and تويم Kouim; and those belong to كوه قارن Karen Kouh.

The most considerable city of those we have mentioned is ري
Rey. After Baghdad there is not in the eastern regions any city
more flourishing. Its gates are much celebrated: one of them
is called the دروازه ناطان Derwazeh Natan, facing the mountainous country, or the كوهستان عراق Kouhestan of Irak;
another leads to Cazvin: another, called the دروازه كرهك
Derwazeh Gurhek, is in the direction of قم Kom. And there
are many remarkable streets and quarters in this city; such as
روده Rudeh, and قليسان Kelisan, and دهك نو Dehek Nou,
and نصراباد Nasrabad, and ساربانان Sarbanan, and Bab al
Jebal باب الجبال or the Mountain Gate; and the درهشام
Der-i-Hesham, or Hesham's Gate; and the درآهنين Der-i-
Ahenin, or the Iron Gate; and the gate called درعتاب Der-i-
Ithab; but the quarter of Rudah is the most populous and flour-
ishing of all.

In this place are many bazars, and caravanseras, and market-
places. In the suburbs there is a mosque. The citadel is in good re-
pair, and there is a wall round the suburbs, which is, however, falling to decay, and almost desolate. Here they have both river water

and water brought by canals or trenches: one of these is called the كاريز شاهي *Kareiz Shahi*, or Royal Aqueduct; it passes by Sarbanan: another, called كيلاني *Gilani*, also passes through Sarbanan. For the most part the inhabitants drink the water of these aqueducts. There are many canals besides. Here they cultivate the land, and practise husbandry, and traffick for gold and direms. The people of this place are hospitable and polite. Here they manufacture fine linen, cotton, and camelots, which are sent to all parts of the world.

خوار *Khar* is a small town, supplied with water by a river which runs from دماوند *Damavend*. دهمه *Dehmeh**, and شلينه *Shelineh*, are two towns belonging to the territories of Damavend; they are smaller than Khar.

Dehmeh is larger than Shelineh; it abounds in cultivated fields, gardens, and orchards, and fruits. There is not any place in the whole country of a more cool temperature.

In the territory of Rey there are villages larger than those towns; such as وامیز *Vameiz*, and ارينو *Arinou*, and درسين *Dersein*, and درا *Dera*, and توسين *Kousein*, and سيست *Seist*, and خسرو *Khosru*, and others: and I have heard that in every one of these villages there are two thousand inhabitants or more.

* Or وهمه *Wehmeh*.

From the territory of Rey, cotton and linen clothes are sent to Baghdad, and into Azerbaijan; and in those places which we have spoken of, there is not any navigable river: a stream flows from the summit of Damavend; and all round this mountain are considerable villages, such as دبیران *Debiran*, and درمیه *Dermeyah*. Of this place was علي بن شروين *Ali ben Sherouin*, who was taken prisoner on the banks of the river جيحون *Jihoun*.

The mountain of Damavend is the most eastern of all the mountains in Taberistan, and may be seen from all parts of the country: they call it افترع*, because that on it there are not many trees.

But تومس *Koumes* belongs to Damavend; دامغان *Damghan* is larger than خوار *Khar* of Rey; سمنان *Semnan* is smaller than Damghan; and بستام *Bustam* is smaller than Damghan: it is remarkable for excellent fruit.

قزوين *Cazvin* has two suburbs, with walls. The chief mosque is situated in the great suburbs. Here are two small canals or aqueducts, of which the water is used for drinking, and for the purposes of agriculture; yet, with this scarcity of water, the city is pleasant, and abounds in provisions: It is the pass into

† Or اقترع

Deilman; and there are constant quarrels between the people of these places. It produces fruits, such as grapes and almonds, &c. so plentifully that they are carried to other parts of the country. This city is one mile by one mile.

ابهر *Abher* and زنكان *Zengan* are two small, but pleasant and well supplied towns; of which Zengan is the larger: but its inhabitants are idle and not industrious.

طبرستان *Tabaristan* is a considerable province. The buildings in it are of wood and reeds. It adjoins اران *Aran*.

ساري *Sari* is larger than Cazvin, well inhabited, and supplied with provisions. Silk is produced in great quantities throughout all quarters of Tabaristan; it is sent, for the greater part, to امل *Amol*. The people of Tabaristan have very thick and long hair, with heavy eye-brows; they speak very fast, and their usual diet is bread made of rice: they eat much fish, rice, and milk: they manufacture garments of silk and wool. In all Tabaristan there is not a river on which boats can be employed; but the sea is near.

كركان *Gurkan* is a small place, less liable to rain and damps than Tabaristan. The people of Gurkan are amiable in their dispositions, of a generous and manly nature. Without the city is a piece of ground called بكرابان *Bekrabad*, through which runs a considerable stream; it produces much silk. This district is very well watered and cultivated: after you pass Irak, no spot is more abundant than Gurkan: it yields the fruits both of warm and cold climates; and snow is to be found even in summer. Many eminent men have come from this country. Dinars and direms are current in Tabaristan; and the من‎ *mun* of that land is six hundred direms.

استراباد‎ *Asterabad* is situated near the Caspian Sea; from that you go to ابسکون‎ *Abisgoun*, and by the sea to خزر‎ *Khozr*, and دربند‎ *Derbend*, and دیلمان‎ *Deilman*, and other places: in all this country there is not any port or harbour more commodious or larger than Abisgoun. Here is a place called دهستان‎ *Dehestan*, very fertile; and the Turks * come here from خوارزم‎ *Khuarezm*.

ذکر مسافات این دیار‎

The Stages and Distances of this Country.

From ری‎ *Rey* to قزوین‎ *Cazvin*, four merhileh; from Cazvin to دهر‎ *Deher*, two short merhileh. Whoever desires to go from Rey to زنکان‎ *Zengan*, without going to Cazvin, must

* ترکان‎ Turks of Khorasmia, or Turkestan, Tartars, Scythians, &c.

take the road by a village near Rey, called بردآباد Berdabad, one of the villages of the waste or desert. From Rey to قسطانه Kestaneh, one merhileh; from Kestaneh to مسکوبه Meskoubeh, one merhileh; from that to ساوه Saveh, nine farsang. Saveh is sometimes reckoned as belonging to the province of جبال Jebal, and sometimes to Rey.

From Rey to مهین Mehein, a merhileh of nine farsang [*]; from Mehein to بلور Belour, one merhileh; from Belour to کلازل Kelazil, a merhileh of six farsang (or one merhileh, six farsang); from Kelazil to the Castle of Lauzer قلعه الزر, one merhileh; from that to قهرست Kehrest, one merhileh, six farsang (or a merhileh of six farsang); and from that to امل Amol, one merhileh.

مسافات از ری بخراسان

Stages and Distances from Rey to Khorasan.

From Rey to مربدین Merbedein, one merhileh; from that to کهنده Kohendeh, to خوار Khar, one merhileh; from Khar to دهیه نمک Dhey Nemek, one merhileh; from that to *Ras al Kelb* راس الکلب (or the dog's head), one merhileh; from Ras

---

[*] Or a merhileh and nine farsang مرحله نه فرسنگ...

al Kelb to سمنان Semnan, one merhileh; and to علي اباد Ali Abad, one merhileh; from جرم جري Jerm Jery, one merhileh; to دامغان Damghan, one merhileh; from Damghan to خداوه or خلاوه Khelawah or Khedaweh, one merhileh; from that to بدليس Bedlis, one merhileh; from Bedlis to مورجان Mourjan, one merhileh; from Mourjan to هفت در Heft Der (or the seven gates) one merhileh; and from Heft Der to اسداباد Asedabad, one merhileh. Asedabad belongs to the borders of Nishapour.

راه از طبرستان بكركان

Road from Taberistan to Gurkan.

From امل Amol to مسله Mesleh, two farsang; from that to ترجي Terjy, one merhileh; from that to ساري Sari, one merhileh; from بامیه Bamieh to مراسك Merasik, one merhileh; from that to طبيشه Temisheh, one merhileh; from Temisheh to استراباد Asterabad, one merhileh; from Asterabad to Rebat Hafs رباط حافص one merhileh; from Asterabad to كركان Gurkan, one merhileh. Whoever desires to go forth from Asterabad must go to the رباط وداره Rebat Wedareh, one merhileh; from that to جرهان Jerhan, one merhileh. Whoever will go from Amol must go to مالط Malet, one merhileh; and from Malet to ساري Sari, one merhileh.

راه از امل بديلم

Road from Amol to Deilem.

From Amol to بابل *Bayel*, one merhileh; from that to سالوس *Salus*, one short merhileh; from that to کلار *Gullar*, one merhileh; from Gullar to ديلم *Dilem*, one merhileh; from Amol to عين الهم *Aien Alehem*, one short merhileh. From کرکان *Gurkan* to دمارزاري *Demarzari*, one merhileh; from that to امرويلو *Amrouilou*, one merhileh; from that to اجع *Ajaa*, one merhileh; from Ajaa to سنداىست *Sendanest*, one merhileh; and from Sendanest to سراىن *Serain*, one merhileh; from Gurkan to جهىنه *Jehineh*, one merhileh; from Jehineh to بسطام *Bustam*, one merhileh.

ذكر درياي خزر

Of the Sea of Khozr, or the Caspian.

The western side of this Sea belongs partly to ديلمان *Deilman*, and طبرستان *Taberistan*, and کرکان *Gurkan*, and its borders; and part of it is bordered by the deserts of خوارزم *Khuarezm*. On the western side is اران *Aran*, and موقان *Moukan*, and the territories of سرير *Serir,* and part of the deserts of عزيه *Azziah:* and on the north it has the desert of Azziah, to the territories of سياه كوه *Siah Kouh;* and on the south, باكيل *Bakeil,* and ديلمان *Deilman,* and the neighbouring places. This sea is not connected with any other; and if a person wishes to make a tour completely round it, nothing will impede him but a few rivers which fall into it from various quarters. The waters of this sea are bitter and dark-coloured; its bottom is a blackish clay, differing in this respect from the Sea of قلزم *Kolzum,* or of عمان *Oman,* or of پارس *Pars.* This Sea of Pars is of such clear water that one may see the white stones at the bottom; but the waters of this Sea of Khozr are dark-coloured, and in it there are not found any such things as pearls, or coral, or similar marine productions. It is, however, much frequented by the ships of merchants who traffick from one town to another; and it affords much fishing. In this ocean there are not any inhabited islands, as in the Sea of Fars and of Roum; but there are many trees and forests *.

(صورت دریا خزر)

(Blank Page for a Map of the Caspian Sea.)

* لیکن درختان وبیشه بسیاراست It is not clear whether those trees occupy the islands of this sea, or skirt its borders.

One island is considerable, with a fountain of water and many trees; and there is another large island on the borders of لكذان Lekzan, which has also fresh water. To this island they bring cattle from برذع Berdaa in boats, and turn them out to graze, and leave them until they become fat.

Near ابسكون Abisgoun is a place called دهستان Dehestan, with very sweet and wholesome water. Here the people of the neighbouring places assemble for the purpose of fishing. It is said that there is a race of Turks (تركان) dwelling in the vicinity of سياه كوه Siah Kouh (or the black mountain.)

After one passes موكان Moukan to دربند Derbend, for two days journey the country is شيروان Shirwan; from that to سمندر Semender, fourteen days journey; and from Semender to اتل Atel. This Atel is a certain river which comes from روس Rous and بلغار Bulgar. One half of this river belongs to the western side, the other to the eastern. The sovereign of Atel resides on the western side: he is styled King, and surnamed بال Baul. Here are many tents; and in this country there are but a few edifices of clay, such as bazars (market-places) and bathing houses. In these territories are about ten thousand Mussulmans. The king's habitation is at a distance from the shore: it is constructed of burnt bricks; and this is the only building of such materials in all the country: they will not allow any body but the king to erect such a dwelling.

The city of اتل *Atel* has four gates. One of those gates faces the river; another looks towards Iran, in the direction of the desert. The king of this country is a Jew: he has in his train four thousand Mussulmans, and خزري *Khozrians* (Christians), and Idolaters; but his principal people are Jews: And this king has twelve thousand soldiers in his service, of whom when one dies, another person is immediately chosen into his place; and they have no other commander but him. And this king has under him nine magistrates or judges (قاضي): these are Mussulmans, Jews, Christians, and Idolaters. The smallest in number of the inhabitants of this country are the Jews; the greatest in number are the Mussulmans and Christians: but the king and his chief officers are Jews. There are magistrates of each religion; and when they sit in the tribunal of justice, they are obliged to report to the king all that passes, and to bring back his answer and opinion, and put his sentence into execution.

This city has not any suburbs; but the cultivated fields and grounds extend for near twenty farsang. Agriculture is much practised, and the husbandmen carry the produce of their labour in boats and carriages to the city. The chief diet of this people is fish and rice: they bring honey and wax from the borders of روس *Rous*. The principal persons of Atel are Mussulmans and merchants: their language is like that of the Turks (ترك or Tartars), and is not understood by any other nation.

The river of Atel comes from the borders of جرجیر *Jerjir*, and from that goes on to کیماک *Kaimak*, and to غز *Ghuz*, and so on to بلغار *Bulgar*, and falls into the sea near برطاس *Bertas*. It is said that this river, at the season when all its waters are collected, is greater than the river جیحون *Jihoon*; and that it rushes into the sea with such a body that it seems to conquer the water of the Caspian; and one can see its stream unmixed with the sea water, as far as a journey of two days.

In خزر *Khozr* there is a certain city called اسمید *Asmid*, which has so many orchards and gardens, that from دربند *Derbend* to سریر *Serir* the whole country is covered with the gardens and plantations belonging to this city. It is said that there are above forty thousand of them. Many of these produce grapes. In this town are many Mussulmans, who have mosques; and their houses are built of wood. The king is a Jew, in friendship with the Padshah of Khozr, and on good terms with the Padshah of سریر *Serir*. From this place to the borders of Serir, is two farsang.

The inhabitants of Serir are ترسا *Tersas* or Christians. It is said that in this Serir was a throne, and that there was a certain king of the kings of Pars, who, when he gave a principality to one of his sons, sent him here with a golden throne; which principality has continued established to this time. A son of Behram Chopin is said to have first-possessed it [*]. The inhabitants of Serir are on good terms with the Mussulmans. In this part of Khozr I know not of any other town than سمید Semid (before written Asmid.)

برطاس Bertas is a people near Khozr, on the banks of the river of اتل Atel. They are called برطاس; but the region is also styled in general خزر Khozr, روس Rous, or Serir.

The people of Khozr are near the Turks (ترکان), whom they resemble. They are of two classes; one of blackish complexions, and such dark hair that you would suppose them to be descended from the Hindoos: the other race fair complexioned; these sell their children; but it is not allowed among the Jews and the Christians to sell, or make one another slaves.

They bring from other countries those commodities which Khozr does not produce, such as tapestry or curtains, honey, candles, and similar articles. The people of Khozr have not materials for making garments or clothes: they therefore import them from کرکان Gurkan, Armenia, Azerbaijan, and Roum. Their king is styled the خاقان خزر Khacan of Khozr:

---

[*] Behram Chopin is said to have flourished in the latter end of the sixth century of the Christian æra. See D'Herbelot's *Bibl. Orient.* Art. *Baharam* and *Serir*.

When a prince is to be raised to the Khacanship, they bring him forth, and tie a piece of silk about his throat, so tight that he can scarcely draw his breath. At that moment they ask him, how long he will hold the sovereignty? He answers, "so many years." He then is set at liberty, and becomes Khacan of Khozr. But if he should not die before the expiration of the time he mentioned, when that space is fulfilled, they put him to death.

The Khacan must be always of the Imperial race. No one is allowed to approach him but on business of importance: then they prostrate themselves before him, and rub their faces on the ground, until he gives orders for their approaching him, and speaking. When a Khacan of Khozr dies, whoever passes near his tomb must go on foot, and pay his respects at the grave; and when he is departing, must not mount on horseback, as long as the tomb is within view.

So absolute is the authority of this sovereign, and so implicitly are his commands obeyed, that if it seemed expedient to him that one of his nobles should die, and if he said to him, "Go and kill yourself," the man would immediately go to his house, and kill himself accordingly. The succession to the Khacanship being thus established in the same family; when the turn of the inheritance arrives to any individual of it, he is confirmed in the dignity, though he possesses not a single dirhem. And I have heard from persons worthy of belief, that a certain young man used to sit in a little shop at the public market-place, selling petty articles; and that the people used to say, " When the present Khacan shall have departed, this man will succeed to the throne." But the young man was a Mussulman, and they give the Khacanship only to Jews.

The Khacan has a throne and pavilion of gold: these are not allowed to any other person. The palace of the Khacan is loftier than the other edifices.

In the district of Bertas the houses are built of wood. The people are of two tribes or classes; one near the extreme confines of غز *Ghuz*, near بلغار *Bulgar*, about two thousand in number, under the dominion of the Bulgarians; the other next the Turks. The language of Bulgar and of Khozr is the same. Bulgar is the name of a city, where there are Mussulmans and mosques; and near Bulgar is another town called سو *, where there are also Mussulmans and mosques.

In these two cities there are about ten thousand inhabitants. Here the length of a summer's night is such that a man cannot go more than the distance of one farsang—rather, not so much; and in winter the day is equally short as the night in summer.

---

* Doubtful in the Eton MS. and mine.

Of the روس *Rous,* there are three races or tribes: one near Bulgar; their king dwells in a town called كونابه *: this is larger than Bulgar. Another race is called ارثاني *Orthani* or *Arthai*; their king resides in a place called ارثا *Artha*: but the other tribe, called جلابه *Jellabeh,* is superior to those; but no one goes for the purposes of traffick farther than Bulgar. No one goes to ارثا *Artha,* because that there they put to death any stranger whom they find. Artha produces lead and tin, and the animal called (سمورسياه) Black Martin or Scythian Sable. The Russes burn their dead; and it is an established rule amongst them not to shave one another's beards. Bulgar is next to Roum. It is a powerful and numerous people, for the greater part Christians.

ذكر مسافات خزر

Of the Roads and Stages of Khozr.

From ابسكون *Abisgoun* to the borders of Khozr, three hundred farsang; from Abisgoun to دهستان *Dehestan,* about six merhileh; and, when the wind blows fair, one goes on latitudinally (تريهناي دريا) in the sea to Derbend; from امل *Amol* to ستبدر *Sutemder* is eight days journey, or Sumteder, or ستبدر

---

* Gounaieh or Gounabeh. No point under the last syllable, or over.

Sumsider *; and from Sutemder to Derbend, four days journey; (چهار روزه) from Derbend to the Region of Serir (مملکت سریر), is three days journey; and from Amol to the extreme boundary of Bertas, twenty days journey; from Bertas to جبال *Jebal* or Bejebal, ten merhileh; and from Amol to بجبال *Bejbal*, one month; also one month from Amol to Bulgar, by way of the desert, or, if one goes by water, it may be two months. From Bulgar to the borders of Roum, ten merhileh; and from Bulgar to Gunaieh, or کونابه *Gunabeh*, &c. twenty merhileh. From Bejebal to تشرث † *Toshereth*, or Bashkouth, or تشخرث *Tothkereth*, about ten days journey; and from بشخوث *Bashkouth* to Bulgar, twenty merhileh.—God knows the truth.

ذکر بیابان میان پارس و خراسان

Of the Deserts between Pars and Khorasan.

On the east the desert of Khorasan partly borders the province of مکران *Makran*, and partly سیستان *Seiestan*; to the south it has کرمان *Kirman*, and Fars, and part of the borders of Isfahan.

In this desert there are not many habitations of men, as in

---

* Obscure. † No point.

the (بادیه) desert, where the Arabs have their dwelling; or the other desert between Oman and Yemameh (or هیامه Hemameh), towards the sea, on the borders of Yemen, where also they reside; or the deserts of Makran and سند Sind, in which, likewise, are the habitations of men, and meadows for the pasture of cattle. But this desert of Khorasan is almost totally uninhabited and waste. To the north it has Khorasan and part of سیستان Seiestan; to the west it borders on تومس Koumis, ری Rey, and قم Kom, and قاشان Kashan.

This desert is the haunt of robbers and thieves, and without a guide it is very difficult to find the way through it; and one can only go by the well-known paths. The robbers abound in this desert, because it is situated on the confines of so many different provinces. Part of this desert belongs to Khorasan, part of it to Sejestan; parts also to Fars, Kirman, Isfahan, Kom, قاشان Kashan, Rey, and the borders of تومس Koumis, and its vicinity.

صورت بیابان میان فارس و خراسان
(Map of the Deserts between Fars and Khorasan.)

One of the mountains in this desert is called کوه کرکس Karges Kouh, with its four sides towards the desert. The circumference of this mountain is not more than two farsang: in the middle of this mountain there is a spring called آب بیده Aub Beideh.

سياه كوه *Siah Kouh*, or the Black Mountain, belongs to the province of Jebal.

In this desert are some springs; but I never heard of any towns, except, perhaps, one little city (پنم*) of Kirman, on the road to Seiestan.

In this desert, on the road from Isfahan to Nishapour, there is a place called جرمه *Jurmeh*. On the confines of this desert are some well-known towns: on the borders of Pars, Mabin or *Mahin* ماهين, Yezd, عقده *Akedeh*, اردستان *Ardistan* of Isfahan; and on the Kirman side, خبيص *Khubeis*, and روزي *Ruzi*, and برماشير *Bermashir*. On the borders of توهستان *Kuhestan* are قم *Kom*, قاشان *Kashan*, and دره *Durreh*: so on to the borders of Rey and of خوار *Khar*, also سمنان *Semnan*, and دامغان *Damghan*, on the borders of تومس *Koumes*.

The principal roads through this desert are those from Isfahan to Rey, from Kirman to Sejestan, from Fars and Kirman to Khorasan; the road of Yezd, on the borders of Fars; the road of روزي *Ruzi*, and خبيص *Khubeiz*, and another called راهنو, or the new road from Khorasan into Kirman. These are the best known roads.

* Obscure.

از ري باصغهان

Route from Rey to Isfahan.

FROM Rey to دره *Durreh*, one merhileh; all this way, except two farsang, is cultivated and inhabited.

From Durreh to ديركحين *Deir Kahein*, (no distance marked): the well-water here is bitter, and they drink rain-water, and have two cisterns or reservoirs without the town.

From Deir to كاح *Kah* is all desert; two farsang to قم *Kom*; this is a village; and then two farsang are desert. From Kom to دهيه كيران *Dehieh Giran*, (or Guebran, كبران) one merhileh; cultivated and inhabited. From Dehieh Giran to قاشان *Kashan*, two merhileh; well peopled, and cultivated on the edge of the desert. From Kashan to رباط بدره *Rebet Bedreh*, two merhileh; cultivated and inhabited on the borders of the desert. Rebat Bedreh contains about fifty houses; the inhabitants are good husbandmen.

From Bedreh to رباط علي بر رستم *Rebat ali ber Rustam*[*].

[*] Perhaps for رباط علي بن رستم

one merhileh;—desert. To the borders of this desert belongs the كوه كركس *Kouh Karges*. At this Rebat are men stationed, who guard the road: they have reservoirs, into which they bring running water from other places.

From this to دانچی *Danchy*, one merhileh: this is a large village, and well inhabited. Thence to Isfahan, one short merhileh. In going from Rey to Isfahan, the Karges Kouh is on the left hand, and the سیاه کوه *Siah Kouh* on the right: The Siah Kouh is a notorious haunt of robbers. From Karges Kouh to دیر کحین *Deir Kehein* is a journey of four farsang; from Deir Kehein to Siah Kouh, five farsang; and from Siah Kouh to Karges Kouh, nine farsang.

Road from Mabein to Khorasan.

FROM مابین *Mabein*, or بابین *Babein*, to مزرعه *Mezraieh*, which is situated on the skirts of the desert, one merhileh: here are fountains and running water, and but a few inhabitants. From that to حرمه *Harmeh*, four merhileh: at every interval of two farsang is a vaulted building and reservoir of water. From Harmeh to نوخانی *Nu Khani*, four merhileh: at every four farsang is a vaulted building, with a cistern of water. From نو احی خانی *Nu ahi Khani* to رباط حوران *Kebat Houran*, one merhileh. From this Rebat to the village of مسکهان

Muskehan, one short merhileh: thence to طليس *Telis*, one merhileh; from that to بردسير *Berdsir*, two merhileh: thence to Nishapour, five merhileh; and the road to the village of كزي *Gozi* is altogether three farsang. طليس *Telis* is a large village, containing one thousand inhabitants.

راه شور

Road of Shour.

شور *Shour* is the name of a stream of water in the desert. This road begins at the village of برہ *Bereh**, on the edge of the desert toward the Kirman side. From that village the road winds to the fountain, one merhileh: In this journey there is not any building seen. Thence to *Omru Bersereh*, بعمر و برسرح one merhileh: here are great pits of red clay, and wells from which the water runs into a reservoir. And in this desert of شور *Shour*, as you go from Khorasan to Kirman, " on the right hand, at the distance of two farsang, is a grove of trees: they say that here are trees and statues of men †." From that to the آب شور *Ab Shour*, one merhileh: some

---

* No point being marked; it may be Nireh, Tireh, Yereh, &c.

† سوئ دست راست بر دو فرسنكي درخنستاني هست كويند انجا درخت هست و صورت مردم

vaulted buildings are erected over this fountain of Shur. From this to كزي *Gozi*, one merhileh; and in this day's journey, at four farsang from كزي *Gozi*, is a reservoir of rain-water.

ذكر راه راوان

Of the Road of Ravan.

THIS road begins at the village of Ravan, on the borders of Kirman. From راوان *Ravan* to دكوخوي *Deku Khoui*, one merhileh, where a stream flows. Thence to سور دوارده *Sur Duardeh* (probably سور دوازده or شور), one merhileh. Thence to رباط ويران *Rebat Viran* (or the ruined Rebat deserted, &c.), one merhileh: this place is never free from robbers. Thence to دير برتان *Deir Berkan*, one merhileh: there are about twenty houses in this place, where is a fountain; the people here are good husbandmen, and they have date trees. At the distance of two farsang is likewise a fountain, with date trees; but no one lives there, as it is the haunt of robbers. At every two farsang is a cistern or reservoir of water, as far as بيرشك *Bireshk*: The water of Bireshk is sweet. From Bireshk to جور *Jawr* is one merhileh: from Jawr to لست *Lest* or يست *Yest*, two merhileh; and from Jawr to كزي *Gozi*, three merhileh.

ذکر راه خبیص

Road of Khebeis.

KHEBEIS is a town on the borders of this desert, with running water and date trees. From that to دوراك *Durak* is one merhileh; and during this stage, as far as the eye can reach, every thing wears the appearance of ruin and desolation; for there is not any kind of water. One merhileh to شور *Shour,* where is a broad water-course of rain water: the stream of Shour waters these grounds, and torrents fall into this water-course. Thence to ارسل *Arsel,* where is a small hill, one merhileh: thence to a pond, or reservoir of rain water, one merhileh: thence to a Rebat, two merhileh; here is a fountain of running water, and about two hundred inhabitants, who live by husbandry. Thence to كوكور *Kou Kour,* one merhileh; this is a populous village on the borders of كوهستان *Kouhistan.* From Kou Kour to خوست *Khust,* two merhileh: and on this road of Khebeis, when one goes two farsang from the Rebat, where is the fountain on the way towards Khorasan, there are, for about four farsang, black stones. From Arsel to *Kur* (كورخاوچي or كوكور) are small stones, some white, some blackish, like camphor (كانور), and some greenish, like glass.

مسافات از یزد بخراسان

Stages and Distances from Yezd to Khorasan.

FROM Yezd to جهر *Jehr*, or حمر *Hamr*, one merhileh: in this stage are fountains and reservoirs of rain-water, but no inhabitants. From حمره *Hamreh* to خوانه *Khouaneh*, one merhileh: this is the desert; but at Khouaneh are about two hundred inhabitants, who cultivate the fields, and keep four-footed creatures. From Khouaneh to (تل سیاه و سپید) the black and white *tel*, or heap, one merhileh; in this day's journey are not any buildings to be seen; at this place is a reservoir of rain-water. From Tel-i-Siah ve Sepeed to سباعید *Sebaaid*, one merhileh: this Sebaaid is a large village, containing four hundred and seventy inhabitants.

From the Rebat to ریک *Rik*, one merhileh: at this stage is a reservoir of rain-water, and a caravansera, but no inhabitants. From this to the رباط کوران *Rebat Gouran*, one merhileh: this Rebat is constructed of stone and mortar; and there are three or four persons residing in it, who take care of it: here also is a spring of water.

From Rebat Gouran to رباط کره *Rebat Gurreh*, one merhileh.

At the caravansera of زاداخور *Zadakhour* is a well of water; but there are not any inhabitants. From زاداخرت *Zadakheret* (before زاداخور) to بیشا داران *Beisha Daran*, one merhileh: this is a village containing three hundred inhabitants; they have water in trenches or ditches, and cultivate their lands. From Beisha Daran to another village, دهیه دیکر *Dhey Digur* (perhaps a proper name), one merhileh: this is a well cultivated and inhabited place, containing about five hundred persons, who are husbandmen; here they have running water. Hence to *Bernaraduieh* برنارادویه, one merhileh. At this stage is a caravansera with a well; but there are not any inhabitants. From this to Rebat زنکی *Zingy*, one merhileh: at this Rebat are three or four persons; there is also running water.

From Rebat Zingy to استلشت *Astelesht*; here is a reservoir of rain-water, also a caravansera, but without any inhabitants. From استلشت *Astelesht* to بریر *Berir*, one merhileh: this Berir is on the borders of لست *Lest*, belonging to Nishapour: at two farsang of this stage they have erected khans (inns), and reservoirs of water; and the roads of this desert are here mentioned together, viz. the road of Isfahan; then the road of Rey; then the road of Mabin; then the road of Khorasan; then that of Shour; then the road of Khebeis; and after that the road called *rah nuh* (new road), which is that of Kirman.

ذکر راه نو

The New Road.

From برماسیر Bermasir to رسنان Resnan, one merhileh: here are date trees. From this, passing into the desert, no buildings appear. Thence to چشمه سیراب Cheshmeh Sirab (a spring of clear water), one merhileh. From that to the village of Salm, سلم دهیه four merhileh of desert; they say this village belongs to Kirman: thence to هرات Herat, two days journey (دوروزه راه)

But the road of Seistan is this: From برماسیر Bermasir to بسح Basekh, on the borders of Kirman, five days journey. From Besekh to Seiestan, seven merhileh, which appears from the map of Seiestan and Kirman.

(Blank page for the Map.)

ذكر سيستان

Account of Seiestan or Sejestan.

THE east of Seiestan is bounded by the بيابان مكران desert of Makran, and of the land of Sind زمين سند, and partly by the territories of مولتان Multan. To the west it has Khorasan and part of the territories of Hind: To the north it has Hindoostan; it is bounded on the south by the deserts of Seiestan and Kirman.

زنج Zarinje is fortified, and has a castle, with walls and ditches: the water which supplies these ditches, springs up in them; and it has other supplies of water. It has also five gates. One gate is called در اهن Deri Ahen (iron gate); another, the درواز كهن Dervazeh Kohen: a road passes through each of these gates. The third gate is that of كركونه Gurkouneh, on the Khorasan road. The fourth, called در بلسكي Der Beleski, (perhaps for بستي Bosti) leads to بست Bost: this is the most frequented of any of these gates. All these have gates of iron.

The fortifications have thirteen gates: one called درواز رمينا Dervazeh Remina, or مينا Meina, which leads to Pars; another, the درواز كركان Dervazeh Gurkan; the third, Dervazeh Ashirek درواز اشيرك; the fourth, در سان Deri San; the

fifth, در خویک دروازه شعیب Dervazeh Shaieb; the sixth, در خویک
Deri Khouiek; the seventh, در کار Deri Kar; the eighth,
در بلیسکی Deri Belbiki, or Beliski; the ninth, دروازه طعام
Dervazeh Taam; the tenth, is در ایریس Deri Aireis; the
eleventh, در عنجوه Deri Anjoueh; the twelfth, دروازه رستان
Dervazeh Restan; the thirteenth, is در زنکیان Deri Zingian. All these gates are built of earth or clay, because wood
becomes rotten, and decays.

Here is a mosque, situated without the Dervazeh Pars. The
Governor's palace is situated between the دروازه طعام Derwazeh Taam and Dervazeh Pars.

Between these two gates, also, is a lodge or dwelling, erected
by یعقوب بن لیث Yacoub ben Leith; and the Governor's palace is one of those which belonged to عمرو بن لیث Omru ben
Leith.

Near the Der Gurkouneh, and the Dervazeh Biseky, there is a
large building, which was the treasury of Omru ben Leith. The
bazars of the town are situated about the mesjed or mosque: they
are ample, and well supplied; as are those of the citadel, one of
which was built by order of Yacoub ben Leith, who also bequeathed a legacy to the mosque, and another to an infirmary
(بیمارستان) or hospital for the sick. And from this bazar there
is a daily revenue of a thousand direms.

In this city are streams of running water: one passes by the Dervazeh Kohen; another by the Dervazeh Nu; and another by the gate of Taam: where these three meet together, they turn a mill. Near the mosque is a large reservoir of water; from which a stream flows, and enters the gardens belonging to the principal houses. The greatest number of houses are about the suburbs; the citadel, however, has its gardens and running streams.

Some land in the vicinity of this city is barren and sandy. The air is very warm. Here they have dates: there are no hills. In winter there is no snow: in general there is a wind, and they have windmills accordingly.

Between Kirman and Seiestan there are some considerable buildings, the remains, it is said, of the antient city called رام شهرستان *Ram Shehristan*; and they say the river of *Seiestan* رود سیستان runs through this place. The city of Zerenje was built by men originally of this Ram Shehr.

ذكر روديهاي اين ديار

Of the Rivers of this Country (Sejestan.)

THE most considerable river of Sejestan is called the رود هیرمند *Rudi Heirmend*, which comes from غور *Ghaur* to the city of بست *Bost*, and from that runs to Sejestan, to the lake *Zareh* درياي زره. This lake is very small, when the waters of the river are not copious; when the river is full, the lake increases accordingly. The length of this lake is about thirty farsang from the quarter of كويد *Gouid*, on the Kouhistan road (كوهستان), to the bridge of *Kirman* پول كرمان, on the road of Pars. In breadth this lake is about one merhileh. Its waters are sweet and wholesome, and afford abundance of fish. All about this lake are situated villages and small towns, excepting on that side next the desert, where there are not any habitations or buildings.

The رود هيرمند *Heirmend* is a large river, and goes one stage (يك منزل) from Seistan. There are some other streams, as that which runs to لسكر *Lesker*; another called سبيرود *Sebirud* or سيبود *Seibud*; and another called سياره رود *Siareh Rud*, or Sibareh: and in the seasons that these streams are full, boats come down the Heirmund from Bost to Seistan; and the rivers of Seistan all proceed from the سياره *Siareh* Rud.

There is another stream called رود شعبه *Rud Shaabeh*, which affords water to thirty different villages. There is another river here, called رود ميلا *Rud Meila*, which is said to fall into the lake Zareh. On the road to بست *Bost*, over this river, they have constructed a bridge of boats, like those bridges which are in Irak. Of the streams which fall into the lake Zareh, one is the روڏ عامل *Rud Aamil*, which comes from the low grounds of فره *Fereh*; and روڏ یسک *Rudi Sek*, which comes out of غور *Ghaur*: its waters are almost consumed in passing through the land; but what remains of it falls into the Zareh lake.

Sejestan is a fertile and fine country: it produces dates in abundance. Most of the inhabitants are wealthy and opulent. In the district called رحج *Reheje*, they apply themselves very much to farming and husbandry. In this district are the towns of تل *Tell*, and درغس *Darghes*, on the banks of the هیرمند *Heirmend*; and تغهي *Toghahi*, and خلج *Khilje*, and کابل *Kabul*, and غور *Ghaur*, are of the colder climate.

The Khiljians are of a Turkish (ترکن *Tartar*) race, who, in ancient times, settled in this country, between Hindoostan and the borders of Sejestan. They resemble the Turks or Tartars in personal appearance, and retain the dress and customs of that nation; and all speak the Turkish language.

بست *Bost* is one of the principal cities in the province of Sejestan; except زرنج *Zirenje*, no city is larger than it. The inhabitants of Bost are polite and generous, resembling, in dress and manners, the people of Irak. It is a city well supplied with provisions, fruits, and dates: they trade from this city with Hindoostan.

غزنين *Ghaznein* is a small city, one merhileh from Seiestan. From the vicinity of this place came the * ضغاريان *Soffarians*, who conquered Pars, Sejestan, Khorasan, and Kirman: they were four brothers, يعقوب عمرو طاهر علي فرزندان ليث *Yacoub, Omru, Taher*, and *Ali*, the sons of *Leith*. Taher was killed at the gates of Bost. Yacoub died at his return from Baghdad, and his tomb is at Nishapour. Ali spent some time in كركان *Gurkan*; then settled in دهستان *Dehestan*. Yacoub, it is said, had originally been the servant of a coppersmith; and Omru, a camel-driver.

طاق *Tauk* is a small town near Bost: it has a suburb, or neighbouring village, which supplies fruits and grapes for all parts of Seiestan: it has also reservoirs of water. فره *Fereh* is a large town. In the neighbouring villages there is much farming carried on; and there, also, are dates in great abundance. داور *Daver*, and طالقان *Talecan*, are at two menzils distance from them: they are small towns near فيروزمند *Firouzmend*, with running water and cultivated grounds.

* For anecdotes of this extraordinary family, see the *Bibliotheque Orientale* of D'Herbelot, articles *Soffarian*, and *Leith*, &c.

ذكر مسافات سيستان

Distances and Stages of Sejestan.

The first merhileh from Sejestan to Herat is called كركونه Gurkouneh, three farsang. From Gurkouneh to پیر Peir, four farsang: thence to حریر Herir, one merhileh: thence to the bridge of the river of فره Fereh, one merhileh; and from the bridge to Fereh, one merhileh: from دره Dereh to کوسان Kousan, one merhileh: this is the boundary of Sejestan. From Kousan to اسفران Asferan, one merhileh: from اسفرار Asferar to کاریز Kariz, one merhileh: from Kariz to Siah Kouh, one merhileh.

راه از سيستان به بست

Road from Sejestan to Bost.

The first merhileh of this way is called رسوق Resouk: to سرور Serur, one merhileh; to the Dhey حروري Heruri, one merhileh. A narrow river (تنك perhaps the river's name) crosses this road: over it there is a bridge constructed of brick. From this bridge of Heruri to Rebat دهك Dhehek one menzil: thence to Rebat ازسور *Azsour*, one menzil: then another Rebat; also the Rebat هستان *Hestan*; from Rebat Hestan to Rebat عبدالله *Abdallah*; and from Rebat Abdallah to Bost; and from Rebat دهک *Dhehek* to within one farsang of Bost, the whole is desert.

راه از بست بغزنی

Road from Bost to Ghizni.

FROM Bost to Rebat فیروزمند *Firouzmend*, one menzil: thence to Rebat معون *Maaun*, one menzil: from Maaun to Rebat کر *Kur*, one menzil; thence to the place called شهر رح *Roha* or *Rohaje*, one menzil: thence to نسکین آباد *Nuskeen abad* (or Tuskeen), one menzil: thence to خراسانه *Khorasaneh*, one menzil: thence to رباط سیراب *Rebat Sirab*, one menzil; thence to ادفی *Audafi*, or Adeki, one menzil; thence to Rebat چنکلاباد *Chungalabad*, one menzil; thence to دهیه عوم *Dhey aoum*, one menzil; thence to Dhey خاست *Khast*, one menzil; thence to Dhey جومه *Jumah*, one menzil; thence to خابسار *Khabsar*, one menzil.

The boundary is the village or Dhey خساجی *Khesajy*; and the Rebat هزار دهي *Hezar Dhey* is very large, and the first within the borders of غزنی *Ghizni*; thence to غزني *Ghizni* is sixteen merhileh.

راه از سیستان براه بیابان

Road from Sejestan by the Desert.

FROM رح Rohah to Rebat سنکین Senkin, one menzil: thence to Rebat بم Bom; thence to سیجان Sehijan: total, fourteen merhileh.

راه از سیستان بکرمان و فارس

Road from Sejestan to Kirman and Fars.

THE first stage on the Fars road is خاوران Khaveran: the second, Rebat دارک Daruk; from Daruk to برین Berin, and thence to کاو پلنک Gau Pelenk; thence to رباط ماسی Rebat Masi; thence to Rebat قاضی Cazi; thence to Rebat کرامحان Keramhan; which five stages, altogether, are eight merhileh. There are five towns on the borders of Kirman, belonging to Seistan, built by عمرو لیث Omru Leith: here is the تنطره کرمان Kantereh Kirman, which is a bridge; and طاق Tauk, on the road of کویر Gouir, five farsang. From Seistan to حره Hareh, (or فره Fereh), one merhileh; between Fereh and قرین Kurreen, and between *** and فره Farreh, three merhileh; and this Farreh is opposite Kurneen or تربیین Kerbin, near the desert. طاق Tauk is on the road of کویر Gouir. From Bost to سروان Sirvan, two merhileh; on the road of دوار Duar, cross the river Heirmend, one merhileh: thence to درغش Durghesh, one day's journey: from نعس Naas to هجراي Hejrai, about one farsang; from هجراي Hejrai to اسفجاي Asfjai, three merhileh.

Now we proceed to describe the region of Khorasan.

ذکر دیار خراسان

Account of the Province of Khorasan.

KHORASAN, on the east, is bounded by part of Sejestan and Hindoostan; because all that lies beyond Ghaur may be esteemed in Hindoostan. To the west lie the desert of غزنه Ghazneh, and the borders of کرکان Gurkan. To the north of Khorasan, ماوراللنهر Maweralnahr, and some towns of ترکستان Turkestan. To the south the deserts of Fars and تومس Koumis, part of which extends towards the borders of کرکان Gurkan, طبرستان Tabaristan, ري Rey, and the hills of دیلم Dilem.

Now it is time to exhibit a Map of Khorasan, and to describe its various divisions.

(Blank Page for the Map.)

From the borders of کرمان *Kirman* to the coast of the Caspian دریای خزر, and to the boundary of خوارزم *Khuarezm* is all well inhabited, and cultivated, and fertile.

The cities of chief note in Khorasan are these four: مرو *Meru*, and بلخ *Balkh*, and نیشاپور *Nishapour*, and هراة *Herat*. The others belong to the various Kourehs (کوهان) or districts; as قهستان *Kuhestan*, نسا *Nesa*, and سرخس *Sarkhes*, and اسفرین *Asferin*, and بوشک *Boushek*, and بارغیس *Barghis*, and کنج رشاق *Kunje Reshak*, and مروالرود *Meru-al-roud*, and کورکانان *Gourkanan*, and غرجستان *Ghurjestan*, and بامیان *Bamian*, and تخارستان *Tokharestan*, and زم *Zam*, and آمل *Amol*. We speak of خوارزم *Khuarezm*, as belonging to ماورالنهر *Maweralnahr*, or Transoxania.

The city of Nishapour is situated on a level ground, and extends one farsang in every direction: the buildings are of clay. There are two considerable suburbs, well inhabited, with mosques. Here is a place which they call لشکرگاه *Leshkur gah* *; and the go-

---

* Station of the army.

vernor's palace is situated in the ميدان حسين *Meidan Hosein,* near which is also the prison. The governor's palace was built by order of Omru ben Leith.

There are four gates. One is called دَرپول *Der-i-poul;* another, دروازه كوي معضل *Derwazeh Goui Moasel;* the third is called در تهندز *Der-i-Kohendez;* and the fourth, *Derwazeh poul Nekein* دروازه پول نكين. Kohendez is without the suburbs. The gate which leads toward Balkh and Maweralnahr is called دروازه خبك *Derwazeh Khebuk;* and the gate towards كركان *Gurkan* and عراق *Irak* is called دروازه عشاب *Derwazeh Ishab.* On the road leading to Pars and Kuhestan there is a gate called دروازه سيرپس *Derwazeh Seirpes.* In the suburbs are two market places, or bazars, and fountains of water.

The city of Nishapour is watered by a subterraneous stream, which is conveyed to the fields and gardens, and falls into cisterns and reservoirs without the town; and there is a considerable stream, that waters the city and villages about it: this stream is called سقا *Seka.* In all the province of Khorasan there is not any city larger than Nishapour, nor any blessed with a more pure and temperate air. Here they make garments of silk and fine linen, which are in such esteem that they send them to all quarters.

The places depending on, and bounding Nishapour, are numerous and extensive; as بوركان Bourkan, and ماان Maan, and سلوتک Selutek, and تركان Turkan, and زوزن Zozen, and كندروحان Kanderuhan, and داون Daven, and اردوار Ardvar, and خسروكرد Khosrugird, and بهمناباد Bahmanabad, and خرينان Kherinan, and ساروان Saruan, and رمواده Remvadeh, and مهرجان Mihrjan, and اسغرابن Asferin, and زيدين Zeidin, and كركان Gurkan, and Tous, to the north of Nishapour, where is the *meshid* of Ali ben Mousa al Redha, on whom be the blessing of God! There, also, is the burial-place of Haroun *.

In the mountains of Nishapour and Tous they find Turquoises. In former times the governors of Khorasan resided at Meru, or at Balkh; but the Taherian † family made Nishapour the capital. Many illustrious personages and learned men, as is well known, have issued from this place.

The city of مرو Meru, which is also called مرو شاهجان Meru Shahjan, is very ancient. Some say it was originally built by Tahmuras, or by Dhul Kernein (Alexander the Great). Here are three celebrated mosques: one which was erected at the first introduction of Islam, they call the old mosque. Four streams

---

* The Khalif Haroun Arrashid died in the year of the Hegira 193, (A. D. 808.)

† The Taherian Dynasty began in the year of the Hegira 225, (A. D. 839), and lasted fifty-six years: it consisted of five princes.

water this city: near one of these the ancient walls and buildings were situated, of which some vestiges may yet be seen. There are four gates: one, the در شارسان *Deri Sharistan,* near the great mosque: the second is called در شهجان *Deri Shehjan;* the third, در بر *Deri Ber;* the fourth, در مشکان *Deri Mishkan;* this is the gate of Khorasan. Near this gate was the camp and palace of Mamoun, where he resided until his succession to the khalifat. The رود امل *Rudi Amol* is a considerable river: those streams which we have mentioned, all proceed from it; and it is called the مرغاب *Murghab* or the *Water of Meru* آب مرو

Here Yezdegird, the last Persian monarch, was slain in a mill; which circumstance gave to the Mussulmans possession of Farsistan. From Meru also rose the splendour of the Abbassides; and Mamoun was at Meru when he became heir to the Khalifat. Various gallant generals and illustrious learned men has Meru produced; so that in more remote times, it was remarkable above all other places of Iran. برزویه *Barzouieh,* the physician who excelled all others of his profession, and باربد *Barbud,* the musician who composed such delightful airs, were of this place. The melodies of Barbud are still imitated in this country.

The fruits of Meru are finer than those of any other place; and one cannot see in any other city such palaces, with groves, and streams and gardens. They manufacture silk at Meru; and I have heard that the art of making it was originally transferred from Meru to Taberistan, and that they still send to Meru for the eggs of the silkworms, from the other cities. The cotton and linen of Meru are also highly esteemed.

هرات *Herat* * is the name of a city to which belong the following places: مالف *Malef*, حسان *Hessan*, اسرينان *Aserinan*†, اوبه *Aubeh*, مارابا د *Marabad*, داشان *Dashan*, كروخ *Kerukh*, شكر كواران *Sheker Kuaran*, ادر *Ader*, ماشران *Masheran*, حست *Hust*, كوسف *Kousef*, اشران *Ashran*. The city of Herat has a castle with ditches. This castle is situated in the center of the town, and is fortified with very strong walls. قهندز *Kehendiz*, with its mosque, belongs to this city. The governor's palace is situated in the suburb called خراسان ابان *Khorasan Abad*.

Herat extends about half a farsang on the road of Busheng or *Pusheng* بوشنگ. There are four gates; one on the road to Balkh; another, on the Nishapour road, called زيادي *Zeyadi*; another, which they call دروازه خشك *Derwazeh Khushk*. All the gates are made of wood, except that on the road to Balkh, which is of iron, and situated in the midst of the city. In all Khorasan and Maweralnahr there is not any place which has a finer or more capacious mosque than Heri (or Herat). Next to it

---

* Or هري *Heri*.   † *Aserinan* or اسربنار *Aserbenan*.

we may rank the mosque of Balkh; and, after that, the mosque of سیستان Seiestan.

At the distance of two farsang from Herat there is a mountain, between which and the city there is not any garden, orchard, nor water, except the river of the city and a bridge. In all the other directions there are gardens and orchards. This mountain, of which we have spoken, produces not either grass or wood, or any thing but stones, which serve for mill-stones. Here is a place inhabited called سکه *Siccah*, with a temple or church of Christians.

The most flourishing quarter of Herat is that in the direction of the gate called در پیروز *Deri Pirouz* (or Firouz). The water here rises in the vicinity of the رباط کردان *Rebat Kirdan*; and when it approaches Herat, other streams branch off from it. One of these is called رود یرخوي *Rud Yarkhoui*, and it waters the district of سپید اسنک *Sepid Asenk*: another stream runs through the villages of کراسان *Kirasan* and سیاوشان *Siaveshan*. The river called کبک *Kubuk*, waters the villages of عریان *Aarian*, and کریکر *Gurigur*. There is also the river سعوکی *Saaveki* running towards پوشنگ *Pusheng*; and the river اردنجان *Ardenjan*, which runs towards the village of سیرشیان *Seirshian*; and the river نسکوکان *Neskukan*, which waters the village of وریِن *Verin*; and the river خرکی *Khehrki*, which runs amidst the gardens and orchards of the city of Herat. On the Seiestan road the whole way is planted with gardens.

مالان *Malan* is a smaller place than كروخ *Keroukh*; it has many orchards and gardens. حسان *Hessan* is smaller than Malan, and has but few gardens, and little running water. اسرينان *Aserinan* is more remarkable for pasture and tillage, than for orchards and gardens; and the inhabitants of this village are hereticks or schismaticks*. مارابان *Marabad* is well supplied with water, and abounds with gardens. اسفران *Asferan* has four towns belonging to it.

پوشنك *Pousheng* is about half the size of Herat, and built on the same plan. The towns depending on Pousheng are, خسروكرد *Khosrugird*, كوسري *Kouseri* and حره *Hereh*. Pousheng produces such a number of *arar*† trees, as is not to be found in all Khorasan beside: they are sent to all parts. The river of Pousheng comes from Heri, and runs on to سرخس *Sarkhes*; but in a season of excessive heat the water does not run so far. Pousheng has a castle, with a ditch: it has three gates.

كوسري *Kouseri* is a smaller town than Pousheng; but it is well watered, and has gardens, groves, and orchards.

بادغيس *Badghis* has several places within its territory: The

---

* خوارج

† I find in the MS. Dictionary Borhan Kattea, that عرعر is the Arabick for mountain cypress, سرو كوهي

بست Kouh Seim, كوه سيم عباباد كوي Koui Ummabad, and
Best, and حارور Hharur, and كابرون Kaberoun, and كالون
Kaloun, and دهستان Dehestan. The inhabitants of Koui Ummabad are of the Shian * sect. The Kouh Seim contains mines of silver. There are running streams at Koui Ummabad, and at Harur; but for the purposes of husbandry rain water is used there; also at Kaloun and Kaberoun, where they have well water. The silver mines are on the road to Sarkhes.

كيف Keif is a smaller place than بين Bein. Bein is larger then Pousheng. Both Keif and Bein are well-watered, and abound in gardens and orchards.

مروالرود Meru-al-rud † is a larger town than Pousheng, with a considerable river, which is the same that runs to Meru (Shahjan). Here are extensive gardens and orchards. The town of كوشك احف Koushek Ahef is also well watered, and has gardens, but not equal to those of Meru-al-rud. The air of طالغان Talkan is wholesomer than that of Meru-al-rud. The river runs between these, and is crossed over by a bridge. Here are many gardens and plantations. Talkan is about the same size as Meru-al-rud: it is situated amid hills; but has running water, and orchards that produce good fruit.

* شاهبان .   † Or Meru'rud.

کورکام *Gourkam* is the name of a district, where there is a colony of Jews. شیورکان *Shiur Kan* is a district, with a village called کندرم *Kanderm.* سان *San* is a small town, the inhabitants of which are of the Shian sect; it is smaller than Meru-al-rud: it has running water with some cultivated grounds, and gardens, and orchards. In the district of Gourkan the *Sekhtian Gourkani* سختیان کورکانی (a kind of Morocco leather) is prepared, which they send to all parts of Khorasan. From Shiurkan to امار *Amar* is one merhileh; and from Shiurkan to باراب *Barab*, two merhileh; and from Shiurkan to Kanderm, four merhileh.

Two towns belong to غرجسان *Ghurjestan*, one called, نشین *Neshin*, the other سورمین *Surmin*, nearly of equal size. Neshin produces great quantities of rice*; and Surmin of dried grapes. From Neshin one goes to the دره *Derreh* of Meru-al-rud; and from Neshin to Surmin is the distance of one merhileh. غور *Ghaur*, which is a considerable district, I shall enumerate among the regions of Islam, or Mohamedanism: because many True Believers dwell there. It is a mountainous country, well inhabited, with running streams, and gardens,

سرخس *Sarkhes* is a city between Meru and Nishapour, situated on a level, without any running water but that which

---

* برنج In the MS. برنج without points, may also be *oranges,* ترنج

(222)

comes from Pousheng*. It is computed that Sarkhes is as large as Meru-al-rud: It is a populous and thriving city: the air is wholesome: the inhabitants drink well-water, and they employ horses or asses in their mills.

نسا *Nesa* is a city of the same magnitude as Sarkhes: it is pleasant and well supplied with water running amidst the houses and streets, and various orchards, groves, and gardens.

تاين *Kaein* is as large as Sarkhes; all the buildings are of clay; it has a fort, with ditches, and a mosque, and a governor's house: the water which they drink there is conveyed in trenches; it has but a few orchards or gardens, and the air is cold.

طيسين *Teisin*† is smaller than Kaien: it has some trees, and the water is conveyed in trenches.

چون *Chun* is smaller than Teisin; it has fine gardens, and very little water: the inhabitants have sheep and other beasts.

كبابه *Kubabeh* is larger than Chun, and has two villages belonging to it: the water which they use is brought in trenches. Of all these places which we have just mentioned the air is cold; and an ample desert stretches out between them, where shepherds reside.

* See page 219.   † Doubtful.

(223)

In the district of Kaien, on the road leading to Nishapour, is found such excellent chalk, that it is sent into all parts. Throughout all the region of كوهستان *Kouhestan* there is not any river water: the inhabitants, therefore, drink water preserved in trenches, or well-water. Here they manufacture very fine linen, hair-cloth, and similar stuffs.

بلخ *Balkh*.—Of Balkh these are the various districts and divisions: تخارستان *Tokharestan*, خلم *Khulm*, سمنكان *Semengan*, بغلان *Baghelan*, سكلكند *Sekilkend*, زوالين *Zualein*, راور *Rawer*, طايقان *Taikan*, سپكبست *Sehekemest* ارهر *Arher*, اندراب *Anderab*, حشب *Hesheb*, سراي عاصم *Serai Aasim*, ورو *Werwa*, مدر *Mudr*, and كاه *Kah*. The towns in the hilly part of this country are, شهران *Shehran*, هلاورد *Hellaverd*, and الوكند *Lavakend*, كاويل *Kaweil*, هليل *Helil*, سكندره *Sekandereh*, كابل *Kabul*, پنجهر *Penjehir*, which is also called ساطير *Satir*: but we descibe these cities of the hilly country as belonging to Maweralnahr; but some may be esteemed rather in the territory of بدخشان *Badakshan*.

The city of بلخ *Balkh* is situated on a level ground, at the distance of four farsang from the mountains: it has ramparts, with a castle and mosques; and extends about half a farsang: the buildings are of clay. There are six gates. The first of these is called در نوبهار *Deri Nubehar*; another, the در رحبه *Deri Rehabeh*: another, the دروازه هندوان *Derwazeh Hindouan* (the gate of the Indians): another is called در جهودان *Deri Jehudan* (the Jew's gate): another, در شصت بند *Deri Shestbend*; and one called در یحیی *Deri Yahia*. Through the town runs a stream called the رود هاس *Rudi Ḥaas*, which passes out at the gate of the Nubehar: this stream turns ten mills, and waters several villages and districts, and flows as far as سیاه کرد *Siahgird*. In the direction of every gate there are gardens and orchards. The walls of Balkh are made of clay, and there is not any ditch.

Of تخارستان *Tokharestan* the largest city is طایقان *Taikan*, situated on a plain, in the vicinity of mountains. It is watered by a considerable river, and has many orchards and gardens. اندرابه *Anderabeh* is situated between the mountains and پنجهیر *Penjhir*. There are two rivers, one the رود اندرابه *Rud Anderabeh*; the other رود کاسان *Rud Kasan*; with gardens and orchards. The other towns of Tohkarestan are nearly of the same size as these; but Taikan is the largest of all.

زوالین *Zualein* and دراب *Derab* are two towns, with running water, and considerable plantations of trees. اسکندره *Iskandereh*, or Sekandereh, is situated in the midst of the mountains. خش *Khesh* is the largest town of this mountainous country; also, the towns of منک *Mank* and ملنک *Melenk* are amongst the hills, where there are various streams, which, as they approach ترمد *Termed*, are collected together, and fall into the river جیحون *Jihoon*, (the Oxus.)

منک *Mank* is a larger town than Melenk; but the houses of both are made of clay. بدخشان *Badakhshan* is smaller than Mank. The neighbouring grounds are well cultivated, and the district populous, with many gardens on the banks of the river. The hills here abound in excellent cattle; and Badakhshan produces the ruby (لعل) and lapiz lazuli (الجرد). The mines are in the mountains; and there is also much musk at Badakhshan.

پنجهیر *Penjhir* is a town situated on the mountains, containing about ten thousand inhabitants, people of bad character: here are gardens and running water, but husbandry is neglected. جاربانه *Jarianeh* is a smaller town than Penjhir. Between these two places are the mines of ore, in which the people dwell, without gardens, orchards, or tilled lands. The river of Penjhir runs through the town, and passes from Jarianeh till it comes to فروان *Ferouan*, and so proceeds into Hindoostan.

بامیان *Bamian* is a town about half as large as Balkh, situated on a hill. Before this hill runs a river, the stream of which flows into غرجستان *Gurjestan*. Bamian has not any gardens nor orchards, and it is the only town in this district situated on a hill: all the others have gardens and orchards, except غزني *Ghizni*, which has not any. A stream runs through Ghizni, than which of all the towns in the districts of Balkh, none is more wealthy or commercial, being the pass or frontier of Hindoostan.

كابل *Kabul* is a town with a very strong castle, accessible only by one road: this is in the hands of the Mussulmans; but the town belongs to the infidel Indians. They say that a king is not properly qualified to govern, until he has been inaugurated at Kabul, however distant he may have been from it. Kabul is also (like Ghizni) a pass into Hindoostan. The fruits of a warm climate, which abound at Balkh, are brought to Kabul, except dates, which do not grow at Balkh, where snow falls. Kabul is situated in a warm climate, but does not produce date trees.

غور *Ghawr* is a mountainous country. In the places about it there are Mussulmans; but Ghawr is mostly inhabited by Infidels. Here are great mountains. The dialect of Ghawr is like that of Khorasan. It is populous, containing many running streams; and I have described it as belonging to Khorasan, because it borders on that province; in like manner including Bamian, and Penjhir, and Maweralnaher, as far as Turkestan. The mountains of these places all abound with mines.

But the جيحون *Jihoon* (or river Oxus) and خوارزم *Kharezèm*, and امل *Amol*, and زم *Zam*, we reckon as belonging to Maweralnahar (Transoxania); and shall speak of them accordingly. Kharezem is situated on the borders of the (Caspian) sea; and the bounds of it, from Balkh and Meru and its other extremities, are all a desert, in which there is not any thing but sand. This desert affords not any running stream: the people use well-water until you come as far as Meru.

Sheep are produced in Ghizni, and Ghaur, and Khilje. Garments of silk and linen are brought from Balkh and Nishapour. The best sheep are those of Ghizni; and the best water, that of the river Jihoon. The men of Balkh are ingenious, and learned in religion and law, and of polite manners. Nishapour is the pleasantest part of Khorasan, and the inhabitants of the most amiable and chearful disposition. The warm parts of Khorasan are, قهستان *Kouhestan,* and the borders of كرمان *Kirman* and پارس *Pars* (or Farsistan). The cold part of Khorasan is about بامیان *Bamian*; for I speak of those places bordering on Kharezem as belonging to Maweralnahar.

مسافات خراسان

Of the Roads and Stages of Khorasan.

WE shall not here particularly describe the roads and stages of Khorasan, because they are already sufficiently known. We shall content ourselves with mentioning, that from the borders of Nishapour, to the village or دهیه کردان *Dhey Kurdan,* on the confines of تومس *Koumes,* near اسدآباد *Asedabad,* is a distance of seven stages or منزل *menzils*; and from Dhey Kurdan to دامغان *Damghan,* five menzil; from Nishapour to سرخس *Sarkhes,* six menzil; from Sarkhes to مرو *Meru,* three menzils: and from Meru to امل *Amol,* on the banks of the river Jihoun, two menzil: from Nishapour to بوزکان *Bouzgan,* and to پوشنک *Pousheng,* four merhileh; from Pousheng to هرات *Herat,* one merhileh: from Herat to Asferin, three merhileh; from Asferin to دره *Derreh,* two merhileh. This is the boundary of Herat.

From قاین *Kaien* to Herat, six merhileh: from Meru to هري *Heri* (or Herat), twelve merhileh: from Meru to باورد *Baverd,* six merhileh; from Meru to نسا *Nesa,* four merhileh; from Herat to مروالرود *Meruar'rudd,* six merhileh; from Heri to سرخس *Sarkhes,* five merhileh; from بلخ *Balkh* to the bank of the river جیحون *Jihoun,* by the way of ترمد *Termed,* two days journey (دو روزه راه); from Balkh to اندرابه *Anderabeh,* nine merhileh; and to بامیان *Bamian,* ten merhileh: from Bamian to غزني *Ghizni,* eight merhileh; from Balkh to بدخشان *Badakhshan,* thirteen merhileh. "From Balkh to the banks of the Jihoon, and to the sea (or lake) of Kharazm (Deriay Kharazm), from Badakhshan Termed, by way of the river Jihoon, thirteen merhileh*: From Termed to زم *Zam,* five merhileh; from Zam to Amol, four merhileh: from Amol to Kharazm, twelve merhileh: and from Kharazm to the sea (دريا) six merhileh.

These are the well-known stages and routes of Khorasan.

From Nishapour to بوزكان *Bouzgan,* four merhileh: from Bouzgan, going by the left towards Nishapour, to مالز *Malez,* one merhileh; (this is not the Malez belonging to Heri:) from Malez to جام *Jaum,* one menzil; and to سكان *Sekan,* one menzil: from سلومد *Selumed* to روزن *Ruzen,* leaving Sekan * * * * *(some words here illegible),* one day's journey (يك روزه راه): from Ruzen to قاين *Kaein,* three days journey. From Nishapour to برشير *Bershir,* four merhileh; from Bershir to كندرم *Kanderem,* one day's journey; from Kanderem to ** سا *Sa*** two days journey; from Sa** to قاين *Kaien,* two days journey: from Nishapour to Khosrugird, four merhileh; from Khosrugird to بهمناباد *Bahmenabad,* one merhileh; from Bahmenabad to مرسان *Mersan,* by the Koumis road, about one farsang: From Nishapour to خاوران *Khaveran,* six merhileh; from Khaveran to مهرجان *Mihrjan,* two days

* This passage seems so obscure, that I shall present it to the reader in the original Persian:

از بلخ تا كنار جيحون تا درياي خوارزم از بدخشان ترمد بر سمت جيحون سيزده مرحله دارند

journey; from Mihrjan to اسفراین *Asferein,* two days journey: and when you go from Bahmanabad to Mihrjan, the first day brings you to a منزلگاه *menzilgah,* or halting-place; the second, to Mihrjan.

ذکر مسافات مرو

Account of the Stages and Roads of Meru.

From Meru to کسہر *Keseher,* one menzil: from Keseher, by the skirts of the desert of Kharazm, and from Meru to دندالقان *Dendalekan,* two merhileh. The road of سرخس *Sarkhes,* the road of باورد *Baverd,* and سوسیقان *Susikan,* and غزنین *Ghaznein,* or غرنین *Ghurnein,* go to Dendalekan. چون *Chun* is a town of three farsang distance between the roads of Sarkhes and Baverd; and Susikan is one menzil farther.

Roads and Stages of Balkh.

From بلخ *Balkh* to خلم *Khulm,* two days journey (دو روزه); from Khulm to والین *Valein,* two days journey; from طایقان *Taikan* to بدخشان *Badakhshan,* seven days journey; from Khulm to Sebenjan* or سنجان *Senjan,* one day's journey;

* Doubtful.

from Sebenjan to اندرابه *Anderabeh,* five days journey; from Anderabeh to جاریانه *Jarianeh,* three days journey; from Jarianeh to Penjhir, one day's journey; from Balkh to بغلان *Baghalan,* six merhileh; to که *Kah,* one menzil; from Balkh to شیوقان *Shiukan,* three merhileh; from قاین *Kaien* to طبسین *Tebsein* * * * three merhileh; to طالقان *Talkan* (or Taikan), three merhileh; and from Talkan to مروالرود *Meruar'rudd,* three merhileh.

ذكر مسافات شهرهاي قهستان

Account of the Distances and Roads of the Towns in Kuhestan..

FROM قاین *Kaein* to روزن *Ruzen,* three merhileh; from Kaien to طبسین مریان *Tebsein Merian,* two days journey; from Kaein to چون *Chun,* one day's journey; from Chun to خوست *Khust,* one farsang; from Kaien to Tebsein, three merhileh.

ذكر ماوراءَ النهر

Account of Maweralnahr, or Transoxania.

To the eastern side of Maweralnahr are, the borders of Hindoostan. To the west it has the land of غزنين Ghaznein, and the borders of طوران Touran, and down to فاراب Farab, and مرکند Markand, and سغد Soghd, and سمرقند Samarcand, and the district of بخارا Bokhara, as far as خوارزم Kharazm, and the banks of the sea (دريا Deria).

On the north of Maweralnahr are the borders of ترکستان Turkestan, as far as فرغانه Ferghanah, and down towards ختل Khotl, on the river حريات Heriat. To the south, Maweralnahar begins from بدخشان Badakhshan, along the river جيحون Jihoon, up to the sea or lake of Kharazm (دریای خوارزم Deriay Kharezm) in a straight line. We place Kharazm and Khotl in Maweralnahar, because Khotl is situated between the river Heriat and the river *Wekhshab* رود وخشاب; and the town of Kharazm is on that side of the river, and nearer to Maweralnahr than to Khorasan.

This is the delineation of Maweralnahr.

(Here one page is left blank for a Map.)

The province of Maweralnahr is one of the most flourishing and productive within the regions of Islam or Mahommedanism. The inhabitants are people of probity and virtue, averse from evil, and fond of peace. Such is the fertility and abundance of this country, that if the other regions were afflicted by a scarcity or famine, the stock laid up on the preceding year in Maweralnahr would afford ample provision for them all. Every kind of fruit and meat abounds there; and the water is most delicious. The cattle are excellent: the sheep from Turkestan, غزنین Ghaznein, and Samarcand, are highly esteemed in all places.

Maweralnahr affords raw silk, wool, and hair, in great quantities. Its mines yield silver, and tin or lead (ارزیز), abundantly; and they are better than the other mines, except those of silver at پنجهیر Penjhir; but Maweralnahr affords the best copper and quicksilver, and other similar productions of mines; and the mines of sal ammoniac (نوشادر) (used in tinning or soldering) in all Khorasan, are there*. Like the paper made at Samarcand, there is not any to be found elsewhere. So abundant are the fruits of سغد Soghd, and استرشینه Astersheineh, and فرغانه Ferghanah, and چاج Chaje (or Shash), that they are given to the cattle as food. Musk is brought from تبت Tibbet, and sent to all parts. Fox-skins, sable, and ermine skins, are all to be found at the bazars of Maweralnahr.

* I have translated this passage literally,

ومعدن نوشادر در همه خراسان انجاست

Such is the generosity and liberality of the inhabitants, that no one turns aside from the rites of hospitality; so that a person contemplating them in this light, would imagine *that all the families of the land were but one house**. When a traveller arrives there, every person endeavours to attract him to himself, that he may have opportunities of performing kind offices for the stranger; and the best proof of their hospitable and generous disposition is, that every peasant, though possessing but a bare sufficiency, allots a portion of his cottage for the reception of a guest. On the arrival of à stranger, they contend, one with another, for the pleasure of taking him to their home, and entertaining him. Thus, in acts of hospitality, they expend their incomes. The Author of this work says, " I happened once to be
" in Soghd, and there I saw a certain palace, or great building,.
" the doors of which were fastened back with nails against the
" walls. I asked the reason of this; and they informed me, that
" it was an hundred years, and more, since those doors had been
" shut: all that time they had continued open, day and night:
" strangers might arrive there at the most unseasonable hours, or
" in any numbers; for the master of the house had provided
" every thing necessary both for the men and for their beasts;
" and he appeared with a delighted and joyful countenance when

---

* If the simplicity of this beautiful eulogium should please the reader as much as it has delighted the translator, he will, perhaps, derive additional satisfaction from perusing this part of it in the original:

و اکر کسی تامل کند پندارد که همه ورا' ماورا'النهر باینمعنی یک خانه است

" the guests tarried a while. Never have I heard of such things
" in any other country. The rich and great lords of most other
" places, expend their treasures on particular favourites, in the
" indulgence of gross appetites and sensual gratifications. The
" people of Maweralnahr employ themselves in a useful and
" rational manner: they lay out their money in erecting caravan-
" serais or inns, building bridges, and such works. You cannot
" see any town or stage, or even desert, in Maweralnahr, with-
" out a convenient inn or stage-house for the accommodation of
" travellers, with every thing necessary. I have heard that there
" are above two thousand rebats or inns in Maweralnahr, where
" as many persons as may arrive shall find sufficient forage for
" their beasts, and meat for themselves."

The Author of the book further says, " I have heard from a
" respectable person who was with ناصر احمد *Nasser Ahmed*,
" in the war of Samarcand, that of all his immense army, the
" greater part were men of Maweralnahr; and I have heard that
" معتصم *Motasem* wrote a letter to عبدالله بن طاهر *Abdallah
" ben Taher*, and sent a letter to نوح بن اسك *Noah ben
" Asek*. The answer of Abdallah was, that in Maweralnahr
" there are three hundred thousand كلاب *Kulabs*: each Kulab
" furnishes one horseman and one foot-soldier; and the absence
" of these men, when they go forth, is not felt, or is not per-
" ceptible in the country. I have heard, that the inhabitants of
" چاج *Chaje* and فرغانه *Ferghaneh* are so numerous, and so

" well disciplined, and furnished with implements of war, that
" they are not to be equalled in any region of Islam. And among
" the lower classes there are farmers, who possess from one hun-
" dred to five hundred head of cattle. Notwithstanding all this,
" there are not any people more obedient to their kings; and at
" all times the ترک *Turk* soldiers had the precedence of every
" other race, and the Khalifs always chose them on account of
" their excellent services, their obedient disposition, their bravery,
" and their fidelity."

Maweralnahr has produced so many great princes and generals, that no region can surpass it. The bravery of its inhabitants cannot be exceeded in any quarter of the Mussulman world. Their numbers and their discipline give them an advantage over other nations, which, if an army be defeated, or a body of troops lost at sea, cannot furnish another army for a considerable time; but in all Maweralnahr, should such accidents happen, one tribe is ready to supply the losses of another without any delay.

In all the regions of the earth, there is not a more flourishing or a more delightful country than this, especially the district of Bokhara. If a person stand on the قهندژ *Kohendiz* (or ancient castle) of Bokhara, and cast his eyes around, he shall not see any thing but beautiful green and luxuriant verdure on every side of the country: so that he would imagine the green of the earth and the azure of the heavens were united: And as there are green fields in every quarter, so there are villas interspersed among the green fields. And in all Khorasan and Maweralnahr there are not any people more long-lived than those of Bokhara.

" It is said that in all the world there is not any place more
" delightful (or salubrious) than those three: one, the Soghd of
" Samarcand; another, the Rud Aileh; and the third, the Ghu-
" tah of Damascus *." But the Ghutah of Damascus is within one farsang of barren and dry hills, without trees; and it contains many places which are desolate, and produce no verdure. " A
" fine prospect ought to be such as completely fills the eye, and
" nothing should be visible but sky and green †." The river Aileh affords, for one farsang only, this kind of prospect; and there is not, in the vicinity of it, any eminence from which one can see beyond a farsang; and the verdant spot is either surrounded by or opposite to a dreary desert. But the walls, and buildings, and cultivated plains of Bokhara, extend above thirteen farsang by twelve farsang; and the سغد Soghd, for eight days journey, is all delightful country, affording fine prospects, and full of gardens, and orchards, and villages, corn fields, and villas, and running streams, reservoirs, and fountains, both on the right hand and on the left. You pass from corn fields into rich mea-

---

* To this passage the *Tarikh Tabari* alludes, in a chapter relating the Virgin Mary's flight from Jerusalem with Christ.—The original Persian is given in the Preface.

† وتماشاکاه چنان باید که چشم از و پر شود که جز اسمان و سبزی نتوان دید

dows and pasture lands; and the Soghd is far more healthy than the Rud Aileh, or the Ghuteh of Dameshk (or Damascus); and the fruits of Soghd are the finest in the world. Among the hills and palaces flow running streams, gliding between the trees. In Ferghanah and چاج *Chaje*, in the mountains between Ferghanah and Turkestan, there are all kinds of fruits, of herbs, and flowers, and various species of the violet: all these it is lawful for any one who passes by, to pull and gather. In سیروشته *Siroushteh* there are flowers of an uncommon species.

We have placed, as first of the borders of Bokhara, from the banks of the Jihoon, the Kourehs and Districts of Maweralnahr. From the Jihoon is the territory of Soghd, and Samarcand, and Siroushteh, and Chaje, and Ferghaneh, and back, from the borders of Samarcand to کش *Kish*, and چغانیان *Cheghanian*, and ختلان *Khotlan*, till one comes to the river Jihoon. ترمد *Termed* and قبادیان *Cobadian*, as far as خوارزم *Kharezm*, and باراب *Barab*, and سنجان *Sinjan*, and طران *Teran*, and ایلاق *Ailak*, are reckoned as belonging to Chaje, and included in Ferghanah. Khuarezm we have assigned to Maweralnahr; and we must reckon as part of Soghd, Bokhara, and Kish, and نخشب *Naksheb*: but our design in this was to render the description more easy. We begin with Maweralnahr, and the district of Bokhara; and then we speak of the river Jihoon.

This river rises within the territories of بدخشان *Badakshan*,

and receives the waters of many other streams. The river وخش
Wekhesh joins it: then the river نومان *Nouman*, which is the
river of منک *Menek*. The third is the river فارغی *Farghi*;
the fourth river is that of اندنجاراغ *Andenjaragh*; the fifth, the
river وخشاب *Wekhshab*, near قبادیان *Kobadian*. All these rivers
fall into the Jihoon: the river Wekhshab comes out of Turkestan,
into the land of وخش *Wekhsh*, near a mountain, where there is
a bridge between Khotlan and the borders of ویشکرد *Weishkird*.
From that it runs towards Balkh, and falls into the Jihoon at
Termed. The Jihoon then proceeds to کالف *Kalef*, and from
Kalef to زم *Zam*, and from Zam to آموي *Amoui*, and from
Amoui to خوارزم *Khuarezm*, and flows into the lake of Khuarezm. There is not any town watered by the Jihoon, until you
come to Zam: there the inhabitants derive some benefit from it;
still more at Amoui: but the chief advantage of the Jihoon results
to Kharezm.

The first district of Maweralnahr, situated on the river Jihoon,
is Khotlan: there are also Wekhsh, and other districts. Near
Wekhsh there are some districts, such as دخان *Dekhan*, and
سقینه *Sekineh*: these two belong to the Infidels. Boys and girls
are brought from these places. There are mines of gold and
silver in Wekhshab. The mountainous country, bordering upon
Tibet, is very populous, well cultivated, abounding in fruits, and
excellent cattle; and the climate is very pure and healthy.

تِرْمِذ *Termed* is a city situated on the banks of the Jihoon: it has a castle and suburbs, and ramparts: the government palace is in the kohendiz, or castle; the prison is in the town; the mosque, and the bazars, in the suburbs. The buildings are of clay; all the streets and bazars are paved with burnt tiles. They drink the water of the Jihoon; and use, for the purposes of agriculture, the water of the river *Cheghanian* رود چغَانيان.

قبادیان *Kobadian* is smaller than Termed. ویشکرد *Weishgird* is about the same size as Termed. From the borders of Weishgird to شومان *Shuman*, to near Cheghanian, they cultivate saffron. قبادیان *Kobadian* produces madder (روناس). Cheghanian is larger than Termed; but Termed is more populous, and better supplied. اخسیک *Akhseik* is opposite زم *Zam*. Zam is on the borders of Khorasan, but reckoned among the territories of Maweralnahr: it is a small town, and the inhabitants deal in cattle. Zam, and Akhseik, on the banks of the Jihoon, are both at the extremity of the desert.

Khuarezm is the name of a region distinct from Khorasan. All round Khuarezm the desert extends. One side of it borders on غزنين *Ghaznein*; that is the western side. The western and southern sides are bounded by Khorasan and Maweralnahr. After Khuarezm and Jihoon, there is not any town until you come to the lake. Khuarezm is situated on the northern side of the Jihoon. On the southern side of the Jihoon is کرکانج *Korkanje*: it is a smaller town than Khuarezm; but it is the pass into various parts: from it the caravans set out for Khorasan and کرکان Gurkan, and غزنی Ghizni, and خزر Khozar, and other places.

It so happens, that one half of Khuarezm should appear in the map of Khorasan, and the other half in the map of Maweralnahr: but we have wished not to separate those parts, or render the reference to the map more difficult.

These are the other cities of Kharezm: درعن Deraan, ساڅزون Hesarasp, چہرہ Chereh, اردجر Ardejer, هزاراسپ Safzoun, کردر Nouran نوران, کردان Kirdan, خواس Khouas, Kirder. The villages are, نکین Nekin, مردا Merda, جغان Jefan, مہما Memha, دحا Deha, حاسکر Hasker, کانجسك Kanjesk. The chief place of that territory is called کاب Kab; it has a castle now in ruins. There was a town here which the water destroyed, and the people built another higher up; and the water has approached the castle, and, it is feared, will ruin it also. The mosque is in this castle, and near it is the palace of the خوارزم شاه Khuarezm Shah: near the castle is the prison: and in the midst is a little river called خردور Kherdour, and the bazar is on the banks of it; the length of it is about three farsang. The gates of the city are, for the greater part, demolished; but they have prepared new ones.

The first border of Khuarezm is called طاهریہ Taheriah, in

I I

the direction of Amoui, an inhabited country on the south of the river Jihoon. On the north side of Khuarezm there is not any population or cultivation, until one comes to the village which they call غار الحیه *Ghar-al-haiah*; from that to Khuarezm there is some appearance of inhabitants and of buildings. At six farsang distance, before you come to this village, there is a river which joins the Jihoon, and on the banks of this are many villages and hamlets; this river is called كاوخواره *Gaw-Khareh*; in breadth it is about five كز *guz*; boats ply on it. After runing two farsang, there is another river branching from it, which they call *Gurbah* رود كربه; it waters many villages, but is not very broad: from this, for about one merhileh in breadth, the villages and buildings become more numerous; and when you come to كركنج *Korkanje*, at two farsang back, there is the extremity of the borders of Khuarezm; and at five farsang a ruined village, called كراغ *Koragh*, near a mountain: from which, and from Hezarasp, on the western side of the Jihoon, there are streams running from that river: Here is Amoui; and there is another river about half as large as the Gaw Khareh, on which boats ply at within two farsang of Hezarasp. This river is called رود كرد خواس *Rudi Kurd Khouas*, and is larger than the river of Ḥezarasp. There is also the river حبیره *Heireh*, on which boats ply.

From the river دال *Dal* to Khuarezm is two farsang: The river بوه *Bouh* is in the district of Korkanje. The water of the river Dal comes to the village of اندرباز *Anderbaz,* where there is a bridge that admits boats; from this place to Korkanje is a distance of one merhileh.

From the river Gaw Khareh to *the city* is twelve farsang; and there is another river below Khuarezm four farsang, which receives its waters from four different places; when they are united, they form a stream about as large as that of the river Bouh. It is said that the Jihoon crosses this river; and that, when the waters of the Jihoon sink, the stream is also diminished. There are many streams on the northern side of the Jihoon, at one farsang from the town called مكمينيه *Medeminiah*; and all the villages along have small streams. The Jihoon falls into the lake at a place called خليجان *Khiljan,* where there is not any village, nor any buildings; the people live by fishing. On the banks of this lake is the land of غز *Ghuz*; from this, when they are at peace, they go from this side to the village of آب‌کیر *Aubgir,* and from the other to Korkange; both of these are on the banks of the Jihoon.

Before one comes to the the river Gaw Khareh there are some mountains, amidst which the Jihoon runs: this place is called بوقسه *Boukeseh*; and from the place where the Jihoon falls into the lake or sea (دریا), to that place where the river of Chaje falls into it, is a journey of ten days. The river Jihoon is frozen in winter, so that loaded carriages pass over it. The ice begins at Khuarezm, which is the coldest place upon the Jihoon.

On the banks of the sea or lake of Khuarezm (دریای خوارزم) there is a mountain called چغاغر *Cheghagher:* here the ice continues from winter till near the end of summer. The circumference of this sea or lake is an hundred farsang: its waters are salt or bitter; and the river Jihoon, the river چاج *Chaje,* and many other streams, flow into this lake: yet this increase of water is not perceptible; and it is generally supposed that there is a communication between this lake and the Caspian Sea (*Deryai-i Khozr* دریا خزر): between these two is a distance of twenty merhileh.

Khuarezm is a town well supplied with provisions, and abounding in fruits; it affords not any walnut-trees. Linen and wool are manufactured there, and also brocade. The inhabitants are people of high reputation and polished manners: the men of Khuarezm are great travellers; there is not any town in Khorasan without a colony of them. The lower parts of the land of غز *Ghuz* belong to Khuarezm: the inhabitants are active and hardy. The wealth of Khuarezm is derived from its commerce and merchandize. They have carpets of سقالب *Siklab,* and of خزر *Khozr,* and they bring to Khuarezm, from Khozr, the skins of foxes, and martens, sables, and ermines.

Of the other places on the river Jihoon, we shall place بخارا *Bokhara* in Maweralnahr first: at all times it has been the seat of government. Bokhara is called بونحكت *Bounheket*: it is situated on a plain; the houses are of wood, and it abounds in villas, and gardens, and orchards; and the villages are as close one to another as the groves and gardens, extending for near twelve farsang by twelve farsang: all about this space is a wall, and within it the people dwell winter and summer; and there is not to be seen one spot uncultivated, or in decay. Outside this there is another wall, with a small town and a castle, in which the Samanian[*] family (آل سامانیان), who were governors of Khorasan, resided. This kohendez, or castle, has ramparts, a mosque, and bazar.

In all Maweralnahr or Khorasan, there is not any place more populous and flourishing than Bokhara. The river of Soghd (رود سغد) runs through the midst of it, and passes on to the mills and meadows, and to the borders of بیکند *Beikend*; and much of it falls into a pond or pool near Beikend, at a place called سام کوس *Sam Kous*.

Bokhara has seven gates: one is called the در شارستان *Deri Sharestan*; the second, در درو *Deri Derou*; the third,

---

[*] For some account of this dynasty, and of Nasser Ahmed, mentioned in page 235, see the Appendix.

درکنده *Deri Kandeh*; the fourth, دراهنین *Der Ahenin*; the fifth درقهندز *Deri Kohendez*; the sixth is called the درواز مهرکی *Derwazeh Mihrgy*, or درواز بنی اسد *Derwazeh Beni Ased*; and the seventh is the درواز سغدیان *Derwazeh Soghdian*. The kohendez, or castle, has also two gates; one the درریکستان *Deri Rikestan*; the other the درواز مسجد *Derwazeh Mesgid*. The ramparts also have some gates, such as the درمیدان *Deri Meidan*, leading towards Khorasan; the درواز ابراهیم *Derwazeh Ibrahim*, towards the east; the درواز بروقسه *Derwazeh Khedik*; the درواز کلاباد *Derwazeh Beroukeseh*; the درواز کلاباد *Derwazeh Gulabad*; the درواز سبرتند *Derwazeh Nubehar*; the درواز نوبهار *Derwazeh Samarcand*; the درواز امینه *Derwazeh Amineh*; the درواز حد سرور *Derwazeh Hedi Serour*, which is on the Khuarézm road; and the درغنج *Deri Ghunje*.

There are, besides, some gates among the bazars, such as the درپول حسان *Der Ahenin*, or iron gate; the درآهنین *Deri Pool Hesan*; and a gate near the mosque of ماج *Maje*; and between these two gates there is another called دررجیه *Der Rejieh*: there is also a gate near the villa of ابوهاشم *Abu Hashem*, and near the bazar; and one near the کوی مغان *Goui Moghan* (or the magi's dwelling), and the درسبرتند *Deri Samarcand*.

There is not any running water between the city and the gate of the kohendez: they bring water from the main river; and this river furnishes some other streams: one is a considerable river called نسرده *Feserdeh,* coming from the river of Bokhara, at a place which they call ورع *Wera*; and it descends by the gate of *Seroukeseh* درسروقسه, till it comes to the lands of ابو ابراهیم *Abou Ibrahim*; and thence proceeds to the gate of ابو لغضل Sheikh *Aboul Fazel,* and falls into the river *Nukendeh,* رود نوکنده. On this river are situated near two thousand villas and gardens, exclusive of corn fields and meadows; from the mouth of this river to the place where it falls into the Nukendeh is a course of about half a farsang.

There is another stream, called the رود باسکان *Rud Basegan,* proceeding from the main river through the middle of the city near the mosque called تزازان *Kezazan*; and there is another stream which comes from near the mosque called عارض *Aarez,* and flows into the Nukendeh; this is called the جویبار عارض *Jouibari Aarez.*

There is another stream, called برکند *Berkend,* which waters part of the fortifications, and falls into the Nukendeh. This river Nukendeh comes from the main river, near Nubehar, and runs among palaces, and houses, and mills, till it comes to the mills on the lands of بیکند *Beikend,* and affords water to them. The river کینه *Keiseh* runs on to غاران مرغ *Gharan Murgh.* The river *Rebah* رود ربا issues from the main river near ریکستان *Reikestan,* and flows on to the villa of Rebah, and waters a thousand summer-houses, and gardens, and groves. The river of Reikestan passes through that place to which it affords water, and to the kohendez, the suburbs near the ramparts, and the government house; and after that it proceeds to the villa of جلال دیزه *Jelal Deizeh.* The river sinks into the ground near the bridge of *Hamdounah* پول حمدونه, and flows subterraneously till it comes to the ponds of حوضهاي بني اسد *Beni Asad*; and the remainder of it runs into the reservoir or cistern of the kohendez. There is another river proceeding from the main one, at the place called ورع *Wera,* which passes by the gate of رحیه *Rehieh,* proceeds to the Derwazeh Samarcand, and from that goes on one farsang.

The villages Ferghaneh and دروفن *Derufen,* طوابس *Touabes,* بورق فرغانه *Bourek Ferghaneh,* سفلي *Sefli,* بومه *Boumeh,* روستاكا *Roustaka,* بخاجمر *Bekhajemr,* حشوان *Heshwan,* اندیدان *Andidan,* كندمان *Kendaman,* سامجر *Samjir,* مادون *Madoun,* سامجر ماوراالنهر *Samjer Maweralnahr,* فرازن السفل *Ferazen al Sefl,* اردان *Ardan,* and فرازن العلیا *Ferazen al Aalia*; all these districts are included within the walls. Those without the walls are, مباخس *Mebakhes,* چند *Chend,* ویس *Veis,* كرمیده *Kurmeideh,* جرغانه *Jerghaneh,* غلیار *Gheliar,* شاق *Shak,* عرقند *Arkand,* سكند *Sekend,* and فرین *Ferin.*

Near the district of طواويس *Touaveis*, before you come to the gate of Bokhara, there are many streams which water the villages and meadows. One of these is the river *Kaferi Kam* روذ كافري كام which runs to وركانه *Werkaneh*; and the river جرغان *Jerghan*, which waters another district and goes on to جرمش *Jermesh*, and falls into the main river. The river نوكنده *Nukendeh*, which waters a district, runs on to the village of فرانه *Feranah*, and the river برجد *Berjed*, on which is a hamlet; and the river بسته *Besteh*, and the river امنيه *Ameniah*, and the river فرازن السفلى *Ferazin al Sefli*, and the river تلنكان *Telengan*, which runs to برقاع *Berkaa:* every one of these affords water to its particular district, without the inclosure of the wall of Bokhara; the remainder runs among the suburbs and fortifications of that city.

Of the rivers we have heretofore enumerated, the greater number proceeds from the river of Soghd, on which boats ply. The inclosure or wall round Bokhara contains twelve gates. There is not any hill or desert; all is laid out in castles, villas, gardens, corn-fields, and orchards. The wood which they use for fuel is brought from their gardens, and they burn also reeds and rushes. The grounds of Bokhara and of Soghd are all in the vicinity of water; whence it happens that their trees do not arrive at any considerable height; but the fruits of Bokhara are more excellent than the fruits of any part of Maweralnahr. Corn is brought to Bokhara from Maweralnahr and other places.

There is a mountain called ذرکه *Zarkah*, in the vicinity of Bokhara; it goes between Samarcand and کش *Kesh*, and joins the border of Ferghaneh, and اطرار *Atrar*, and goes on towards the confines of Cheen; and this mountain is skirted by a desert in the borders of Ferghaneh and ایلاق *Ailak*, as far as جرجره *Jerjereh*.

In Ferghaneh there are mines of sal-ammoniac, and of copperas or vitriol, of iron, and quicksilver, and brass; also of gold, and of turquoise stone; and in this mountain there are springs of naphta, and of bitumen, and resin; also a stone that takes fire and burns. There is, likewise, water, which in summer is frozen, and in the depth of winter is warm. There are some districts of Bokhara within the walls, and some without: of those within the walls, طواویس *Touaveis* is the most considerable town; it is walled, and at a stated time, once every year, the people assemble in it from Maweralnahr: it has pleasant gardens, and orchards, and running streams, and an ancient castle, with suburbs, and a mosque: the inhabitants manufacture linen.

The other towns within the walls are nearly of equal size one with another. کرجینت *Kerjinet* is a large town; جرغانکت *Jerghaneket*, and مدماحلت *Medmamehelet* are of equal size. Every town of the territories of Bokhara has a district belonging to it, except بیکند *Beikend*, which has not any village, but contains near a thousand Rebats.

The town of تربن *Kerin* is near the river Jihoon. The people of Bokhara speak the language of the people of Soghd: they are ingenious: and in business they use direms: their silver is عذرتي *Azerki*, or غدرتي *Ghederki*; and the mode of purchasing used in Maweralnahr does not pass among them. For the greater part they wear the *tunick* تبا and the *cap* كلاه.

At Bokhara, within the city, there are bazars, where, on certain appointed days, the merchants assemble in great numbers, and transact much business. Bokhara and its territories produce fine linen. I have heard a peculiar circumstance mentioned, concerning the Kohendiz or castle of Bokhara; which is, that they never have brought out of it the bier or coffin of any prince, and that any person once confined there is never seen again. " It " is said that the inhabitants of Bokhara are originally descended " from an ancient tribe, which emigrated from Istakhar and " settled there*." The Samanian princes resided at Bokhara; the territories of which and Maweralnahr were under their jurisdiction: the people of Bokhara were so obedient, and so observant of their treaties, that the sovereigns chose to reside among them. The kings of Khorasan were descended from the race of Saman. اسمعيل بن احمد *Ismael ben Ahmed* resided there: the people of Khorasan had behaved treacherously towards him; and his children also resided at Bokhara. Before that, the governors of

---

* و کویند که اصل مردم بخارا در قدیم قومی بوده اند از اصطخر انجا انتقال کرده‌اند

Maweralnahr dwelt in Samarcand, at چاج *Chaje*, or فرغانه *Ferghanah*; but since that the seat of government has been removed from Khorasan to Bokhara.

دنجاره *Denjareh* is situated near the road of بیکند *Beikend*: between that, and between the road, is a distance of one farsang. مغکان *Moghkan* is five farsang distant from the city, on the right hand of Beikend, and from it to the road is a space of three farsang. رندیه *Rendieh* is at four farsang from Bokhara. بومحکت *Bumeheket* is on the road of طواویس *Touaweis* at a distance of four farsang.

From کرمنیه *Kermeniah* to Beikend is one farsang in the borders of Soghd. Bumeheket is situated on the river of Soghd. Soghd is adjacent to Bokhara. After passing Kermenieh one comes to دبوسی *Debousi*.

The capital of Soghd is سمرقند *Samarcand*; it is situated on the southern side of the river of Soghd. It has a castle, and suburbs, and fortifications, with four gates; one, the در چین *Deri Cheen*, or the China gate, on the east; the در نوبهار *Deri Nubehar*, or the spring gate, on the west; on the north, the در بخارا *Deri Bokhara*, or Bokhara gate; and on the south, the دروازه کش *Derwazeh Kesh*, or Kesh gate.

There is running water through the streets and bazars of Samarcand. The city is surrounded by a deep ditch, and a dyke, by which water is conveyed. The most flourishing and populous quarter of Samarcand is that called the سر طاق *Seri tauk*, where there is the fountain of ارزيز *Arziz*: and the shops of the bazar in this place are very numerous; for many legacies and gifts have been appropriated to the buildings about this fountain, which are in the charge of Guebres (or Fire-worshippers) who watch winter and summer.

There is a mosque in the suburbs, near the قهنديز *kohendiz*: and in the river Arziz there are springs, and rivulets from it water the gardens and orchards. The government palace is in the kohendiz; and the citadel is near the river of Soghd; and the walls of these fortifications are about two farsang in extent. There are many villas and orchards, and very few of the palaces are without gardens: so that if a person should go to the kohendiz, and from that look around, he would find that the villas and palaces were covered, as it were, with trees; and even the streets and shops, and banks of the streams, are all planted with trees.

Samarcand is the great pass into Maweralnahr; and the seat of empire was at Samarcand until اسمعيل بن احمد *Ismael ben Ahmed* removed it to Bokhara.

The walls of the fortifications have several gates; such as the در عبد *Deri Abed*, the در افشينه *Deri Afsheineh*, the

در کوهک Deri Kouhek, the در روسین Deri Rousein, the در دیوود Deri Diwoud, and the در نوجند Deri Foujend.

The author of this work says, " I saw a gate at Samarcand,
" of which the front was covered with iron; and there was
" written on it, in the *Hamiri* language; that " Senaa is distant
" from Samarcand a thousand farsang ;' and the people preserved
" the explanation of this writing, in hereditary tradition. After
" that I had been at Samarcand, a tumult or insurrection happen-
" ed; and this gate was burnt, and the inscription mislaid
" or destroyed. Afterwards, Abu Mozaffer Mohammed ben
" Nasser ben Ahmed ben Ased, caused the gate to be again
" constructed of iron, but the writing was lost.*"

The houses of Samarcand are made of clay and wood: the inhabitants are remarkable for their beauty: they are gentle and polite in their manner, and of amiable dispostions. From Samarcand to the mountain (کوه) is one merhileh: and there is close to the city a small eminence which they accordingly call کوهک *kouhek* (a diminutive of کوه) the little mountain: that mountain is about half a mile in length ; it produces clay, and marble, and stones of various kinds; and I have heard that in it were also mines of gold and silver, but they are not worked.

* The reader will find the original Persian of this passage in the Appendix, No. I. See also the Preface and Appendix, No. III.

(255)

The water of Samarcand is all from the river which comes from the mountains above چغانیان *Cheghanian*. There is a reservoir for that water, which they call برغر *Bergher*; from this that water flows till it comes to a place called بیحکت *Biheket*, and thence to ورغس *Warghes*, where there is a bridge; from that the rivers of Samarcand are divided to the east and west. Those on the eastern side proceed from near Warghes, at the place called سمه*, because the mountains there are fewer, and the cultivated fields more numerous: from this the river flows; and the river بوس *Bous* also comes to Samarcand, to which, with the villages, it affords water.

The river بارمس *Barmis* rises in the vicinity of that river, in the southern territory, and waters many villages there. The Bous and Barmis are the largest of all those rivers; they both are navigable for boats, and many streams branch off from them, which water many villages and meadows. From the territory of Warghis to the village called زرغم *Zarghem*, ten farsang in length, and from four to one farsang in breadth; from the district of برغس *Barghis*, and مانغرنج *Manferenje*, and Zarghem, and بیخرو *Bikheru*, above Zarghem, and the rivers which flow from the *desert of Gherban* صحراي غربان, the river استنخر *Istakhar*†, and the river ساوات *Sawat*, and the river

* I have given this word as it appears in my MS. In that of Eton a blank space is left for the name.

† Istakhar of Pars, is generally written اصطخر but sometimes like this استنخر.

مورماجز *Mourmajez*; the river Sawat passes near the Mourmajez and waters many places, and proceeds to the village of وڈان *Weddan*, and to the borders of the district of Istakhar: the river, in all, runs about two merhileh.

The rivers Sawat and Mourmajez run towards the city, and water near seven farsang of territory, till they come to Samarcand; from the mouth or entrance of this valley, or water-course, to Samarcand, is a distance of twenty farsang. After passing Samarcand about two merhileh, a river branches off called روڈقي *Rudeki*, which waters one of the most fertile and populous tracts of land in all Soghd: other streams branch off from this channel, until it approaches the territory of Bokhara, a journey of near six days, watering so many gardens and orchards, that if any person were to look from a hill along the valley of Soghd, he could not behold any thing but trees and green herbage, with here and there a villa and an old castle.

In the district of Barghis are many gardens and dykes. From this valley (or channel) come the rivers above mentioned, and pass under the bridge of Kouhek پول کوهک, at the Samarcand gate درسرتند. The waters of this valley are augmented in summer by the snow from the mountains of غرجستان *Ghurgestan* and the vicinity of Samarcand.

In the territory of فامرغ *Famurgh* there is a certain place called

ربود *Reboud,* in which dwelt اخشيد *Aksheid,* king of Samarcand; and his villa or palace yet remains.

The village of زرغم *Zerghem* is adjoining to that of Famurgh. Famurgh is the most populous and fertile of all the villages of Samarcand.

ساروان *Sarouan* is a mountain on the south of Samarcand: it enjoys a pure air, and the inhabitants of it are healthier and handsomer than those of the other territories. The extent of this hill, and the villages on it, is about ten farsang. At Sarouan is a place which the Christians have built for religious worship, and which is richly endowed*. (This place is called زروكرد *Zarukird.*)

The district of برمر *Bermer* is without water, but is well inhabited, and produces much cattle; the air is good, and the inhabitants are wealthy. The length of this district is two merhileh; and every village in it is above two farsang in extent. The pasture lands are better here than those of Maweralnahr.

Those are the territories of Samarcand, on the right hand of this valley. These on the left hand are, اولاد *Aulad,* and باركيت *Barkeit,* near ستروسته *Setrushtah*; the village of

و انرا وقف بسيار است *

تورغد *Kourghed,* on the borders of Setrushtah, adjoining to Barkeit.

The village of بورماخر *Bourmakher* is large and well inhabited, on the borders of Samarcand. From the borders of Gherban to those of Samarcand is about one merhileh.

ودان *Weddan* is a populous and fertile district, with hills and plains. The towns of Weddan and of كش *Kish* are situated near each other: these two places have belonged to tribes of Arabians, called سباعيان *Sebaaians.* This people had dwellings at Samarcand. مرزبان بن كشغي *Merzeban ben Kashfi* was a man of this district, whom all the illustrious and chief persons invited to the sovereignty of Irak.

There are six villages of Samarcand on the right side of the valley of Soghd, and six on the left. In former times the village of لعيان *Laian* was annexed to the territories of Samarcand, but afterwards became a district of Setrushtah. Pecuniary affairs are transacted in Samarcand by means of gold, and of direms of Ismael, broken, درم اسماعلي شكسته; and there is another coin, called محمدي *Mohammedi,* which is not current in any other place besides the territories of Samarcand. This country abounds in gardens, and orchards, and corn fields, and pleasant prospects; and the Soghd is a delightful and fertile region. كيسانه *Keisaneh* is the eye of all the towns of Soghd; it is inhabited by rich and powerful people.

ذکر شهر کش

Account of the City of Kish.

کش Kish is a city with a kohendiz and ramparts, and two suburbs, one of which (the interior) and the kohendiz are ruined; the mosque also, which was here, is in ruins; the bazar is on the ramparts, and the extent of this city is three farsang by three farsang. The climate here is warm: the buildings are of wood and clay. Here are four gates; one, the در اهنین Der Ahenin, or Iron Gate; another, the دروازه عبید الله Derwazeh Abeid Allah; the third, the در تصابان Deri Kesaban; the fourth, the در شارستان Deri Sharestan. The inner town has two gates; one called the در شارستان درونی Deri Sharestan Deruni; and the other the در ترکستان Deri Turkestan. Turkestan is the name of a certain village. Near this gate are two rivers; the رود تصابان Rudi Kesaban, which comes from the town of سیام Siam. The two rivers pass by the gates of the city; and there are other streams in the vicinity; such as the چاج رود Chaje Rud, on the Samarcand road, at the distance of one farsang from the city; and the river خبک رود Khebek Rud, on the Balkh road, also at one farsang distance from the city; and another, called the river جران Jeran, on the Balkh road, at a distance of eight farsang from the city. These streams fall into the valley of نخشب *Nakshcb*, and water all the palaces of this city; and the gardens and villas of this place extend near four days journey. From this city of كش *Kish* much fruit and wood is produced: there are many villages belonging to Kish; such as ورد *Werd*, and بلاندرين *Belanderin*, and راسيمان *Rasiman*, and كنك *Kenk*, and ارو *Arou*, and حران *Heran*, and سورودە *Surudeh*, and سنك كردە دروبين *Senk Kerdeh Deroubein*, and سنك كردە بروبين *Senk Kerdeh Beroubein*. Those are the territories of Kish.

ذكر شهر نخشب

Account of the City of Naksheb.

The city of Naksheb has a ruined kohendiz. The ramparts have four gates; one, the دروازه بخاري *Derwazeh Bokhari*; another, the دروازه سمرقند *Derwazeh Samarcand*; the third, the دوروزه كش *Derwazeh Kish*; and the fourth, the *Deri Ghaznin* در غزنين. Naksheb is situated on the high road to فاراب *Fareb*, and to بلخ *Balkh*: it stands on a level ground; from the city to the hills is a journey of two days, in the direction of Kish; from Naksheb to the river Jihoon the intermediate space is all desert. In the middle of the city is a considerable river, which comes from the collection of streams at Kish, and waters the territories of Naksheb. The palace of the chief governor is situated near this stream, at the place called سر پول *Seri Poul*, near which, also, is the prison. The mosque is near the Deri Ghaznein, or Ghaznein gate; and an oratory near the Derwazeh Bokhari, or the Bokhari gate: the bazars are on the ramparts, between the governor's palace and the mosque.

Naksheb possesses many territories: two very considerable are بردة *Berdeh* and کشتة *Keshteh*; and there are some villages as large as cities: but in Naksheb and all its territories there is not any river besides that above mentioned; and even that river, in a very hot summer, becomes dry, and they use well-water for their gardens. Naksheb is abudantly supplied with provisions.

ذکر ستروشنة

Description of Setroushteh.

ستروشنة *Setroushteh* is the name of a tract, or country like Soghd; there is not any city or village in this country that bears the name of Setroushteh. It is a mountainous region, bounded on the east by part of Ferghanah; on the west, by the borders of Samarcand; on the north, by چاج *Chaje*; on the south, it lies near Kish and چغانیان *Cheghanian*, and شمان *Sheman*, and دلشکرد *Dileshkird*, and راست *Rast*. The chief town of Setroushteh is called, in the language of that country, بوحکت

Boumheket; and the districts of it are, اران Aran, سامكت Sameket, كوكب Koukib, غرق Gherk, وعكث Waakes, ساباط Sabat, رامين Ramin, دبزك Debzek, بومحكت Boumheket, and حرتانه Herkanah. Boumheket is the residence of the governors; it contains ten thousand inhabitants: all the buildings of this town are made of clay and wood. The inner town has two gates; one called the دروازه بالامين Derwazeh Balamein; and the other, دروازه شارستان Derwazeh Sharestan. There is a mosque in this inner town, and a kohendiz: there is also a considerable river, which turns mills; its borders are planted with trees: there are also bazars; and the extent of this town is one farsang. The water of the ditch runs among the villas, and gardens, and meadows, and corn-fields. The citadel has four gates; one, the Derwazeh رامين Ramin; another, the Derwazeh ابن سمندر Ebn Samender; another, the Derwazeh ابن حكت Ebn Heket; and the fourth, the Derwazeh كهلبان Kehilban. This town has six streams or rivers; the سارين Sarin, which runs into the suburbs, the برجين Berjin, the رسماجين Resmajin, the اسكنكجر Iskenkejr, the رولجي Rouleji, and the سحكر Seheker: all these six streams proceed from one fountain, and turn ten mills. From this fountain to the town is not so much as half a farsang.

رامين Ramin is about the same size as Setrushteh, situated on the Ferghaneh road, in the direction of Soghd: the people here call this place, in their language, سليسده بليس Selisedeh Belis.

This town has walls. The caravans on the high road from Ferghaneh to Soghd pass through it. There are many running streams and gardens, and much tilled land; and the back of this town extends to the hills of Setroushteh, and the front is towards the desert of the country of غز *Ghuz*.

The town of دبزک *Debzek* is built on level ground; it is the chief town of a district: at two farsang distance from it there is a Rebat, which they call the رباط خديش *Rebat Khedish*: it was built by افشين *Afshin*, and is the best Rebat; the people of Samarcand have not one better. In the midst of the Rebat there is a spring of water, over which a dome has been erected.

دېرک *Deirek* (or *Debzek*) is a pleasant and well-supplied town, with running water, gardens, and orchards. All the towns of this region, which we have spoken of, are nearly equal to and resemble one another, but سمنده *Semendeh*, which has running water, but has not any gardens, the cold being excessive. It is, however, a large town, and in summer has pleasant meadows.

رامين *Ramein* and سباط *Sebat* are on the road of Ferghaneh and Chajc. If you wish to go the road of خجند *Khojend*, by the way of کوکت *Kouket*, (or *Koukib*) you must go to Ferghaneh, nine farsang from Samarcand.

In all Setroushteh there is not any river considerable enough to admit of the plying of boats; but there are running streams, and fountains, and meadows, and groves. The villages of the mountainous part of Setroushteh are these: بشاغر *Beshagher*, فرغور *Ferghour*, بالعام *Baloam*, مسک *Mesek*, لسکن *Lesken*, بسنک *Besenk*. These are situated on steep hills: and the cold part of the country, also, has many strong fortresses. Here also are mines of gold, and silver, and copperas, and sal ammoniac. The mines of sal ammoniac (نوشادر *Nushader*) are in the mountains, where there is a certain cavern, from which a vapour issues, appearing by day like smoke, and by night like fire. Over the spot whence the vapour issues, they have erected a house, the doors and windows of which are kept so closely shut and plastered over with clay that none of the vapour can escape. On the upper part of this house the copperas rests. When the doors are to be opened, a swiftly-running man is chosen, who, having his body covered over with clay, opens the door; takes as much as he can of the copperas, and runs off; if he should delay, he would be burnt. This vapour comes forth in different places, from time to time; when it ceases to issue from one place, they dig in another until it appears, and then they erect that kind of house over it: if they did not erect this house, the vapour would burn, or evaporate away.

In the territory of سمندة *Semendeh* they make excellent iron. Iron is also manufactured at فرغانه *Ferghaneh*. At Semendeh there are market-days established, when people come from a great distance; these days occur once every month.

نشامين *Neshamein* and ايلاق *Ailak* are two districts, the extent of both which is two days journey by three. In all Soghd and Maweralnahr there is not any country equal to this in populousness and in buildings: one of its borders is the valley or watercourse of چاج *Chaje*, which falls into the lake of *Khuarezm* درياي خوارزم; it is bounded also by the كار اهن *Kar Ahen* (or iron-works) on the confines of سنخاب *Sinkhab*; another of its boundaries extends to the mountains, adjoining the territories of نشامين *Neshamein*; and another extends to Benagur of the Christians بناكر ترسايان (*Benagur Tersaian*.) All the land is flat.

Chaje is the most considerable of the frontiers of Turkestan: it has many fine buildings. Every palace in it has running water, and delightful verdure. All the buildings are of clay. The capital of that district is called سكت *Seket*; and the other towns are, ديوماكت *Divemaket*, حدينكت *Hedinket*, كنكوان *Kankouan*, نحاكت *Nehaket*, ساكت *Saket*, حوسكت *Housket*, سعودات *Saoudad*, والنكت *Welanket*, كلنجك *Kelenjek*, جنودر *Jenuder*, عاج *Aaje*, الودكت *Alaudket*, غزل *Ghuzl*, عرصل *Arsel*, وردل *Werdil*, كرنه *Kerneh*, عددالك *Adedalek*, حانزكت *Hanzket*, بوحكت *Bouheket*, لعبك *Laabek*, بركوس *Berkous*,

Hanerket, جغركت Jegherket, مرنكت Merinket, كدال Kedal, and كالك Kalek : all these are towns of Chaje.

The towns of ايلاق Ailak are these: بونكت Bounket, the chief town; سكاكت Sekaket, ازنكت Azenket, حمرل Hamerel, بسكت Besket, كهشم Keheshm, وحكت Weheket, خاص Khas, حركات Herkat.

Bounket, the capital, has a kohendiz without the city; but the walls of the town and of the kohendiz are the same. There is a citadel with a wall, and another fortification outside that, with gardens and palaces. The kohendiz has two gates, one of which is towards the town. The town has a wall, and three gates, one of which is called the دروازه ابو العباس Derwazeh Abou al abas; the second is the دروازه كش Derwazeh Kish; and the third is the در آهنين Deri Ahenin, or iron gate.

The citadel has ten gates on the inside; one, the Derwazeh جمدين Hamdein: the second, the Derwazeh اهنين Ahenin; the third, the Derwazeh مير Mir; the fourth, در فرخان Deri Ferkhan; the fifth, Deri كده Kedeh; the sixth, Deri كوافح Kouafah; the seventh, Derwazeh كوي سهل Kouy Sohel; the eighth, Deri اشدبحاق Ashedbehak; the ninth, Deri خاتان Khakan; and the tenth Derwazeh, در كوشك دهقان Der Koushek Dehkan.

On the outer side, the citadel has seven gates; one, the Derwazeh دغكت *Deghket*; the second, Derwazeh خاكت *Khakhet*; the third, Deri بيكند بحاق *Beikend Behak*; the fourth, Der اهنين *Ahenin*; the fifth, Deri كرنجان *Kerenjan*; the sixth, Derwazeh شكر *Sheker*; and the seventh, Derwazeh ثغربان *Segherbad*. The governor's palace and the prison are in the kohendiz; and the chief mosque is on the walls of the kohendiz. In the inner town is a small bazar; but there are great bazars in the citadel. The length of this city is one farsang. The inner town and the citadel are watered by a running stream. There are extensive and fine gardens; and there is a great wall, reaching from the hill called سايلع *Sailaa*, to the brink of the channel or water-course of Chaje. This wall was erected, to separate the country from Turkestan, and prevent incursions. It was erected by order of Abdullah ben Hamid. From this inclosure, to the ditch or fosse, is a distance of one farsang. Here is another river, called the رود تركستان *Rudi Turkestan*, which partly comes from نسكان *Neskan*, and partly from the country of چكرل *Chekrel*: it reaches the town of بحاكت *Behaket*.

There is in ايلاق *Ailak* a river called by the same name (Ailak): this also rises in Turkestan; and runs, for the greater part, into the river of Chaje. بومكت *Boumeket* is the chief town of Chaje. Chaje and Ailak border one upon the other. The buildings, and gardens, and orchards of Ailak, are continued to the valley or water-course of Chaje, without any interval. In the mountains of Ailak there are mines of gold and of silver: these mountains are on the borders of Ferghaneh. دینکت *Deinket* is the largest of all the towns in Ailak. In all Maweralnahr there is not any mint, except at Samarcand and at Deinket.

سنجات *Senjat* is a town, with a kohendiz and citadel; the former now in ruins. The town is in a flourishing state; the inner part of which extends for near a farsang. Near the citadel are gardens and running streams; from the town to the foot of the mountain is three farsang. The town has four gates: the در بوچک *Deri Bouchek*, the در فرخان *Deri Farkhan*, the در سایرانه *Der Sakeraneh*, and the در بخارا *Deri Bokhara*. There is a bazar both in the town and in the citadel. The mosque, and the governor's palace, and the prison, are situated in the inner town.

The towns in the territories of Senjat are, بدحکت *Bedheket*, and سامکت *Sameket*, طراز *Teraz*, اطلح *Atlah*, بیلی *Beily*, کزر *Kezr*, and غرسیران *Ghersiran*; but Sameket is the chief town of the *Koureh of Kunjideh* کوره کنجیده. Kezr is the chief town of فاراب *Farab*. میان *Mian* is a town to which the people of غز *Ghuz* come for the purposes of traffick; and as there are not any hostilities carried on at Mian, the town flourishes, and abounds in all the necessaries of life.

فاراب *Farab* is the name of a district, the extent of which is near one day's journey; all the places in it are very strong: it is a hilly country, and contains much land sown with grain. In the eastern part there is a valley with a water-course, which is supplied by the river of Chaje, and runs towards بيكند *Beikend* to the west.

چاج *Chaje* is a city flourishing and populous, and the inhabitants are Mussulmans of غز *Ghuz*, and of خلج *Khilje*, all of the غازي *Ghazi* sect. Between Farab, and Kenjideh, and Chaje, there are many fields sown with grain: the people live in tents, and are all Mussulmans; but they are not powerful.

طراز *Teraz* is on the extreme border, between the land of the Turks and Mussulmans; and all about there are strong castles, called in general after Teraz. The region of Islam extends as far as this spot.

In the territories of اذركند *Azerkend* there is a city, with a kohendiz, and a mosque, and ramparts, on which is situated the governor's house; and the prison is in the kohendiz: this is a pleasant town, affording good fruits, and inhabited by a courteous and handsome race. Corn is brought to this place from Ferghaneh, and Setroushteh, and other countries, in boats, by the river of Chaje, which is a considerable stream.

The عمود *Amud* rises in Turkestan, in the borders of Azerkend; also the river خرساب *Khersab*, and the river اویس *Aweis*, and تبا *Keba*, and the river حدعلي *Hedali*, and other streams.

The people of غز *Ghuz* are for the greater number Mussulmans. Ghuz is the capital, where the kings of this country reside during the summer. The kingdom of Ghuz extends in a straight line ten merhileh from Khuarezm to this place; and from this to باراب *Barab*, twenty merhileh.

فرغانه *Ferghaneh* is the name of an ample and fertile province, which contains many towns and villages: the capital is called اخسیکت *Akhsiket*: it is situated on a level ground, on a river; and has a kohendiz, and suburbs, and a castle. The governor's palace and the prison are in the kohendiz, and the mosque is in the town: There is an oratory on the banks of the river Chaje. The extent of this city is near three farsang. The castle is walled; and the inner town has five gates: the citadel has runing water: and there are gardens and groves at each of the gates; and there are rivers at the distance of about two farsang.

تبا *Keba* is one of the pleasantest places in this country; it has suburbs, and a kohendiz, and a citadel: the kohendiz is fallen to decay; but the mosque is there. The bazars, and the governor's palace, and the prison, are in the citadel. The citadel is walled round; and has gardens, and orchards, and running water.

اوش *Awesh* is about the size of Keba, with suburbs and a kohendiz, in which are the governor's palace and the prison: it has also a citadel, with walls which are connected with the mountain. On this mountain are stationed the sentinels who watch the motions of the Turkestan army. Awesh has three gates: the دروازه کوه *Derwazeh Kouh*, or the mountain-gate; the دروازه آب *Derwazeh Ab*, or the water-gate; and the دروازه مغکده *Derwazeh Moghkedeh*, or the gate of the temple of the magians.

اورکند *Awerkend* enjoys the warmest climate of any place in the province of Ferghaneh: it is next to the enemy, and is twice or thrice as large as Awesh; it has a kohendiz and suburbs, with groves, and gardens, and running streams. In all Maweralnahr there is not any village more considerable than that of Ferghaneh; it extends one farsang in length, and in breadth; it is well inhabited; the people are good husbandmen, and possess much cattle. The territories of Ferghaneh are, *Bestay Zeirin* بستای زیرین, *Areh* اره, *Touan* توان, *Memaroujan* مهاروجان, *Hed Ali* حد علي, *Awrest* اورست. The first of these territories is Bestay Zeirin, as one comes on the road from خجند *Khojend*. The towns of this district are, وانکت *Wanket*, بسوخ *Besoukh*, جواکند *Jouakend*, رسبان *Resban*;

and the towns of Bestay Zeirin are, مرغنبان *Merghenban,*
اندوکان *Asbekan,* اسبغان *Debel,* دبل *Rendwames,* رندوامس
Andukan. This territory consists of both hilly and level ground,
کیماخس *Kaimakhes,* مامکاخس *Mamkakhes,* سوخ *Soukh.*
There is a certain city called مدوانه *Medouaneh.* اورکند
Awerkend is also the name of a city, and there is not any other
city in the territory. اره *Areh* is the name of a territory, the
chief town of which is called خنلام *Khenlam;* this was the
birth-place of امیر حسن نصر الله *Emir Hassan Nasser
Ullah.*

کروان *Kerouan* is the name of a city, all around which are
many villages. اوراست *Aurast,* سلیکند *Selikend,* سلاب
Selab, are towns which belonged to Turkestan, but have lately
fallen into the power of the Mussulmans.

In the territories of Ferghaneh there are mines of gold and
silver, and the district of Bestay Zeirin affords springs of bitumen
or pitch; and they say that in the mountains of اشهره *Ashehreh*
there are fountains of naphta, and mines of copper, and of turquoise stone, of lead, and of iron: all these are in the borders of
Ferghaneh.

In the mountains here they burn a kind of coal, and, having
moistened the ashes with water, use it as soap in washing their
clothes. In these mountains, also, is a certain stone, part of

which is red, and part green, and part white. From Turkestan to Awerkend there are mines of sal ammoniac, as in the mountains we have before described.

راه از جیحون تا فرغانه

Road from the River Jihoon to Ferghaneh.

FROM تربن Kerin to بیكند Beikend, one merhileh; and from that to طواویس Towaweis; from Towaweis to کرمنیه Kermeniah; and from Kermeniah to دیوسی Divesy, to ازینجر Azinjer; from that to زریان Zerian, and from that to Samarcand; from Samarcand to اباركت Abarket, and from that to رباط سغد Rebat Soghd; in all ten merhileh. From the Rebat of Soghd to مزرغه Mezrgheh, one merhileh; from that to رامین Ramin, one merhileh; from that to سباط Sebat, one merhileh; from Awerkend to ساوكت Saweket, one merhileh; from that to Khojend, one merhileh; from اوش Auesh to Awerkend, one merhileh. If one wishes to go from Khojend to خسكبت Kheskeit, he must proceed from كند Kend to خواتند Khuakend, one merhileh; and from Khuakend to Kheskeit, one long* merhileh. From تربن Kerin, which is the first place of Maweralnahr, to Awerkend, on the extremity of the borders, is a journey of twenty-three merhileh.

یک مرحله بزرک *

مسافاتهاي راه چاج

Distances of Stages on the Road of Chaje.

From Chaje to the extreme boundary of the land of Islam: from اباركت *Abarket* to قطران *Ketran,* the road of Chaje and of Ferghaneh is the same, as far as the رباط احمد *Rebat Ahmed;* there it turns off on the right hand : if one wishes to go to Ketran it is one merhileh ; and if one wishes to go to جرمايه *Jermaiah,* it is likewise one merhileh ; from that to ديرک *Deiruk,* from Deiruk to شق کنند حسين *Shuk Hosein;* from that to شق کنند *Shuk Kenend;* from that to فيک *Feik;* from that to اشورکت *Ashourket;* from that to بيکت *Beiket;* from that to the *Rebat Abou al Abbass* رباط ابو العباس, which is called ايکرن *Aikeren;* from that to the village of عبدکرد *Abdikerd;* from that to سنجان *Senjan;* from that to تاجکت *Tajeket;* and from Tajeket to طراز *Teraz,* two days journey ; during which there is not any inhabited place. If one wishes to go the road of بناکت *Benaket,* he must proceed from ابراکت *Abraket* to زامين *Zamin;* from that to حاوس *Hawes;* from that to سلکت *Selket;* from that to سور *Sour;* from the banks of the Jihoon to طراز *Teraz,* is a distance of twenty-two merhileh ; from that to فراجون *Ferajun,* one merhileh ; from مسالکال *Mesalkal,* one merhileh ; from مابربوعر *Maberbouaar,* one merhileh ; to نجب

(275)

Nejeb, one merhileh; to نسوخ *Nesoukh*, one merhileh; to دیرکن *Deirken*, one merhileh; to رباط ازبک *Rebat Azik*, one merhileh; to نخشب *Nakhsheb*, one merhileh; from Bokhara to Balkh, thirteen merhileh.

راه از سمرقند تا بلخ

Road from Samarcand to Balkh.

It is a journey of two days from Samarcand to کش *Kash*; from Kash to کندل *Kendil*, is three merhileh: as far as this stage, the road of Bokhara and of Balkh is the same. Road from Bokhara to Samarcand: From Bokhara one merhileh to فرجنه *Ferjeneh*; from that, for eight menzils, or stages, the road is a desert and uninhabited; but there are some pasture-lands and water. When one wishes to depart from the river Jihoon, from اموي *Amoui* to ویره *Veireh*, is one merhileh; from Veireh to مردومین *Merdumin*; from Merdumin to اساس *Asas*; from Asas to مغانه *Moghaneh*; from that to طاهریه *Taheriah*; from that to درغان *Derghan*; from that to جربند *Jerbend*; from that to سدون *Sedoun*; from that to هزاراسپ *Hezarasp*; from that to خوارزم *Khuarezm*: the whole, by the inhabited road, twelve merhileh.

مسافات شهرهاي معروف ماورالنهر

Distances and Routes of the principal Cities of Maweralnahr.

FROM Samarcand the road to Setroushteh is the same as that to Ferghaneh, which we have described; wherein, as soon as one comes to زامین *Zamin,* he ceases to be in the territories of Setroushteh. We commence the stages of Maweralnahr with ختلان *Khotlan*; from منک *Menek* to the bridge (پولي), which we have before described, is six merhileh; to وخشاب *Wekshab,* two merhileh; from Wekshab to ابرکند *Aberkend,* two merhileh; and from that to هلارود *Hallarud,* two merhileh; from کند که *Kend Gah* to ملنک *Melenk,* two days journey; and from Melenk to حبک *Hebek,* two days journey; and the heights of the pass of آرهن *Arhen* are at one farsang from Khotlan, from the stone bridge (پول سنکبین) four farsang; from the pass of بدخشان *Badakshan* to the village of حیله *Heileh,* is two merhileh.

مسافات ترمد و چغانیان

Distances and Stages of Termed and Cheghanian.

FROM Termed to حرمیکان *Hermigan,* one merhileh; from that to دار زنكی *Dar Zingi,* one merhileh; from Dar Zingi to Cheghanian, two merhileh; from Cheghanian to جبال *Jebal,* and from that to شومان *Shouman,* two merhileh; from Shouman to الوبان *Alouban,* one day's journey; from Alouban to ویشکرد *Weishgird,* one day's journey; from Weishgird to ابلاق *Ailak,* one day's journey; from Ailak to دربند *Derbend,* one day's journey; from Derbend to كاوكان *Kaukan,* to the castle (قلعه), two days journey; from Cheghanian to زیتون *Zeitoun,* one merhileh; from Cheghanian to كوراست *Kourast*,* one merhileh; from Cheghanian to ریگ دشت *Rik Desht* (the sand-desert), six merhileh; from ترمد *Termed* to قبادیان *Kobadian,* two merhileh; from Kobadian to Cheghanian, three merhileh; from Weishgird to پول سنكین *Pool Senkin* (the stone bridge), one day's journey.

These are the roads and distances between Cheghanian and كوهستان *Kouhestan:* from Cheghanian to ختل *Khetl,* from

---

* In the Eton MS. it appears to be (for it is negligently written) *Lourast.*

Khuarezm to خيوه *Kheiweh*; and secondly, to وركان *Werkan*; and thirdly, to كركانج *Korkanje*; from Hezarasp to *Kirdan Khas* كردان خاس, is three farsang; and from Kirdan Khas to حيره *Heireh*, five farsang; from Heireh to سافرون *Saferoun*, five farsang: and from Saferoun to the city (شهر), three farsang; from Khuarezm to درخاس *Derkhas*, two merhileh; from Derkhas to كردان *Kirdan*, one merhileh; from Kirdan to the village of برانكين *Berankein*, two days journey. The city and the village of Berankein are near each other: from the city to the river Jihoon is a distance of four farsang; from مردانكان *Murdangan* to the Jihoon is two farsang.

مسافات شهرهاي بخارا

Distances and Routes of the Towns of Bokhara.

FROM بومحكت *Boumheket*, which is the chief place of Bokhara, to بيكند *Beikend*, one merhileh; from Boumheket to حجاره *Hejareh*, three farsang; from the city (شهر) to مغكان *Moghkan*, five farsang on the right of Beikend: زبديه *Zebediah* is situated within four farsang of the city; طواويس *Towaweis* at four farsang also. مدماحكت *Medmameheket* is situated in the direction of سغد *Soghd*, at one farsang distance; and وعايكت *Waaiket* is near Medmameheket.

مسافات شهرهاي سغد و سبرقند

Distances and Stages of the Towns of Soghd and Samarcand.

FROM Samarcand to اماركت *Amarket,* four farsang; from that to درغس *Derghes,* four farsang; from that to بيحكت *Beiheket,* five farsang; from the city of Samarcand to Beiheket, nine farsang; from Samarcand to ودان *Weddan,* two farsang; from that to كبون محكت *Keboud Meheket,* two farsang; from Samarcand to اسحر *Aseher,* seven farsang; from Aseher to كاسان *Kasan,* five farsang; and from سحر *Seher* to ارقان *Arkan,* three farsang; from Kasan to ارنحر *Arenjer,* two farsang.

Distances between كش *Kash* and نسف *Nesef:*—From Kash to نخشب *Naksheb,* three merhileh; from Kash to Cheghanian, six merhileh; from Kash to بوكت *Bouket,* five merhileh*; from Kash to Sunekh†, two merhileh; from Naksheb to كشته *Kishteh,* four farsang; and from Naksheb to برده *Berdeh,* six farsang: these are the distances of the territories. The distances of the cities of استروشنه *Asteroushteh:* from حرقانه *Herkaneh* to

---

* I have used the Eton MS. in my translation from this place to the end, my copy wanting the last page.

† سودنح Doubtfully written.

درکت *Derket**, five farsang; and from Herkaneh to زامین *Zamin*, nine farsang: from Zamin to ساباط *Sabat*, three farsang; and from بوحکت *Bouheket*† to Ferghaneh, two farsang; from بیکت *Beiket* ‡, which is on the borders of Ferghaneh, and from ستروشته *Setroushteh* to that place, seven farsang; from Setroushteh to وعکث *Waaketh*, three farsang; on the road of خجند *Khojend*, and from Waaketh to عرق *Arek*, two farsang; and from Arek to Khojend, six farsang.

Distances of ماح *Mah* § and اسحاب *Isahab* ‖ : بناکث *Benaketh*, is situated on the banks of the river of چاج *Chaje*; from that to خرسلیکت *Kherseliket*, one farsang; from Kherseliket to بنکت *Benket* ¶, one farsang; from that to سبورکت *Sebourket*, three farsang; and from that to دهقان **** *Dehekan* ††, two farsang; and from that to زالینکیت *Zalinkiet* ‡‡, one farsang; and from that to هیکت *Heiket* §§, two farsang.

* Or درک *Derk*.
† I have supplied the points in this name, as they are omitted in the Eton MS.
‡ Doubtfully written.
§ I suspect an omission of some points in this word, and perhaps it should be چاج *Chaje*.
‖ Doubtfully written.
¶ I have supplied the points of B and N in this word. It is so doubtfully written in the Eton MS. as to appear like مکت *Meket*; perhaps it should be بناکت *Benaket*.
†† The name following Dehekan is so written in the Eton MS. as to be capable of various readings; I therefore give it as in the MS. کسـ
‡‡ I have here supplied, by conjecture, all the points, except those of the first and last letter.
§§ Doubtfully written.

Thus terminates the Oriental Geography of EBN HAUKAL, *according to the Manuscript preserved in the College Library at Eton—(My copy wants the last leaf.) However abrupt it may seem, I am induced to believe that this is the proper conclusion of the Work; for a considerable part of the last page in the Eton Manuscript is left blank—a circumstance which could not have happened, had it been intended that any more should follow, as the Eastern Penmen are so scrupulously exact in filling every page with an equal number of lines, that they frequently begin a new Section or Chapter at the very bottom of a page. The Author, besides, appears to have accomplished his design, intimated in the second and third pages of this Volume.*

APPENDIX.

No. I.

THE ORIGINAL PERSIAN OF VARIOUS PASSAGES
REFERRED TO AND TRANSLATED IN THE PRECEDING PAGES.

Passage translated in Pages 70 and 71.

بابل دهی کوچک است لیکن قدیمتر بنا عراق است و
این اقلیم را ببابل باز خوانند پادشاهان کنعان انجا مقام کرده
اند و آثار بناهای عظیم مانده است کهان برم که بروزکار
جای بزرک بوده است و کویند که ضحاک بیوراسپ بابل
بناکرده است و ابراهیم علیه السلام را آنجا بآتش انداختند و
کودی دوی هست از ایشان و جایگاه آن یکی را کودی طریق
خوانند و یکی را کود در باردرین جایگاه هنوز کرد خاکستر هست
کویند که آتش نمرود بوده است که ابراهیم علیه السلام بآن
انداخته است و مداین از شرقی دجله است از بغداد تا انجا
یک مرحله دارند و کویند که ذو القرنین آنجا فرمان یافت و

APPENDIX, No. I.

کهان برم که این خبر درست نیست زیراکه اورا زهر دادند در
آنوقت که از چین باز کشت و تابوت اورا باسکندریه پیش
مادرش بردند و کویند که در مداین بر دجله پولی بوده است
و ما آنرا اثر ندیدیم عکبرا و بردان و نعمانیه و دیرالعاقول و
دجیل و جرجرایا و فم الصلح و نهر سایس و دیکر جاها که بر
کنار دجله یاد کردیم بیکدیکر نزدیک اند و در بزرکی و
کوچکی مناسب

Passage translated in Pages 82 and 83. *

پنج جایکاه است در پارس که انرا بزم خوانند و مراد از آن
قبیله باشد یکی از همه بزرکتر است زم حیلوثه است زم زمیجار
خوانند و دیکر زم احمد بن اللیث زم *** خوانند سه دیکر
زم احمد بن صالح چهارم زم شهریار زم بادنجان خوانند پنجم
زم احمد بن الحسین زم کارما خوانند و آن زم اردشیر است

ذکر جومهای کردان

و جومهای کردان پیش از آنست که در شمار آید و کویند

---

* In the Eton MS. this passage begins with the following words in red ink:
پنج است چند جایگاه and then continues (in black ink) و اما زمومهای فارس
"But the *Zemoums* of Fars are five: these are some places," &c. &c.

APPENDIX, No. I. 285

كه در پارس پانصد هزار خانه پیش باشد که زمستان و تابستان بچراکاهها باشند و کس از ایشان که دویست مرد پیوسته دارد از جوبان و مزدور و شاکرد و غلام و آنچه بدین مانند و عدد ایشان نتوان ساخت

Passage translated in Pages 92 *and* 93.

و یک قبیله باشند که دو هزار سوار بیرون آید و هیچ قبیله کم از صد سوار نبود تابستان و زمستان بر جراخورها کردند و اندک مایه مردم از ایشان بحدود صرور و جرور مقام دارند و از آنجا نروند و الت و عدت و ستور و لشکر ایشان چنانست که با پادشاهان باز تواند کوشیدن و گویند * که اصل ایشان از عرب است ایشانرا کوسفند و مادیان باشد و اشتر کم دارند و شنودم که این مردم صد قبیله زیادت باشند و مارا سی و اند قبیله پش معلوم نبود

---

* گویند Literally, "*they say.*" I have translated this word according to its general sense, "*it is said,*" *dicitur, fertur,* &c. in which it is used throughout the MS.; because the author does not mean that "*the men (themselves) said that their (own) origin,* &c."—he would, to express this, have used, after اصل, the possessive خود or خویش, *their, their own,* instead of ایشان.

APPENDIX, No. I.

Passage translated in Page 96.

و در کبرکي چنانست که هر زني که بوقت ابستني يا بوقت حيض زنا کند پاک نشود تا انکاه که در آتشکده آيد پيش هربد برهنه شود و بکنيز کا و خويشتن بشويد

Passage translated in Page 116.

و کتابهاي کبرگان و آتشکده‌ها و اداب کبرگي هنوز در ميان پارسيان است و بهيچ ولايت اسلام چندان کبر نباشند که در ولايت پارس که دار الملک ايشان بوده‌است

Passage translated in Page 129.

بناحيت اصطخر بناهاي عظيم هست از سنگ صورتها کرده و بر انجا بنشته و نکاشته گويند که مسجد سليمان عليه السلام بوده است و ديوان ساخته اند و مانند آن در شام و بعلبک و مصر هست

APPENDIX, No. I.

وبناحيت اصطخر سيبي باشد نيهى شيرين و نيهي ترش
مرداس بن عمرو اين سخن با حسن رجا گفت انكار كرد
بغرستان تا بياوردند و بوي نبود

Passage translated in Page 141.

و بلوج در بيابان كوه تقص باشند و تقص بپارسي كوج
باشد و اين دو قوم را كوج و بلوج خوانند و بلوج مردمان صحرا
نشين باشند راه نزنند و كس را رنجه ندارند

Passage translated in Page 254.

و مصنف كتاب كويد من دروازه ديدم در سمرقند روي
باهن پوشيده اند و زبان حميري بران بنشته اند كه از صنعا
بسمرقند هزار فرسنك است و مردمان علم اين كتاب ميراث
داشتند پس كه دربن وقت من بسمرقند رسيدم فتنه افتاد ان
دروازه را بسوختند و اين كتاب ضايع شد پس از آن ابو
مظفر محمد بن نصر بن احمد بن اسد آن دروازه همچنان
اهنين بغرمود ساختن ليكن كتاب ضايع شد

No. II.

THE Reader will find, among the passages in the preceding article of this Appendix, a short account of the *Bcloujes*, mentioned in pages 140 and 141 of the work. It is necessary here to point out an incongruity between Ebn Haukal's description of this people, and that of other writers. This, however, may be reconciled, if we suppose (what indeed occurs in every page of the original MS.) an error in the writing. For راه نزنند *(they do not infest the roads)*, we must read راه بزنند " they *do* infest the roads," and alter the remainder of the sentence accordingly. I was induced to adopt this reading, from the concurrent testimonies of various Eastern Authors, who all bear witness against the character of the Bolouches.

It will be sufficient to quote two dictionaries; first, the *Ferhung Borhan Kattea* قاطع برهان فرهنگ, article بلوچ—which thus ascertains the true pronunciation of the name:

بلوچ—بضم اول و ثاني وسكون ثالث و چيم فارسى توبى
باشند صحراني و كم عقل و شجاع

" *Bolouche*—with the vowel accent *damma* on the first and

APPENDIX, No. II.

" second; the third quiescent, with the Persian letter *chim*,
" (*i. e.* with three diacritical points.) A race of people who in-
" habit the desert." (Barbarous, or uncivilized) of very little understanding—fierce, &c.

Under another article, the same excellent Dictionary furnishes more ample information on the subject of this people:

كوچ و بلوچ—نام طايفه باشد از صحرا نشينان كه در كوههاي اطراف كرمان توطن دارند و كويند اينها از عربان حجازند و حرفت ايشان جنگ و خونريزي و دزدي و راهزني باشد اگر احيانا پيكانه نيابند يكديكرا بكشند و مال يكد يكرا تاراج كنند و همچنين برادران و خويشان و قرابتان و دوستان باهم جنگ كنند و اين فعل را بسيار خوب دانند

" *Kouche and Bolouche*—the names of certain races of bar-
" barous people who inhabit the mountains on the borders of
" Kirman. It is said that they are descended from the Arabians
" of Hejaz. Their employments are fighting and shedding of
" blood; thieving, and robbing on the roads. If at any time it
" happens that they cannot find strangers, they murder one
" another, plundering and destroying each other's property.
" Thus, even brothers, near relations, and friends, quarrel;
" and they consider this as a pleasant occupation."

APPENDIX, No. II.

I shall extract a passage, on the same subject, from another very valuable work, the فرهنگ سروري *Ferhung Sururi*.

بلوچ—قومي اند بغايت بيعقل از مردمان بياباني كه قافلها را زنند و اكثر شجاع و تيرانداز باشند و ايشانرا كوچ بلوچ نيز گويند

" *Bolouche*—a people extremely stupid or void of understand-
" ing, who inhabit the deserts and plunder the caravans, and for
" the greater part are warlike and good archers; they are also
" styled *Kouche Bolouche*."

The فرهنگ جهانكيري *Ferhung Jehanguiri* gives the same account and nearly in the same words as the Borhan Kattea above quoted.

If the origin of this extraordinary people were to become the subject of antiquarian investigation, the character of the ancient inhabitants of Hejaz (Arabia the Stony or Rocky) should be compared with that of their reputed descendants; and I believe that such a comparison would in some measure confirm this traditional origin. Of the barbarism which prevailed among the Scenites* or

---

* Strabo (Geograph. Lib. xvi.) describes the Scenite Arabs " as plunderers or robbers, and feeders of cattle."—Σκηνιταί Αραβες ληϛρικοι τινες κὰ ποιμενικοί—who almost totally neglected the arts of agriculture, devoting their attention to the feeding of cattle of all kinds, but especially camels.—γεωργουντες μεν η ουδεν η μικρα, νομας δε εχον]ες παντοδαπων θρεμματων, και μαλιϛα καμηλων.

APPENDIX, No. II.

Nomades, or, as they are emphatically styled by Ebn'olathir[*], the اهل الحجر *people of the rock*, it would be easy to collect a variety of anecdotes. But one quotation from an Arabian author will serve to prove, that if the ferocious Bolouches are descended from the Hejazians, they are not, by any means, a degenerate offspring.

On the subject of these Arabs we are informed, that
من خواصهم الحرب وسفك الدما و محبه القتل و الحقد
" A disposition for war and shedding of blood, a love of slaughter
" and violence, and a spirit tenacious of anger and of hatred, were
" among their peculiar qualities and characteristicks [†]."

To their uncivilized state Sir William Jones alludes in the following passage:

" The manners of the Hejazi Arabs, which have continued, we
" know, from the time of Solomon to the present age, were by
" no means favourable to the cultivation of arts; and as to
" sciences, we have no reason to believe that they were ac-
" quainted with any, &c. [‡]"

It remains to discover at what time any colony of this people

---

[*] See Pocockc's Specimen Historiæ Arabum, 4to, Oxf. 1650, p. 87.
[†] Pocockc, Spec. Hist. Arab. 87.
[‡] Discourse on the Arabs. Asiatick Researches.

established themselves in the confines of Hindustan and Persia: that a commercial intercourse subsisted from the earliest ages between the inhabitants of Arabia and the Hindus, cannot well be doubted. The same learned author, Sir William Jones, declares, that the " ports of Yemen, (or Arabia Felix,) must have " been the emporia of considerable commerce between Egypt and " India, or part of Persia *."

But it was not merely a few traders or merchants that settled in Hindustan; according to a writer † quoted by Pococke, whole bodies of Arabians having emigrated from their own country, invaded and occupied the territories of India, in an age of very remote antiquity ‡.

I have not leisure at present to trace the subject with more minute research; but I think it one that affords matter for interesting and curious investigation.

* Discourse on the Arabs.
† احمد بن يوسف Ahmed the son of Joseph.
‡ " Reliquos Arabiæ finibus egressos Indiæ regiones occupasse," &c. Pococke Spec. Hist. Arab. p. 40.

No. III.

THE following extract from the ancient Chronicle of Tabari is referred to in the Preface, page x, and may serve to illustrate Ebn Haukal's account of the Hamyaritick inscription on the gate of Samarcand. See p. 254, and 287.

The transactions here recorded are said to have happened early in the sixth century, when Cobad, the Persian monarch, was slain, and his dominions invaded and plundered by the Arabs, under Samar, a nephew of the Tobba, or king of Yemen. The account of this invasion, and of Cobad's death, as related by Tabari, with a literal translation, will be found in the Oriental Collections, vol. iii. p. 156; where I have given it as a specimen of the most pure and ancient *Parsi*. The original Chronicle of Tabari was written in the Arabick language; and this Persian translation was made in the year of the Hegira 352, (A. D. 963), by a vizier of the Samanian princes[*], who inserted many curious traditions and observations of his own. See the Preface, p. xii.

---

[*] D'Herbelot, Bibliot. Orient. Art. Tarikh and Thabari.

و سمرنیز از جیحون بکذشت و بسرقند شد و آن حصاری
محکم داشت ملک بحصار اندر شد یکسال بر در حصار اندر
بنشست هیچ چیز نتوانست کردن تا یک شب خود کرد حصار
می کشت از دربانان حصار مردي را بکرفت و بلشکرکاه خود
آورد و اورا کفت ملک این شهر چه مردي است بدین
زیرکي و هشیاري که ازیکسال باز حیلت همي کنم نبي
توانم این حصار کشادن آن مرد کفت این ملک را هیچ
دانایي نیست و سخت ابله کردنده است و اورا جز مي
خوردن و طرب کار نیست و شب و روز مست باشد ولیکن

And Samar also passed from the river Jihoun (the Oxus) and went to Samarcand. This city had a castle very strongly fortified, in which the king resided: one whole year Samar continued before the gates of this castle, without being able to effect any thing against it. At length he himself went the rounds, and took prisoner a certain man, one of the porters of the castle, and brought him into the camp, and said to him: "What kind of " person is the king of this place, whose skill and ingenuity are " such, that, after trying every stratagem for a whole year, I am " not able to take this castle." The man answered, " This king " is not by any means a person of sagacity: he is one of very " foolish conduct; whose only employments are drinking of " wine and festivity: he is intoxicated day and night: but he has " a daughter who manages all these affairs, and takes care of the

APPENDIX, No. III.

اورا دختریست که این تدبیر او همی کند و این سپاه و حصار او نگاه میدارد سمر با خود گفت تدبیر که زنان کنند آن کار آسان بود آن مرد را گفت که این دختر شوي دارد گفت نه سمر مرد را هدیهٔ داد و گفت که مرا بتو حاجتست که پیغامی از من بدان دختر رسانی گفت رواست سمر یک حقهٔ زرّین بیاورد و پر از یاقوت و مروارید و زمرّد بکرد و گفت بدان دختر ده و اورا بگوی که من از یمن بطلب تو آمده ام و مرا آن پادشاهی بکار نیست زیرا که همه خراسان و عجم مراست باید که خود را بزني بمن دهي و با من چهار

" army and of the castle." Samar said within himself, " It is
" easy to defeat the arrangements which women make." Then
he asked the man, Whether this daughter of the king had a hus-
band?—the man informed him, that she had not. Samar having
bestowed him a present, said, " I have occasion for your services;
" you must bear a message from me to this damsel:"—the man
consented. Samar then brought out a golden casket, and filled
it with rubies, and pearls, and emeralds, and said, " Present
" these to that damsel; and tell her, that I have come from
" Yemen in search of her; that the conquest of this kingdom is
" not my object, for all Khorasan and Persia already are mine;
" but she must give herself to me as a wife. There are with me
" four thousand chests full of gold: all these I will send to her;

هزار تابوت زر یست آن همه بدو فرستم و این شهر بپدرش ببخشم چون این کار برآید و تمام شود مکر از وي. مرا پسري آيد که ملکي عجم و چینستان اورا باشد و من بشب ازنخست این تابوتهاي زر بدو فرستم پس آنگاه اورا بخواهم آن مرد همان شب در سمرقند اندر رفت و این سخن مر دختررا بگفت دختر راي کرد و هم آن شب آن مرد باز فرستاد باجابت بردن و سخن برآن بنهادند که فردا شب آن تابوتهارا بغرستد و بشب بشارستان اندر آيد چنانکه کس نداند و سمرقند را چهار در بود گفت کدام در شهر بکشایم دیکر روز سمر چهار هزار

" and I will bestow this city on her father, whenever these
" affairs shall be finally settled: and if she should bear unto me
" a son, the empire of Persia and of Cheenistan shall be his. I
" shall first, as an earnest, send her, by night, the chests of
" gold; and afterwards espouse her."

The man having gone into Samarcand the same night, delivered this message to the damsel, who deliberated on it, and then sent back that person to ratify the bargain; and to desire Samar that he should on the following night send the chests of gold into the city, and come there himself in such a manner that no one might perceive it. Samarcand had four gates, and she told him which of these gates should be opened.

APPENDIX, No. III.

تابوت بیاورد و بهر تابوتی دو مرد اندر نشاند با سلاح تمام
چون شب تاریکی شد هرتابوتی برخری نهاد و برهر تابوتی
مردي موكل كرد با سلاح تمام مقدار دوازده هزار مرد بسمرقند
اندر فرستاد و ایشانرا گفت كه من سپاه برنشانم و همه را گرد
كرد حصار بپای كنم چون شها بشهر اندر شوید سرهاء تابوت
بكشایید و بیرون ایید و جرسها بزنید تا من بدانم و هر مر دیرا
جرسی داده بود پس در بکشایند تا من با سپاه درایم پس
چون نیم شب بود رسولی دختر بیامد که در شهر بکشادند
پس پاره تابوتها بغرست سپر تابوتها برخران نهاد و خود با سپاه

On the next day Samar brought out four thousand chests, and put into each two men completely armed; and when the night became dark, he placed each chest on the back of an ass, and to each he appointed a man as a superintendant, likewise completely armed: thus there were to the amount of twelve thousand men. These he sent on into Samarcand, and told them that he would place his army in proper disposition, and station them all round the castle; and he directed them, that when they should be within the city, they might open the lids of the chests, and come out, and ring bells (for he had given a bell to every man), so that he might know how matters went; and then they were to open the gate and let him enter with the army. When it was midnight, a messenger came from the damsel, saying, "The gate of the city " is opened; let some of the chests be now sent." Samar placed

APPENDIX, No. III.

برنشست چون بحصار رسیدند همه از تابوتها بیرون آمدند و
حربها زدن کرفتند و درهای شهر بکشادند و سمر با سپاه بشهر
اندر آمد و شمشیر اندر نهادند و تا روز می کشتند تا جوی
خون برفت و ملک را بکشت و دخترش را بکرفت و یکسال آنجا
بماند و در کتاب تسمیه البلدان است که سمرقند را آن وقت
چین خواندندی و چینیان در آنجایگاه بودند و کاغذی
چینیان بنهادند و سمر آن شهر را بر نام خویش نهاد پارسی
سمرکند و بزبان ترکی شهر کند بود باز چون بتازی کردانی
سمرقند بود پس سمر سپاه بکشید و بترکستان اندر شد و تبت

the chests on the asses, and took his station with the army. When the chests arrived at the castle, all the men came forth from them, and began to ring their bells, and threw open the gates of the city; and Samar entered with his troops, sword in hand, and they continued to slaughter until it was day; so that blood ran in streams: the king was slain and the damsel taken prisoner; and Samar remained in this city one year. In the book entitled *Tesmiah al Boldan*, it is mentioned, that in those times Samarcand was called *Cheen*, and the *Cheenians* were there; and these people first made the paper of the Cheenians. But Samar called this city after his own name. In Persian Samarkand (with the letter ک). *Kand* (کند) in the Tartar or Turkish language signifies a city. But when this name was used in Arabick, it became Samarcand سمرقند, (with the letter ق.) After this Samar led forth his army and proceeded into Turkestan and to Tibbet, &c. &c.

APPENDIX, No. III.

The ancient tradition, here recorded, is unknown to most of the modern Persian writers, or, at least, unnoticed by them [*]. *Emir Rauzi,* however, in his excellent geographical compilation, the *Heft Aklim,* or Seven Climates, informs us that

شهر نامي که از اهل تبع یمن بود آن شهر را ویران کرده انبیه
چنانکه از آن عمارت اثری نگذشت پس از آن بشرکند
اشتهار یافت عرب معرب ساخته سمرقند گفت

" a person named Shamar who was of the family of the *Tobba,*
" or sovereigns of Yemen, destroyed that city, so that no vestige
" remained of its (principal) building, (a castle of immense extent,
" and said to have been erected by Gurshasp, and repaired, at
" different times, by Lohorasp and Alexander the Great). After
" that it acquired the name of Shamarkand (with the letter ک)
" which the Arabs, according to their idiom, call Samarcand,
" with ة)."

The same account is given in the *Ajaib al boldan* and other manuscripts, which agree in assigning to this city the highest degree of antiquity. If the tradition preserved by Tabari is founded in historical fact, we may suppose the gate on which the

---

[*] I must also acknowledge that in one copy of Tabari, in my possession, it is not found: but the other two preserve it. From the more ancient of these, transcribed A. D. 1446, this extract has been given.

APPENDIX, No. III.

Hamayritick inscription was fixed, to have been that which the avaricious princess opened to the wily Samar; and it is probable that this inscription commemorated in the language of that Arab, the success of his stratagem, although we only learn from Ebn Haukal that it mentioned the distance from Samar to Samarcand. See page 254—287, and Preface, p. ix, x, xi.

The paper of Samarcand, to the manufacture of which Tabari alludes in the preceding extract, is celebrated by various writers. Although the Arabians do not pretend to have known the invention of it before the eighty-eighth year of the Hegira (A. D. 706), yet the use of paper was universal among the Persians and Chinese in ages of more remote antiquity [*]. According to *Ali ben Mohammed* علي بن محمد (quoted by the learned *Casiri*) the art of making paper was introduced at Samarcand in the thirtieth year of the Hegira (A. D. 650); and he adds,

وليس قبل ذكل يوجد القرطاس الا بسمرقند و بالصين

" heretofore the use of paper was only known at Samarcand and " among the Chinese." And Casiri [†] thinks it most probable that the Arabians learned it from the Persians or Chinese. " Unde " verisimile profecto est Arabes hujusmodi usum a Persis et

---

[*] Biblioth. Arabico-Hisp. Casiri, Tom. II. p. 9.
[†] Bibl. Arab. Hisp. Tom. II. p. 9.

" Sinensibus, quorum regiones partim expugnarunt partim per-
" lustrarunt jamdiu accepisse; id ipsum luculentissime demon-
" strant complures codices manuscripti *Escurialensis* Bibliothecæ,
" quorum aliqui exarati sunt anno Egiræ 400 (Christi 1009); alii
" anno 500, Christi vero 1106."

No. IV.

In pages 235, 245, 254, the reader is referred for some account of the Samanian Dynasty to this article of the Appendix; and in the Preface also, p. x. a passage is quoted from Abulfeda, which mentions a prince of this family.

The learned D'Herbelot, in his account of the Samanians[*], (which he collected from a chronicle, expressly written on the subject of their history, and another excellent work, the *Lebtarikh*) notices a difference of calculation in respect to the duration of this dynasty, which commenced in the year of the Hegira 261 (A. D. 874), and terminated in the year 388, (A. D. 998.)

[*] Bibliot. Orient. Article Samaniah.

APPENDIX, No. IV.

I find that, according to the *Tarikh Gozideh*, it lasted 102 years, 6 months, and 20 days: according to the *Tarikh Kipchak Khani*, 103 years, 2 months, and 11 days: there are still greater variations in other accounts; but all may be reconciled by observing that some historians do not consider Ismael as king, although he possessed all the power of one, until his government was acknowledged by the Khalif.

The names of the Samanian princes in the order of their succession are here given according to the Tarikh Gozideh, the Khelassut al Akhbar of Khondemir, and other manuscripts.

1. اسماعل بن احمد
Ismael ben Ahmed.

2. احمد بن اسماعل
Ahmed ben Ismael.

3. نصر بن احمد
Nasser ben Ahmed.

4. نوح بن نصر
Nouh ben Nasser.

5. عبدالملك بن نوح
Abdalmalek ben Nouh.

APPENDIX, No. IV. 303

6. منصور بن عبدالملك
Mansour ben Abdalmalek.

7. نوح بن منصور
Nouh ben Mansour.

8. منصور بن نوح
Mansour ben Nouh.

9. عبدالملك بن نوح
Abdalmalek ben Nouh.

The Tarikh Jehan Ara and some other chronicles add the name of another اسماعيل بن نوح *Ismael ben Nouh*; but the Samanian Dynasty is generally said to consist of nine princes, those who are above enumerated.

The third, *Nasser ben Ahmed*, is the person who, according to our author, Ebn Haukal, rebuilt the Gate of Samarcand (see p. 254), and under whom a respectable person at Maweralnahr is said (in p. 235) to have borne arms. This prince is styled, by Abulfeda (see a passage quoted in the Preface, p. x), *Mohammed Ebn Locman Ebn Nasir ben Ahmed*. And, in the *Tarikh Kipchak Khani*, I find him entitled, *Saied Abou'l'hassan Nasser ben Ahmed* سعيد ابو الحسن نصر بن احمد. He succeeded his father in the year of the Hegira 301 (A. D. 913), and died Anno

APPENDIX, No. IV.

Hegira 330, (A. D. 941.) According to Kipchak Khan, the poets رودكي *Rudeki* and ابو العباس زيچي *Abou l'abbas Zeichi* flourished in the time of Nasser Ahmed.

The Cazi Ahmed al Ghuffari, in his Tarikh Jehan Ara, informs us, that

در معجم البلدان مذكور است كه سامان قريه است در سمرقند و بعقيده بعضي موضعي *&c.*

" in the geographical work, entitled Moajem al Boldan, it is
" observed that Saman was a town belonging to Samarcand, or,
" according to some, a place in the territories of Balkh, from
" which the ancestor of the Samanian family derived his name."

FINIS.

INDEX.

N. B. This Index does not refer to any Articles of the Preface or Appendix.

A.

Alexander the Great, 70, 116, 215
Abbassides, 16, 66
Abraham, 40, 58, 70, 130
Asses not larger than sheep, 37
Animal (uncommon), 25
Altar of David, 39
Apostles, 39
Apple (extraordinary), 129

B.

Babylon, ancient capital of the Persian Empire, 3
Balsam, 36
Bodies of the dead, at Teneis, in Egypt, 36
Bodies of the dead burnt by the Russes, 191
Book purchased for 1000 dinars, 119
Barzouieh the celebrated physician, 216
Bolouches, a people of Kirman, 140, 143
Barbud the musician, 216
Basrah (number of streams at), 63

C.

Curds, 83, 92, 97
Crocodiles, 31, 36, 155
Castles (impregnable), 94
Christians, 13, 14, 23, 26, 36, 42, 43, 52, 53, 56, 58, 59, 160, 161, 186, 187, 188, 191, 218, 257, 265

D.

Daniel the prophet, his bones found, 76
Dolphin, 35

INDEX.

F.

Fertility of Maweralnahr, 233
Fatemites, 20, 21
Fish without bones, 133
——— uncommon, 31
Fire temples, 85, 95, 116
——— worshippers, 116, 146, &c.
——————— extraordinary rites, 95, 173
Fire issuing from a mountain, 77

G.

Grecian philosophers, 41, 52
Gog and Magog, 8, 9
Gypsies, 83
Guebres. See Fire-worshippers

H.

Hospitality of the Transoxanians, 234
Hamyaritick inscription, 254

I.

Idols (worshipped), 13, 146
Idol at Moultan, 148
Jews, 10, 42, 116, 160, 186, 187, 188, 190, 221, 224
Jewish king, 185, 189
Jesus, 39, 67, 127, 237
Israelites, 29, 38, 171
Joseph, 31

K.

Kaaba, 2, 128
Kouche, a people, 140, 143
Kings of Spain, 28
Khacan, or King of Khozr, 189
Kermez, the dyer's worm, 161

L.

Language——Pehlavi, 114
——————Parsi, 114
——————of Khuzistan, 76
——————Pars, 114
——————Ghawr, 227
——————Tabaristan, 174
——————Kirman, 143
——————Makran, 152
——————Derbend, 159
——————Ardebil, 163
——————Bokhara, 251
——————the Kouches and Bolouches, 143
Land of Lot, 46

M.

Mary (Virgin), 39, 127, 237
Magick and sorcery, 130
Mummy, 133

N.

Nimrod, 70, 130
Noah's Ark, 60

INDEX.

Noushirvan, 69, 158

O.

Ommiades, 24, 26, 60, 119, 124

P.

Palace of Noushirvan, 69
Pyramids of Egypt, 33
Pharaoh, 37
———his villa, 36
Paper of Samarcand, 233

R.

Rosewater of Shiraz, 132
Romances of the Persians, 172
Ruins of Baalbek, 43

S.

Shapour or Sapores, 74, 100
Sassanides, 71, 134
Samanides, 121, 245, 251
Sabeans, 42, 58
Scorpions, 20, 56, 77, 171
Sea fights, 54

Soffarian dynasty, 77
Scull set in silver, 123
Statues of kings, 129
———at Bisutoun, 173
———in the desert of Shour, 197

T.

Temple of the Sabeans, 42
———of Solomon at Persepolis, or Istakhar, 129

W.

Wall at Derbend, built by Noushirvan, 158
Water of the Caspian Sea, dark coloured, 181
Wealth of the inhabitants of Siraf, 115, 133

Y.

Yezdegird slain in a mill, 216

Z.

Zohak, 70, 116, 172

PRINTED, *AT THE ORIENTAL PRESS*, BY WILSON & CO.
WILD-COURT, LINCOLN'S INN FIELDS, LONDON.

ERRATA.

Page.	Line,		
28	2, 3	*For* comlexion,	*Read* complexion.
84	12	Derayi,	Deryai.
90	3	after شعب, add بوان,	and read the English Shaab-bouan, as one name.
100	16	ot,	or.
146	8	possessors,	professors.
172	16	never,	not.
196	21	Kebat,	Rebat.
220	10	then,	than.
228	22	بخدشان,	بدخشان.
241	9	Chereh,	Chehreh.

Pages 258, 259, 260, (et passim,) *for* Kish, *read* Kash.

(309)

SECOND INDEX.

N. B. As the preceding Index has not appeared sufficiently copious for this Work, the Names of Places are added in that which follows. The references to the Preface are expressed in Roman numerals.

A.

Aaje, 265
Aalia, 248
Aaneh, 60
Aaien, 109
Aamil, 207
Aarian, 218
Aasim, 223
Aarez, 247
Aayeth, 72
Abadan, 11, 61, 64, 73, 75
Abadeh, 86
Abad, 217
Abarket, 273, 274
Abdikerd, 274
Abyssinia, 4, 13, 14, 22
Abendian, 87
Ablah, xiv, xv, 64, 79
Aberkouh, 86, 102, 103, 108, 111, 130, 132
Abdarrahman, 86, 107, 129
Abdejan, 132
Aboughanem, 139, 140, 143
Abaus, 144
Aberi, 154
Abenjan, 160
Aberkendman, 164
Abher, 165, 169, 170

Abisgoun, 176, 180, 185, 190, 191
Abshour, 197
Abdallah, 210
Aberkend, 276
Abnez, 26
Aden, 14
Adereh, 40
Adeib, 159
Adneh, 45
Aderaa, 49
Adithah, 50
Adeki, 210
Ader, 217
Adedalek, 265
Ægypt. See Egypt
Africa, 2, 4, 5, 7, 15, 16, 19, 21, 28, 132
Afadeh, 30
Afaresk, 133
Agemi, 165, 168
Ahmah, 65
Ahouam, 33
Ahwaz, 74, 75, 80
Ahef, 120
Ainas, 51
Aien al Shems, 36
Aien Zarieh, 54

Aien Arbah, 38
Ailek, 37
Aikan, 139
Aidah, 74
Aidej, 75, 80, 113
Airi, 147
Aien Alhem, 175, 183
Ailak, vii, 238, 250, 264, 265, 266, 267, 268, 277
Aikeren, 274
Ailah, xiv
Ajaa, 183
Akareb, 110
Akereh, 194
Akhseikh, 240
Akebseh, 49
Akhmim, 35
Akrites, 53
Akbera, 71
Aklid, 86
Akdeh, 112
Aljezireh. See Jezireh
Allami, 13
Al Botem, viii
Alsour (lake), 84
Allan, 4, 5, 156
Alexandria, 29, 31, 33, 45, 50, 52, 70

S S

SECOND INDEX.

Allas, 139
Allepo. See Haleb
Almour, 90
Alaudket, 265
Almerasek, 175
Ali Abad, 182
Alouban, 277
Amarket, 279
Amoui, 239, 242, 275
Amad, 270
Amedi, 165
Amadeh, 89
Ameden, 88
Ameniah, 249
Amar, 221
Amol, 175, 179, 181, 182, 183, 190, 191, 192, 213, 226, 228, 229
Amrouilou, 183
Amid, 55, 57
Ambouran, 90
Anbarbanan, 87
Antakiah, 44, 49, 51, 52
Anbas, 50, 51
Anbar, 55, 56, 59, 61
Anar Meherje, 111
Andi, 150
Anderab, 157
Andemesh, 168
Anbereh, 193
Anderabeh, 223, 224, 228, 231
Andenjaragh, 239
Anderbaz, 243
Andidan, 248
Anduken, 272
Andalus, ii, 4, 5, 7, 15, 16, 81, 25, 26, 27, 28, 51, 53
Aoud, 167
Areh, 271, 272, 280
Arenjer, 279
Arkan, 86, 279
Arhen, 276

Arou, 260
Arkand, 248
Ardan, 248
Ardejer, 241
Arher, 223
Ardenjan, 218
Ardvar, 215
Arsel, 199
Arthai, 191
Artha, 191
Arinou, 177
Arjeish, 162, 165
Armi, 162, 165
Armia, 162
Aras, 161, 162
Ardebil, 64, 135, 156, 157, 158, 160, 161, 162, 163
Armen, 4, 5, 156
Aran, 155, 156, 159, 160, 163, 179, 183, 262.
Armenia, xxiii, 78, 155, 156, 157, 159, 160, 161, 162, 163, 188
Armaiel, 151, 154
Arjan, 90, 91, 95, 96, 104, 110
Arghan, 78, 79, 82, 105, 112, 131, 135, 130, 129, 113, 133, 116, 11
Arzen, 99
Arem, 74
Arghan (Koureh), 90
Ardeshir (Khereh), 88, 135
Ardeshri (Koureh), 87, 91, 99
Ardeshir (Dereh), 82, 91, 83, 104, 131
Ardeshir, 82, 83, 91
Arirah, 89
Ardeshirgird, 121
Arzu, 90
Arden, 39, 40, 47, 48, 49
Arhadouh, 26

Armeh, 17
Arbilah, 15, 20
Arjan, 110
Asas, 52, 274
Asker Mokrem, 20, 78, 79
Asijeh, 19
Assat, 13
Asker al mohdi, 67
Asel, 78, 79, 90
Asedan, 87
Aselan, 87
Astourah, 26
Asouan, 29, 35, 37
Ascalon, 48
Ashmouein, 35
Astadan, 90
Aseljar, 90
Astehajan, 113
Asdejan, 88
Astefahaian, 89
Asknoun, 95
Asfendrud, 161
Asedabad, 166, 228, 169, 182
Asterabad, 175, 176, 180
Astelesht, 201
Asferar, 209
Asfjai, 212
Asferin, 213, 215, 228
Aserinan, 217, 219
Ashran, 217
Asenk, 218
Asferan, 219, 230
Ashiket, 270
Asbejan, 272
Ashereh, 272
Ashourket, 274
Aseher, 279
Asteroushteh, 279
Atlah, 268
Atrar, 250
Atel, 185, 186, 187, 188
Audafi, 120

SECOND INDEX.

Aulenjan, 113
Aurd, 97
Auhileh, 162
Auher, or Auhar, 167
Aubgir, 243
Aubeh, 217
Aulad, 257
Aurast, 172
Awlas, 46, 50
Aweis, 109, 270
Awerkend, 271, 272, 273
Awerst, 271
Awesh, 271
Ayoub, 166
Azhaman, 86
Azzeh, 48
Azerbai, 144
Azend, 152
Azerbaijan, xxiii, 3, 60, 62, 155, 156, 159, 161, 162, 163, 165, 167, 172, 174, 178, 188
Azziah, 184
Azsour, 210
Azenket, 266
Azerkend, 269, 270

B.

Babel (Babylon), 3, 10, 70, 130
Basrin, 24
Baghdad, 9, 61, 62, 66, 67, 68, 69, 70, 71, 77, 78, 116, 120, 126, 127, 135, 172, 176, 178, 208
Barab, 9, 221, 238, 270
Bahrein, 11, 119, 128, 138
Barbary, 19, 21
Bajeh, 13, 29, 37

Barkah, 15, 16, 19, 29
Basireh, 15, 17, 20, 51
Bakour, 17, 20, 21
Batileh, 18
Basna, 21
Bab al Tauk Resafeh, 67
Bab-alia Sertheh, 67
Basan, 79, 74, 89
Bazar, 73, 74, 79, 80
Bakhtegan (lake), 84
Baman, 87
Bagheras, 47, 49
Baherah, 89
Baalbek, 48, 49, 129
Balis, 44, 58
Barmah, 48, 57, 73
Balousa, 56
Bardoun, 80
Basrah, xiv, xvi, 61, 62, 63, 64, 65, 71, 79
Barem, 142, 145
Badenjan, 83, 91, 123
Balaien, 90, 196
Bajirem, 88
Bazem, 89, 110
Bahalouk, 90
Bahelsegan, 90
Bazrick, 96, 113
Balkh, 121, 213, 214, 215, 217, 218, 223, 224, 225, 226, 227, 228, 230, 231, 239, 259, 260, 275, 304
Badergan, 106
Bam, 144, 145
Baren, 139
Banias, 49
Bardan, 71
Baloui, 147, 150
Bales, 154
Baku, 160, 162
Bar, 167
Bardestan, 175

Bamieh, 182
Bayel, 183
Bakeil, 184
Bashkouth, 192
Basekh, 202
Barghis, 213, 255, 256
Bahmanabad, 215, 229, 230
Badghis, 219
Baghelan, 223, 231
Badakshan, 223, 225, 228, 230, 232, 238, 276
Bamian, 213, 225, 226, 227, 223
Baverd, 228, 230
Barmis, 255
Barkeit, 257, 258
Baloam, 264
Benat, 79
Beiza, 86, 91, 93, 103, 111, 113, 121, 127, 135
Behour, 39
Beit al Mokeds, 33, 48. See Jerusalem.
Bethlehem, 39, 40
Beniah, 49
Besirin, 51
Beled, 55, 56
Betaiah, 61, 65, 68, 71
Berdan, 71
Bermasir, 139, 194, 202
Besa, 104, 109, 111, 113, 115, 116, 125, 132, 133
Berdoun, 74, 77, 80
Beinoul, 90
Besmeil, 90
Bendil, 110
Beshadour, 100, 113
Behreh, 135, 197
Bend, 103
Berje, 96
Behouleh, 89
Benjeman, 105

SECOND INDEX.

Berm, 113
Behar, 144
Belid, 55, 56
Beher, 105
Besket, 266
Behaket, 267
Bedheket, 268
Beily, 268
Bestay Zeirin, 271, 272
Besoukh, 271
Beiket, 274, 280
Benaket, 274, 280
Berankein, 278
Beiheket, 279
Berdeh, 279
Benaketh, 280
Benket, 280
Beherje, 147, 150
Besmeid, 150, 154, 155
Bein, 153, 154, 220
Beldan, 154
Bervanan, 157
Bezerend, 157
Berdaa, 157, 160, 161, 163, 164, 185
Bektan, 157
Berzenje, 160
Berzend, 163
Berkeri, 165
Bedlis, 165, 182
Berah, 167
Berd, 169
Berdabad, 101
Bertas, 187, 188, 190, 192
Bejibal, 192
Bedreh, 195
Belein, 196
Berdsir, 197
Beisha Daran, 201
Bernaraduieh, 201
Berir, 201
Berin, 211

Best, 220
Bershir, 229
Beikend, 245, 250, 252, 269, 273, 278
Berkend, 246, 247
Beni Asad, 248
Bekhajemr, 248
Besteh, 249
Berkaa, 249
Bergher, 255
Bermer, 257
Belanderin, 260
Berdeh, 261
Berjin, 262
Beshaghir, 264
Besenk, 264
Benagur, 265
Berkous, 265
Bijerm, 11, 112, 119
Bilbileh, 18, 27
Bileroun, 150
Bilkan, 160, 163
Bisutoun, 166, 172
Bireshk, 193
Biheket, 255
Boukeseh, 243
Bour, 168
Bourkan, 215
Bou, 243, 242
Bouzgan, 228, 229
Boushek, 213
Bom, 211
Bost, 203, 206, 207, 208, 209, 210, 212
Bordan, 169
Bouket, 279
Bounket, 266
Bumeheket, 252, 262, 278
Busheng, 217
Bulgar, 185, 187, 190, 191, 192, 5, 7, 9, 10
Bustam, 183, 175

Bourmah, 26
Bosi, 80, 74, 77
Bokhara, 122, 125, 232, 236, 237, 238, 245, 247, 249, 250, 251, 252, 253, 275, 278
Bou (or Abou) Ghanem, 143
Bolouje, or Bolouche, 138, 140, 141, 143, 146, 288, 298, 291
Boudenjan, 107
Boukur 35, 36
Bouheket, 245, 265, 280
Bourmaket, 258
Bous, 255
Boumeh, 248
Bourek Ferghaneh, 248
Bustam, 178

C.

Carcoub, 74, 80, 133
Cazvin, 122
Cazeroun, 82, 95, 108, 111, 112, 113, 132, 133, 135
Canaan, 130, 70
Cadesia, 61, 62, 65, 66
Caaba (or Kaaba) 2
Caspian (or Deryai Khozr). See Khozr
Canouge, 9
Carmourah, 18
Cashmere, 4
Cairo 11, 30
Caisariah, 48
Cazi, 211
Cashan, 168
China. See Cheen
Cheilak, 10
Cheen, 4, 5, 6, 8, 9, 10, 12, 70, 250, 298

SECOND INDEX.

Chekrel, 267
Chaje Rud, 259
Chend, 248
Cheghagher, 244
Chereh, 241
Cheghanian, 238, 240, 255, 261, 277, 279
Chaje, vii. 233, 285, 288, 243, 244, 252, 261, 263, 265, 266, 267, 269, 270, 274, 280
Chun, 222, 230 231
Chungalabad, 210
Cheshmeh Sirab, 202
Chendwar, 150
Cortubah, 18, 27
Costatineh (Constantinople) 9, 10, 51, 52
Corcoub, 80
Cobadian, 238
Curds, 155, 158, 171
Curdistan, xxii
Curdan, 56, 97
Cufah, 61, 62, 65, 66, 67, 68, 71; 132

D.

Darabjerd, 89, 94, 104, 110, 111, 112, 113, 133, 134
Dartak, 89
Darein, 112
Daurak, 11
D. dien, 97
Daibul, 12
Damiat, 34
Damavend, 172, 173, 177, 178
Darenjan, 90
Damascus. See Demeshk
Danbul, 147, 148, 150, 154, 155
Daloui, 150

Damghan, 175, 178, 182, 194, 228
Danchy, 196
Darghes, 207
Daver, 208
Daruk, 211
Daven, 215
Dashan, 217
Dal, 242, 243
Dar Zingi, 277
Dehekan, 280
Derket, 280
Derghes, 279
Derkhas, 278
Derbend, 158, 159, 160, 162, 164, 180, 185, 187, 190, 191, 192, 277
Derghan, 275
Deirken, 275
Deiruk, 274
Debel, 272
Deinket, 268
Debzek, 262, 263
Debousi, 252
Derban, 141, 142, 157
Denjaneh, 252
Desht Varein, 130, 131, 132
Derusen, 248
Derwazeh Samarcand, 248
Deizah, 248
Deha, 241
Deraan, 241
Delouan, 91
Dekhan, 239
Deihan, 97
Deria, 232
Dendalekan, 230
Derab, 224
Dereh, 209, 228, 82
Derman, 142
Deir Berkhan, 198
Deher Houmah, 139

Dehieh Giran, 195
Deir Aber, 96
Deir Kaheim, 195, 196
Derjend, 90
Demarzari, 183
Deidelout, 90
Deher, 180
Dermeyah, 178
Derberan, 178
Dera, 177
Dersein, 177
Derneh, 177
Dehestan, 176, 180, 185, 190, 191, 208, 220
Deheihlour, 168
Deheih Abou Ayoub, 166
Deilman, 165, 172, 174, 175, 178, 180, 183, 184
Deinour, 94, 165, 167, 168, 169
Deir Kherkan, 164
Deinel, 160, 162, 164, 165
Derituk, 160
Derek, 158, 147
Deheireh, 86
Demeshk (Damascus) xiii, xiv, xv, xvi, 40, 43, 44, 47, 48, 49, 237, 238
Deirgan, 87
Dejeil, 71
Dehmeh, 177
Deshkereh, 69, 71
Desht (lake) 84, 88
Deiralaakoul, 71
Deidan, 79
Derjend (River) 64
Deilman, 3, 8
Dejleh (or Tigris) 11, 26, 31, 54, 56, 57, 59, 60, 64, 66, 67, 70, 71, 72, 75, 78, 79, 162
Dehkellan, 110

SECOND INDEX.

Derijan, 88
Dehein Seifomareh, 88
Destekan, 88
Dertek, 89
Dhey Nemeh, 181
Dhey Digur, 201
Dhey, 209, 210
Dhehek, 209, 210
Dheyaoum, 210
Dhey Jumah, 210
Dhey Moured, 93
Dhey Kurdan, 228
Diarbekre, xxiii
Diar Modhar, 58
Divesy, 273
Divemaket, 265
Dileshkird, 261
Dilem, 161, 183, 212
Doumish, 164
Dourek, 72, 79, 80
Doukak, 108
Doubein, 106
Dorenjan, 90
Duzdan, 166
Dur, 169
Durreh, 194, 195
Duardeh, 198
Durak, 199
Duar, 212

E.

Ebher, 175, 122
Egypt (Misr) ii. xxvii, 2, 4, 5, 7, 13, 14, 19, 22, 29, 31, 34, 37, 38, 51, 53, 40, 45, 46, 129, 132, 292
Emessa, 43
Eskanderiah (Alexandria), 33
Ethiopia, 4, 14, 22
Euphrates, 31, 37, 38, 44, 50, 54, 55, 57, 58, 59, 60, 65, 68, 69, 72, &c.

F.

Fars, Farsistan, or Pars, xxiii, 2, 3, 8, 81, 82, 84, 85, 86, 95, 108, 140, 165, 192, 193, 194, 211, 212, 216 227
Fanek, 86
Farkhan, 88
Fardek, 90
Fahas (Alilout), 18, 26
Falestine. See Palestine.
Faz (or Fez) 17, 21
Fataih, 30
Famhel, 150, 151, 152, 154
Faloui, 154
Farab, 232, 260, 268, 269
Farghi, 238
Famurgh, 256, 257
Fetrioun, 153
Feldi, 154
Ferasendeh, 168
Fereh, 207, 208, 209, 211, 212.
Ferouan, 225
Ferghanah, 6, 232, 233, 235, 238, 248, 250, 252, 261, 263, 263, 264, 268, 269, 270, 271, 272, 274, 276, 280
Ferma, 35
Feik, 48, 274
Ferdin, 189
Fertast, 90
Fermoun, 147
Fermouiah, 18
Feikerah, 27
Feserdeh, 247
Ferazan-al-Sefli 248, 249
Ferin, 248
Feranah, 249
Ferghour, 264

Ferajan, 274
Ferjeneh, 275
Firouzmend, 208, 210
Firouz (Kam) 90, 98, 113, 126, 135
Firkh, 110, 112
Fioum, 31
Forat. See Euphrates
Fomapalah, 71
Foruab, River, 84
Fostat, 30, 33, 36
Frat. See Euphrates

G.

Gaza, 33, 40
Gaw Khareh, 242, 243
Gerbadcan, 169
Ghurghaz, 9
Ghurneh, 9
Ghuz, 9, 10, 243, 244, 263, 268, 269, 270, 187, 190
Ghafek, 18, 26
Ghira, 144
Ghour, 39, 40
Ghouteh, xiv, xv, xvi, 40, 48, 237, 238
Gherahelm, 44
Gherasem, 49
Ghersiran, 268
Guhzl, 265
Gherk, 262
Ghurgestan, 256, 213, 221, 225
Gherban, 255- 258
Ghehar, 248
Gharan Murgh, 247
Ghar al Naiah, 242
Ghurnein, 230
Ghaznih, 212
Ghizni, 210, 225, 226, 227, 228, 241

SECOND INDEX.

Ghaznein, 208, 230, 232, 283
Ghaur, 205, 207, 212, 221, 226, 227
Gilan, 174
Giran, 195
Gird, 89
Gibraltar, 7, 19, 20, 25, 51
Gondi Shapour. See Jondi Shapour, 77
Gouz, 109
Goured, 113
Gourkam, 221
Goukanan, 213
Gouvi, 211, 212
Gouid, 206
Gozi, 197, 198
Gounabeh, 191, 192
Gounaieh, 191, 192
Gurki, 158
Gurkan, 8, 9, 110, 121, 159, 174, 175, 176, 179, 180, 182, 183, 188, 208, 212, 214, 215, 241
Gullar, 183
Guebran, 195
Gurkouneh, 209
Guh Pelenk, 211
Gurigar, 218
Gurbah, 242

H.

Hawr, 108
Haneid, 69
Hadithah, 57, 60
Hafieh, 89
Haijan, 88
Habeirah, 68, 71
Hawer Ableh, 64
Harah Rudgan, 86
Hadejan Shapour, 89
Hairah, 62, 66
Hareh, 97
Haran, 86
Hajr, 46, 89
Harouniah, 38, 45, 50
Haleb, 47, 49
Hasirmenje (or Jasirmenje) 55, 59
Hameres, 88
Habbesh (Abbyssinia) 4, 13, 22
Hamrah, 30
Hamadan, 166, 167, 168, 169
Hamdan, 167, 172
Hafs, 182
Harmeh, 196
Hamr, 200
Hareh, 97, 211, 219
Hasker, 241
Hamdounah, 248
Hanerker, 266
Hamerel, 266
Hawes, 274
Hallured, 276
Heiket, 280
Herkaneh, 279, 280, 262
Hejareh, 278
Heireh, 65, 66, 278, 242, 108, 112
Hermigan, 277
Heileh, 276
Hebek, 276
Hezarasp, 241, 242, 275, 278
Hedali, 270, 271
Herket, 266
Hedinket, 265
Heran, 260
Heshwan, 248
Heriat, 232
Helil, 223
Hellaverd, 223
Hesheb, 223

Hessan, 217, 219
Hejrai, 212
Hezar, 26, 109, 210
Hestan, 210
Heruri, 209
Herin, 89, 209
Heirmend, 205, 206, 207, 212
Herat, 121, 202, 209, 213, 217, 218, 219, 228
Hemaneh, 193
Heft Der, 182
Heban, 164, 166
Heilabshar, 159
Hesn Ebn Omareh, 12, 111, 112
Herman, 152
Helbeh, 150
Heidour, 147
Hebab, 144
Hemed, 144
Hey, 61, 63, 64, 74, 77, 119
Hemaigan Sefly, 122
Hedim, 87
Heyaz, 46, 90
Heilouieh, 82, 90
Hesouah, 89
Heran, 86, 260
Heskan, 88
Heir, 110
Herbazan, 107
Herieh, 102
Haifan, 97
Hembeir, 89
Heraje, 112
Hemeid, 88
Herah, 26, 65, 66
Heith, 59
Hejr, 46
Hemess, 43, 47, 48, 49
Hemah, 44
Hejaz, 46, 132, 289, 290, 291

SECOND INDEX.

Hedim, 87
Herdeh (River) 84
Hhoumah, 87, 113
Hharur, 220
Hind, 2, 147, 203
Hindoostan, 3, 4, 5, 9, 12, 18, 203, 207, 212, 225, 226, 232, 292
Hejar, 46, 89
Hije, 89
Homer, xi
Houbakan, 86
Holwan, 61, 62, 69, 71, 162, 167, 168, 170, 172
Houran, 49, 50
Houman, 33, 34
Honadah, 27
Hormuz, 12, 88, 138, 139, 140, 141, 142, 143, 145
Houran, 97
Hormuz Keran, 112
Houmah, 111, 139
Husnabad, 144
Houmah al Net, 74
Houmah al San, 74
Housket, 265
Hust, 217
Humdan, 9
Hysn Mohdi, 11, 74, 75, 78, 79, 80, 129
Hysn Ebn Omarreh, 12, 111, 112
Hysn Mansour, 44, 50
Hysn Moselamah, 60

I. J.

Jawr, 82, 88, 94, 100, 111, 112, 113, 130, 132, 198
Jarin, 86

Jasermenje (or Hasermenje) 55, 59
Jarour, 93
Jarouen, 138
Jarianeh, 225, 230
Jaum, 228
Jezireh, 47, 54, 55, 56, 59, 127, 156, 161
Jesmeden, 160
Jebai, 40, 74, 127, 161, 172, 181, 192, 194, 277
Jehan (River) 45
Jehudistan, 169
Jerth, 173
Jermjery, 182
Jerhan, 182
Jchineh, 183
Jerjer, 187
Jellabeh, 191
Jehr, 200
Jefan, 241
Jelal Deizeh, 248
Jerghaneh, 248
Jerghan, 248
Jermesk, 249
Jerjereh, 38, 250
Jeran, 259
Jerjeir, 38
Jenuder, 265
Jegherket, 206
Jermaiah, 274
Jerbend, 275
Jeladan, 97
Jehrem, 111, 116, 132
Jehreh, 113
Jenabah, 90, 105, 106, 111, 112, 113, 132
Jemgan, 97
Jeran, 113, 60, 259
Jerusalem. See Beit al Mokeds 39, 48, 52
Jezireh Ebn Omar, 57

Jedan, 58
Jebal al Kellal, 53, 54
Jerjeraya, 71
Jireft, 139, 140, 141, 142, 144, 145
Jiroukan, 139
Jirdeh, 139
Jirouan, 145
Jibel (Tarek) 20
Jihoun (River) 155, 178, 187, 225, 226, 228, 232, 238, 239, 240, 243, 244, 245, 251, 260, 273, 275, 278
Jouakend, 271
Jouibari Aarez, 247
Jondi Shapour, 73, 75, 77, 79, 80, 168
Joubendan, 96
Jouim, 89, 85
Joumeh Mesehan, 110
Jouein, 110
Joudi, 60
Jouidan (River) 84
Irak (Arabi) xxiii, 1, 2, 6, 88, 46, 61, 62, 63, 66, 71, 72, 76, 79, 125, 127, 133, 148, 156, 157, 158, 165, 166, 168, 171, 176, 180, 200, 207, 214, 258
Isfahan, 75, 81, 91, 96, 102, 100, 112, 123, 133, 157, 192, 193, 194, 195, 196, 201, 165
Iskandereh, 224
Ispahan, 169, 172, 173, 199
Istakhar, xxv, 82, 86, 91, 93, 94, 98, 99, 100, 102, 103, 107, 108, 111. 113, 116, 119, 128, 129, 134, 135, 137
Iskenkejr, 262
Isashab, 280

SECOND INDEX.

Istakharan, 109
Iskanderiah. See Alexandria
Jurmeh, 194

K.

Kandabil, 147, 151, 153, 154
Kair, 151, .152
Kanteli, 153
Kapchak, 159
Kablah, 160
Kanjah, 160
Kantereh al Naaman, 166
Kashan, 169, 171, 172, 193, 194; 195
Karen, 174, 175, 176
Karges, 193, 196
Kahein, 195
Kah, 195, 223, 231
Kabul, 207, 223, 226
Kariz, 209
Kantueh Kirman, 211
Kanderuthan, 215
Kaberoun, 220
Kaloun, 220
Kankouan, 265
Kalek, 266
Kaimakher, 272
Kankan, 277
Kasan, 279
Kan, 221
Kanderm, 221
Kaein, 222, 223, 228, 229, 231
Kaweil, 223
Kabul, 223, 326
Kasan, 224
Kash, vii, ix, xi, xvi, 258, 259, 260, 279
Kanderim, 229
Kalef, 239
Kanjesh, 241

Kab, 241
Kafer Kam, 240
Kafra al Alia, 87
Kanserin, 44, 49
Kahira (Note) 30
Kakour, 37
Karma, 83
Karcoub, 61
Kattah, 86
Kales, 86
Karma, 83
Karcoub, 61
Kattah, 86
Kas (River) 84
Kales, 86
Karma, 83
Kafra al Sefli, 87
Karzein, 88, 97, 96, 102, 112
Karian, 91, 123
Kattah, 86, 102, 108, 111
Kadban, 94
Kaaba (or Caaba) 2, 128
Karkheh, 74
Kazeroun (Cazroun) 89, 90, 94, 97
Kakan, 90
Kantereh, 89, 122
Kam Firouz, 90, 95, 98, 113, 126, 135
Kashgird, 145
Kahas (Alilont) 18
Kabulistan
Kaimak, 9, 10
Kelaahereh, 147
Keniabeh, 151, 152, 154
Kelwan, 151
Kebr, 153, 154
Kesr, 153, 175
Kesdan, 154
Kerieh, 157
Kenjah, 162, 164

Kendman, 164
Kelkaterin, 164
Kelilgoun, 164
Kerkhan, 164
Keser Dusdan, 166, 169
Kesralberadin, 169
Kellar, 87, 110, 175
Kestaneh, 181
Kelazil, 181
Kehrest, 181
Keramhan, 211
Kerbin, 212
Kemkh, 217
Kehendiz, 217
Keroukh, 219
Keif, 220
Kescher, 230
Keiseh, 247
Kendaman, 248
Kerjinet, 250
Kerin, 251, 273
Kerminiah, 252, 273
Keisaneh, 258
Kesaban, 259
Kenk, 260
Keshteh, 261
Kebout Meheket, 279
Kend Gah, 276
Kendil, 275
Ketran, 274
Kend, 273
Kerouan, 272
Keba, 270, 271
Kenjideh, 269
Kezr, 268
Keheshm, 266
Kedal, 266
Kerneh, 265
Kelenjek, 265
Ketaiah, 30
Kenamah, 27
Kesrbend, 147

SECOND INDEX.

Kesisan, 145
Keraoun, 144
Kellan, 110
Keri, 139
Keles, 86
Kelid, 86, 93
Kesri, 88
Keherjan, 88
Keferisa, 89
Keliwazi, 67
Keliwan, 74, 77
Kefer, 105
Kerar, 112
Kereh, 109
Kehrgan, 109
Kelouder, 107
Keiawem, 89
Kesr Aaien, 109
Kelimah, 52
Kelimiah, 52
Kesr Ebn Hobeireh, 63
Kellal, 53, 54
Kerbela, 68
Kedah, 26
Keisa, 45
Kenisa, 50
Keber, 87
Khemardegan, 87
Khan, 87
Khan Badieh, 106
Khar, 177, 178, 181, 194
Khouf, 36
Khefa, 37
Khefar Kar, 37
Khenaserah, 44
Khabour, 59
Khabouran, 57
Khoshbu, 84
Kawrnak, 65
Khuzistan (Susiana) xxiii, 2, 11, 20, 29, 78, 80, 81, 157, 165, 166, 169

Kharizan, 78
Khorasan, 3, 67, 81, 108, 121, 132, 138, 157, 165, 169, 172, 181, 192, 193, 194, 195, 197, 199, 200, 201, 203, 208, 212, 214, 215, 216, 217, 219, 226, 227, 229, 232, 233, 237, 240, 244, 245, 251, 252, 295
Khouareh, 110
Khemrud, 145
Khozr, xxvi, 3, 5, 8, 9, 159, 162- 180, 183, 187, 188, 190, 191
Khoorsan 88
Khebis, 139
Khan, 87, 106
Khan Daouid, 105
Khosruhein, 130
Kheis, 142
Khanifen, 88
Khem, 88, 107
Kherik, 88
Kheir, 121, 132
Khan Shur, 106
Khan Khamad, 110
Khur Khiz, 9, 110
Khuzn-jiah, 9
Khederge, 9, 10
Kherouje, 152
Khounah, 157, 164, 200
Khoui, 157, 165, 198
Khaberan, 157, 158
Khullat, 165
Khuast, 167, 168, 171, 172, 210
Khan Lekhan, 169
Khosru, 177
Khorasmia, 180
Khelawah, 182
Khedaweh, 132
Khubeis, 194, 199

Khust, 199, 231
Khebeis, 199, 201
Khilje, 207, 227, 269
Khorasaneh, 210
Khabzar, 210
Khesajy, 210
Khaveran, 211, 229
Khuarezm, xxiii, 213, 226, 227, 278
Khosrugird, 215, 219, 229
Kherinan, 215
Kherki, 218
Khulm, 223, 230
Khesh, 224
Kharasm, 230, 232, 238, 239, 241, 242, 243, 244, 246, 265, 270, 275
Khotl, 232
Khoslan, 238, 239, 276
Khozar, 241, 244
Khonas, 241
Kherdour, 241
Khiljan, 243
Khebek Rud, 259
Khojend, 263, 271, 273, 280
Khas, 260
Khersab, 270
Khenlam, 272
Khesehirt, 273
Khetl, 277
Khersaliket, 280,
Kishteh, 278
Kirdan Khas, 278
Kish, 238, 250, 258, 259, 260, 261. 275, 279
Kirdan, 241, 248, 218
Kirman, 2, 12, 46, 53, 81, 86, 61, 98, 99, 102, 107, 111. 118, 153, 166, 193, 194, 196, 198, 201, 202. 203, 205, 206. 208, 211 213. 227, 289

SECOND INDEX.

Kirder, 241
Kisaban, 259
Kishteh, 279
Kihsest, 181
Kirasan, 218, 228
Kibrakanan, 147
Kirkanan, 153
Kipchak, 156
Kipshak, 156
Kirman Shahan, 169, 192
Kirman, 16, 17, 20, 22, 30
Kirouan, 16, 17, 20, 22, 30
Kirdman, 89
Kirdgan, 144
Kibres, 53
Kiasah, 37
Kous, 49, 50, 245
Kouh, 72, 173, 176, 184, 185, 193, 194, 196, 209
Kouhestan, 3, 78, 123, 143, 156, 165, 166, 169, 172, 173, 176, 194, 206, 213, 214, 223, 227, 231, 277
Kouin, 86. 88, 111, 131
Kounein, 145
Kouz, 144
Kouingan, 88
Koum, 89
Kouheftan abu Ghanem, 139
Koumin, 139
Kouje or Kouche, 140, 142, 289, 290
Koureh, 97
Kohendez, 108
Kouar, 105
Koumeſh, 121
Korkh, 67
Kolzum, 4, 6, 13, 29, 39, 184
Kornouifah, 18
Kourieh, 18
Koules, 27

Kousein, 177
Kouim, 176
Koumis, 175, 178, 193, 194, 212, 228, 229
Kom, 168, 169, 170, 171, 172, 176, 193, 194, 195
Koumenjan, 167
Kohhendez, 181
Koukour, 199
Kousen, 209
Koushek Ahef, 220
Kousef, 217
Kouseri, 219
Kouh-seim, 220
Kouh Ummabad, 220
Kobadian, 239, 240, 277
Korkanje, 240, 242, 243, 278
Korasan, 241
Koragh, 242
Kourek, 256
Kourghed, 258
Koukib, 262, 263
Koureh of Kimjideh, 268
Kourast, 277
Kuakend, 173
Kubabeh, 222
Kurmeideh, 248
Kur, 158, 210
Kurge, 159
Kurreh, 167, 168, 169, 170
Kuarezm, 183, 228, 220
Kurreen, 211, 212
Kunje Reshak, 213
Kuaran, 217
Kubuk, 218
Kurkheh, 73
Kumar, 109
Kurich, 108
Kurnah Allas, 93
Kumbuz Malgan, 90
Kushein (River), 84
Kufertouma, 45, 56, 57

L.

Laristan, xxiii
Lattian, 12
Lahout, 31
Lawen, 87
Ladikiah, 38, 49
Lames, 52
Lashgird, 143
Lagheristan. 88
Lahein, 97
Lanjan, 164
Lashter, 167
Lansin, 167
Lawzer, 181
Lavakend, 223
Laian, 258
Laurast, 277
Laabek, 265
Leshkur, 80, 20, 74, 79, 206, 213
Lest, 198, 201
Lekhan, 169, 264
Lebez, 160
Leniran, 159
Lekzan, 159, 185
Lesout, 157
Lebnon, 39
Libnan, 39
Lour, 73, 78, 168, 172
Lourdegan, 87
Louar, 143

M.

Malaca, 2, 19
Mardah, 18
Magreb (Part of Africa), 2, 4, 7, 8, 15, 16, 22, 27, 28, 51, 53, 132
Mansoureh, 2, 4, 12, 147, 148, 150, 151, 154, 155

SECOND INDEX.

Maweralnahr (Transoxania), 3, 4, 9, 121, 212, 217, 223, 226, 227, 232, 233, 235, 236, 237, 238, 239, 240, 241, 245, 248, 249, 250, 251, 252, 253, 257, 264, 265, 268, 271, 273, 270, 303
Madaien, 69, 70, 71
Mahirouian, 11, 72
Macheen, 5, 12
Marouan, 89
Majouge, 8
Madaien, 11, 69, 70, 71
Marsafah, 27
Mardah, 26
Maserm, 97
Mardein, 56
Marhein, 86
Maren, 141
Masmoudah, 27
Marein, 112
Masidan, 58
Malghan, 90
Mazem, 23, 36
Masanan, 89
Masisa, 45, 50
Manein, 88, 95, 96, 109, 112, 113, 134
Matout, 80
Mahein, 86
Masouref, 86
Mahan, 139
Matoub, 80
Makran, 138, 140, 141
Manoui, 147
Maseh, 147
Manah, 151, 152
Majeh, 18
Marend, 157, 164
Maaoun, 145
Mahmud Abad, 162

Marsin, 167
Makran, 146
Maderan Roud, 167
Maset Khouh, 173
Malet, 182
Mabin, 194, 196, 201
Mahiah, 18
Mahin, 194
Maaun, 210, 214
Masi, 211
Malgan, 90
Malef, 217
Marabad, 217, 219
Masheran, 217
Malan, 219
Mank, 224, 225
Malez, 228
Markand, 232
Madoun, 248
Manferenje, 255
Makakhes, 272
Maberbouaar, 274
Mah, 280
Meket, 280
Medmameheket, 278
Mebaderal Kebri, 74, 78
Merdangan, 278
Melenk, 276, 224, 225
Menek, 276, 239
Merdumen, 275
Mesalkal, 274
Mezrgheh, 273
Medina, 66, 117
Medonaneh, 272
Merghenban, 272
Memarujan, 271
Merinket, 266
Mesek, 264
Menunjan, 145
Melakhes, 248
Medeminiah, 243
Memha, 241

Merda, 241
Mersan, 229
Memur-rudd, 228
Meru Shahjan, 220
Meshkan, 86
Merdin, 72
Meroni, 147
Mei, 106
Mesouahi, 147, 150
Meron, 121
Meshari, 147
Meimoun, 147, 151, 164
Mesihan, 142
Mekran, 151, 152, 153, 155, 192, 193, 203
Meshkaneth, 113
Meskeni, 153
Med, 153
Meshkan, 86
Masbah, 154
Meibed, 86
Mehabari, 154
Meraghah, 157, 162, 164, 165
Merah, 166
Memeid, 88, 111, 112
Mehil, 175
Mesleh, 175, 182
Memkan, 88
Meruta, 175
Meskoubeh, 181
Mehein, 181
Merdan, 90
Merasik, 182
Mezraiek, 196
Meila, 206
Meru, 213, 215, 216, 217, 221, 227, 228, 230
Meserkan, 139
Merualrud, 213, 214, 220, 221, 222, 231
Medar, 64
Mentah, 64

SECOND INDEX.

Meki, 87
Mehaian, 86
Meibed, 86
Mesihar, 97
Mebaderal Kaberi, 74, 78
Merzend Khan, 110
Meden beni Salem, 26
Mesoul, 97
Mekianah, 27
Mediounah, 27
Meileth, 56
Mesopotamia, 2, 38, 54, &c.
Medah, 89
Meltiah, 38, 47, 50, 34. 55, 57
Meraash, 38, 41, 49, 50
Merzingan, 139
Menajah, 139
Mehreje, 139
Memehes, 38
Meftah, 73
Mesjed Ibrahim, 40
Medar, 73
Mesres, 44
Mesakenat, 89
Menje, 44, 47, 49, 50
Mecca, 128
Mes, 96
Mediterranean Sea, 2, 6, 7, 8, 15, 19, 25, 29, 37, 51, 51
Mekeh, 102
Mekia, 18
Mehsah, 19
Misr (Egypt), 2, 4, 5, 7, 16, 31
Mihra, 152, 169
Mian, 268
Mihran, 148, 150, 151, 154, 155
Mihrjan, 229, 230, 140, 215
Misan, 157
Mihra, 152, 169

Miougan, 141
Miafarekin, 161, 165
Mires, 164
Mianeh, 164
Mohar wan, 175
Moghken, 252, 278
Moumajez, 256
Moghaneh, 275
Moan, 47
Mousul, 55, 56
Moukan, 183, 162
Mourjan, 182
Mahirooian, 75, 111, 112, 116
Mahrooian, 86, 90, 105
Mourid, 93, 107
Mouje Maiha, 97
Mouje, 97
Mour, 99
Mouronan, 145
Mohdi, 110
Mouekaf, 30
Mourouan, 145
Modhar, 58, 59
Mohediah, 15, 17, 19, 22
Multan, 4, 147. 150, 151, 152, 154, 155, 203.
Muskehan, 197
Mushirkan, 74, 75

N.

Nadonan, 88
Naiel, 153
Nabul, 153
Nader, 90
Nakhjevan, 165
Naaman, 166
Naas, 212
Naksheb, 238, 260, 261, 275, 279
Nat, 78

Nahiah, 18
Nahia, 26
Nabolis, 40, 48
Nasedan, 58
Natdia, 45
Nahr Saies, 71
Nahr Ailah, xiv
Neamaniah, 71
Netirah, 50
Nethenan, 45
Nesrin, 24
Nehr Tiri, 74, 77, 80
Nehrwan, 69
Nebulis, 90
Nedeheh, 146, 151, 154
Nedeh, 154
Neshoui, 157
Nehavend, 167, 170
Nemek, 181
Nesa, 213, 222, 223
Neshkukan, 218
Neshin, 221
Nekin, 241
Neshamein, 264, 265
Nehaket, 265
Neskan, 267
Nejeb, 275
Nesoukh, 275
Nesef, 279
Nishapour, 121, 172, 182, 194, 197, 201, 208, 213, 214, 215, 217, 221, 223, 227, 228, 229
Nile (River), 14, 30, 31, 32, 33, 34, 35, 36, 37
Nisibin, 55, 56, 60
Noah Kherik, 88
Nourman, 239
Nouran, 241
Nubia, 4, 7, 9, 13, 14, 29, 31
Nubehar, 224, 247
Nukendeh, 247, 249

SECOND INDEX.

Nuskeen, 210
Nu Khani, 196
Nubendejan, 90, 103, 105, 110, 111, 112

O.

Oman, 11, 12, 128, 184, 193
Omareh, 12, 88, 94, 111, 112
Omru (Lake), 128
Omru Bersereh, 197
Ord (or Aurd), 97
Orthani, 191
Orden. See Arden.
Oxus. See Jihoun.

P.

Pars, 2, 3, 11, 12, 46, 72, 73, 75, 77, 78, 79, 82, 83, 84, 85, 86, 87, 93, 94, 98, 100, 105, 145, 169, 184, 192, 194, 203, 206, 208, 214, 227
Palestine, 39, 40, 48
Pelenk, 211
Peir, 209
Penjehir, 223, 224, 225, 226, 231, 233
Persian Sea, 2, 4, 5, 6, 7, 8, 14, 81
Persepolis. See Istakhar.
Pirouz, 154
Pir Kurieh, 108
Poul-i-meimoun, 164
Pool-Senkin, 277
Pul Andemesh, 168
Pusheng, 217, 218, 219, 222, 288

R.

Rahouk, 151
Rasek, 147, 152
Rakan, 167
Ramer, 168
Rasi, 169
Rasal Kibb, 181
Ravan, 198
Ram Sheheristan, 205
Rawer, 223, 168
Rasiman, 260
Rast, 261
Rabein, 144
Ram Hormuz, 73, 79
Ramuz, 79, 80
Rasein, 110
Radan, 86, 87
Ramjerd, 86
Rahban, 113
Ramleh, 39, 47, 48
Razika, 58
Raccah, 55, 58
Rus-al-aien, 55, 56, 57
Rahabah-malek-ben Tawh, 59
Ramnan, 11
Raai, 15
Rahey, 17
Rebaiah, 27
Red Sea (Sea of Kolzum), 4, 6, 29
Rebehi, 15, 20, 21
Rebaaia, 59
Remah, 47
Remaa, 39
Rekem, 49
Resajeh, 67
Rey, 122, 127, 157, 161, 165, 167, 168, 172, 174, 175, 176, 177, 178, 180, 181, 193, 194, 195, 196, 201, 212

Remin, 97
Resendgah (Keloudar), 107, 109
Rekisa, 109
Rehan, 89
Reshak, 89, 112, 144
Resasil, 153
Reyan, 160
Renjan, 169
Rengan, 122, 175
Rebat Kass, 482
Rehat Wedareh, 182
Rebat Bedreh, 195
Rebat Aliben Rustam, 195
Rebat Viran, 198
Rebat Gouran, 200
Rebat Gurreh, 200
Reheje, 207
Reha, 210, 211
Remvadeh, 215
Rebat Kirdan, 218
Rebat, 247, 248, 250
Reihestan, 248
Rehieh, 248
Rendieh, 252
Rebond, 257
Resmajen, 262
Rebat Khedifh, 263
Resban, 271
Rendwames, 272
Rebat Soghd, 273
Rebat Ahmed, 274
Rebat Abou Al Abassi, 274
Rebat Azik, 275
Rik Desht, 277
Rik, 200
Roum, 2, 3, 4, 6, 7, 8, 14, 37, 38, 43, 45, 46, 47, 50, 51, 52, 54, 78, 161, 188, 190, 192
Rous (Russia), 4, 5, 10, 185, 186, 188, 190, 191

SECOND INDEX.

Roumiah, 51, 52
Rouad, 40
Roudan Hemed, 144
Roubin, 145
Rondan, 111, 112, 140
Rouz, 113
Roustai Zem, 96
Rouiest, 143
Rouiah, 89
Roustai Reshak, 89, 130
Roustak, 113, 130
Roud, 167
Roha, 210, 211
Rohaje, 210
Roustaka, 248
Rouleje, 262
Rudi Turkestan, 267
Rudi Kesaban, 259
Rudeki, 256
Rud Basegan, 247
Rudi Kurd Khouas, 242
Rud Aileh, 237, 238
Ruzen, 229, 231
Rud Kasan, 224
Rud Anderabeh, 224
Rudi Haas, 224
Rud Yarkhoui, 218
Rudi Amol, 216
Rudi Sek, 207
Rud Aamil, 207
Rud Meila, 206
Rud Shaabeh, 206
Rudi Heirmend, 205
Ruzi, 194
Rudbar, 174
Rudeh, 169
Rud Rawer, 167, 168, 170
Rugird, 167
Rud, 154, 155, 164, 206

S.

Sahel al Arab, 130
Sarsan, 68
Samereh, 68, 69, 71, 72
Saidabad, 94
Samarcand, ix, x, xi, 157, 232, 233, 234, 237, 238, 248, 249, 251, 252, 253, 254, 255, 256, 257, 258, 259, 260, 261, 262, 263, 268, 273, 275, 276, 278
Sahelal Kebri, 86, 107
San, 89, 110, 221
Samgan, 88
Sarour, 93, 103
Sasan, 79
Saf-beni-al Seghar, 85, 88, 91, 118
Saied, 32, 33, 37
Salimiah, 48
Samereh, 60, 62
Salem, 26, 202
Saiheh, 44
Samisat, 44, 50, 54, 55, 57, 59
Sanjan, 56
Sarbanana, 177
Sarrah, 26, 27
Sarfasseh, or Sarkassass, 18
Saveh, 167, 168, 131
Sarien, 175
Sari, 175, 179, 182
Salous, 175, 183
Sarbanan, 177
Sarkhes, 213, 219, 221, 222, 228, 230
Sarnan, 215
Satri, 2, 3
Sa, 229
Safzoun, 241
Sam Kons, 245

Saman, 304
Samjir, 248
Samjer Maweralnahr, 248
Sawat, 255, 256
Sarouan, 257
Sameket, 262, 263
Sabat, 262, 263, 273
Sarin, 262
Saket, 265
Saoudad, 265
Sailaa, 267
Saweket, 273
Saferoun, 278
Sabat, 280
Scythian, 180
Sclavonia (Siklab), 4, 5, 7, 9, 10, 87
Sebourket, 280
Seher, 279
Sedoun, 275
Selket, 274
Senjan, 274
Selab, 272
Selikend, 272
Senjat, 268
Sehaket, 266
Seket, 265
Semendeh, 263, 264
Selisedeh Belis, 262
Senk Kerdeh Beroubin, 260
Senk Kerdeh Deroubein, 260
Setrushtah, 257, 258, 261, 262, 263, 264, 269, 276, 280
Scheker, 262
Senaa, 254
Seif Omareh, 88
Sefli, 87, 122, 248, 249
Seroukeseh, 246
Serigan, 138, 139, 143
Sekineh, 239
Sedreh, 74

SECOND INDEX.

Sebenjan, 230
Serakiah, 116
Serser, 113
Serder, 113
Setouder, 113
Sefareh, 88
Selumed, 229
Selmisa, 43
Sekanat, 88
Sekan, 229
Seghur Sham, 38, 50, 57
Sekandereh, 223, 224
Seif-beni Zoheir, 118
Serai Aasim, 223
Seghur Jezirah, 38, 50
Sehekemest, 223
Senjan, 82, 90, 230, 231, 238
Sekilkend, 229
Senjar, 56
Selsan, 74
Semengan, 223
Sey, 64
Seim, 220
Serskek, 86
Seida, 49
Sejestan, 46, 218
Seradsin, 87
Seirshian, 218
Serden, 87
Semeran, 88, 112
Sepid Asenk, 218
Selutik, 215
Serout, 47
Sehizan, 211
Senkin, 211
Serur, 209
Sek, 207
Seibud, 206
Sebirud, 206
Sebaaid, 200
Seis, 90
Sekan, 106

Seiestan, 3, 138, 139, 140, 192, 193, 194, 202, 203, 205, 206, 207, 208, 209, 211, 212, 218, 283
Semid, 188
Semender, 185
Seruje, 60
Serain, 183
Sendanest, 183
Selimiah, 48
Semnan, 169, 175, 176, 178, 182, 194, 196
Seist, 177
Seilan, 133, 156, 173
Semireh, 73, 169, 170, 171, 172
Seheneh, 167
Serouah, 161
Seirwan, 61, 62
Serir, 159, 184, 187, 188, 192
Servan, 156, 168, 169, 170, 171, 172, 212
Seimereh, 61, 62
Selmas, 157, 164, 165
Senja, 69
Seidan, 147
Sejelmarah, 17, 21
Sedusan, 147, 150, 151, 154
Serin, 4, 5
Serlaier, 33
Sham (Syria), 2, 4, 7, 35, 37, 38, 39, 42, 45, 47, 48, 49, 51, 53
Sherah, 28, 40, 43, 78
Shebirz, 44
Shehrzour, 61, 62. 69, 168, 171, 172
Shateif, 16, 22, 27
Shehr, 145
Shirkan, 144
Shemasiah, 67
Shourab, 105

Shushtêr, 75, 76, 77, 79
Shaab Bouan, xiv, xv, 90, 105
Shekireh, 90
Shek Kirman, 102
Shapour, 82, 89, 90, 91, 95, 97, 99, 103, 129, 135, 168
Shabaleg, vii
Shehran, 88
Shekeir, 88
Shukal-reshak, 89
Shuk-al-masanan, 89
Shehr Leshkur, 73
Shushter, 73, 74
Shir, 108
Sherazu (Zem), 89
Shiraz, 82, 83, 87, 93, 99, 100, 103, 104, 106, 107, 108, 110, 113, 116, 119, 122, 125, 128, 131, 132, 135, 137, &c.
Shahrung, 87
Shehristan, 87, 205
Shadafzai, 97
Shaberan, 159
Shirvan, 160, 163, 164, 185
Shamakhy, 160, 163
Shaberan, 160
Shemkour, 160, 162, 164
Shrousend, 160
Shahan, 166, 169
Sherwend, 167, 171
Shaber Khuast, 167, 168, 171, 172
Shehrud, 169
Shehmar, 175
Shelineh, 177
Shour, 197, 198, 199, 201
Shaabeh, 206
Sheker Kharan, 217
Shiurkan, 221
Shehran, 223
Shebangareh, xxiii

SECOND INDEX.

Shiukan, 231
Shash, vii, 233
Shuman, 240
Shak, 248
Sheman, 261
Shuk Hosein, 274
Shuk Kenend, 274
Shouman, 279
Sheer, 106
Sikaliah (Sicily), 53
Singe, 139
Sir Kouh, 106
Sihan (River), 45
Sirin, 18, 25
Siraf, 11, 82, 88, 104, 105, 111, 112, 113, 115, 133
Sinir, 11, 105
Sind, 2, 4, 5, 12, 147, 153, 155, 193, 203
Siklab (Sclavonia), 2, 5, 7, 9, 10, 97, 244
Siah Kouh (Black Mountain), 8, 184, 185, 194, 209
Sirouab, 87
Sirm Kan, 107
Seif-al Abi, 88
Siareh Rud, 206
Sibareh, 206
Sirab, 210
Siccah, 218
Siaveshan, 218
Siahgird, 224
Siroushteh, 233
Sindiah, 147
Sindan, 154
Sinai, 29
Simreh, 168
Siam, 259
Sinkhab, 265
Sour (Tyre), 40, 48, 274
Soukh, 272
Souaren, 164

Soghd, 232, 234, 237, 238, 245, 249, 251, 252, 253, 256, 258, 262, 262, 263, 264, 265, 278, 279
Sourbah, 154
Souk-al-azim, 67
Soura, 68
Souk Asunbeil, 74
Souk-al-arbaa, 74
Soul-al Khess, 102
Souk, 74, 38
Souanjan, 89
Solymanan, 74, 75
Sourdadi, 90
Sourdan, 145
Sous, 61
Souad, 61
Sodom, 47
Spain. See Andalus.
Spahawn, or Ispahan, 72, 73, 167, 168, 169, &c.
Surudeh, 260
Surim, 262
Sunekh, 279
Sureh, 147
Sutemder, 191, 192
Sum teder, 191
Sumsider, 192
Sur Duardeh, 198
Surmin, 221
Susikan, 230
Sus, 15, 73, 76, 77, 80
Sumbeil, 77, 78
Surmek, 30, 113
Surmeh, 86, 93
Sus Aksi, 17, 20
Syria (Sham), 2, 4, 7, 35, 51, 53, 129, 132, 157

T.

Tarfah, 17
Tarsousah, 19. 51, 53
Tanjah, 20, 51
Tahouth, 15, 17, 21, 22, 27, 28
Tarek (Gibraltar), 19, 20
Tabertha, or Tiberiah, 48, 100
Tab (River), 84
Tangiers. See Tanjah.
Tarkhinfan, 86
Tabaristan, 3, 121, 158, 159, 174, 175, 178, 179, 180, 182, 183, 212, 217, &c.
Taiboul al Kawian, 87
Taberah, 89
Tarsous, 43, 45, 46, 50, 52
Tacrith, 55, 59, 61, 62, 69, 72
Tawh, 59
Tarkhinsan, or Tarjensan, 86, 118
Talat, 89
Tasimoun, 152
Tabriz, 157, 164
Tairberan, 159
Tarem, 162, 174
Tawet Souaren, 164
Takaun, 169
Talekan, 175, 208, 220
Tauk, 208, 211, 212
Taikan, 223, 224, 230, 231
Taheriah, 241, 275
Tejeket, 274
Teb, 74
Teib, 61, 78, 80
Tesouje, 87
Tebisan, 89
Tel Deilemi, 131
Tesoukh, 98
Temisan, 110

SECOND INDEX.

Terkan, 144
Tel beni Seiar, 60
Tehiaihah, 27
Teran, 87
Tencis (Tunis, or Teinise, 34, 36
Terkoum, 36
Tetar, 154
Teflis, 160, 162, 164
Teraa, 162
Temseir, 176
Terjy, 182
Temisheh, 182
Terka, 106
Telis, 197
Tel-i-siah ve Sepeed, 200
Tel, 207
Teisin, 222
Termed, 225, 228, 229, 238, 239, 240, 277
Tebsein, 231
Tebsein Merian, 231
Teran, 238
Telengan, 249
Teraz, 268, 269, 274
Thareb, 49
Themabin, 60
Tirar, 87
Tir Merdan, 90
Tiberiah, 20, 40, 48, 160
Tigris (see Dejleh), 162
Tibet, xx, 4, 10, 12, 233, 239, 298
Tiah beni Israel, 29
Tokharestan, 4, 213, 223, 224
Toletiah, 18
Toletilah, 25, 26, 27
Tour Sina (Mount Sinai), 29
Touje, 106, 112, 132
Touran, 146, 151, 154, 232
Toshereth, 192
Toghahi, 267

Touabes, 248
Tous, 215
Touaveis, 249, 250, 252, 273, 278
Touan, 271
Trabolis, 43, 48, 49
Trablis, 16, 19
Trabzoun, 161
Turezhumeh, 169
Turkestan, 9, 180, 212, 222, 226, 232, 233, 238, 239, 259, 265, 267, 270, 271, 272, 273, 298, &c.
Tuskeen, 210
Turkan, 213
Tuncat, vii
Tyre, 40, 48

U.

Ummabad, 220

V.

Varein (Desht), 130, 131, 131
Vameiz, 177
Valein, 230
Vashir, 145
Vernan, 163
Verin, 218
Veis, 248
Veireh, 275
Viran, 193

W.

Waset, 61, 62, 65, 66, 71, 72, 79, 80
Wazin, 88
Wahh, 22, 29, 84

Wadi al hejar, 18, 26
Wahat, 54
Warghes, 255
Waakes, 262
Wanket, 271
Waaiket, 278
Waaketh, 282
Wehmeh, 177
Wedareh, 182
Werwa, 223
Wekshab, 232, 239, 276
Wekhsh, 239
Weishkird, 239, 240, 277
Wera, 247, 248
Werkaneh, 249
Weddan, 255, 258, 279
Werd, 260
Welanket, 265
Werdil, 265
Weheket, 266
Werkan, 278
Wirdgird, 167, 168, 170

Y.

Yajouge, xxvii, 7, 8, 9, 10
Yar, 167
Yarkhoui, 218
Yemen, 11, 13, 14, 132, 194, 292, 293, 299
Yezd, 86, 102, 111, 113, 132, 139, 194
Yemameh, 193
Yest, 198, 200

Z.

Zareid, 154, 145, 143
Zawieh, 78
Zakoureth, 87

SECOND INDEX.

Zabein, 59
Zaar, 48
Zarieh, 45
Zamin, 274, 276, 280
Zalinkiet, 280
Zadakhour, 201
Zadakherſt, 201
Zarinje, 200
Zam, 213, 226, 229, 239. 240
Zarkah, 250
Zarghem, 255, 237
Zamkird, 257

Zebidiah, 166, 278
Zeitoun, 277
Zerian, 273
Zeirin, 271, 272
Zeidin, 215
Zerinje, 205, 207
Zemgen, 164, 165, 179, 180
Zemgan, 162
Zeitrah, 45
Zeilaa, 14
Zem, 82, 112
Zeif, 33, 37

Zem Shehrazu, 89
Zerend, 189
Zingbar, 14, 31
Zingan, 162
Zingy, 201
Zozen, 215
Zoha, 58
Zouilah, 15, 17, 21, 22, 27
Zouialah, 27
Zubidieh, 166
Zualien, 223, 224
Zyad Abad, 107.

ADDITIONAL ERRATA.

[*See thoſe already noticed in page* 308.]

Preface, Page iv, line 20, for *ie*, read *le*.
———— Page 42, .. 23, for *Molk*, read *Malek*.
———— 68, .. 5, for *Molk*, read *Malek*.
———— 84, .. 7, for *Koshbu*, read *Khoshbu*.
———— 160, .. 16, for *Kaujah*, read *Kanjah*.
———— 279, .. 10, for ارنجر read ارنجر

PRINTED, *AT THE ORIENTAL PRESS*, BY WILSON & CO.
WILD-COURT, LINCOLN'S INN FIELDS, LONDON.